Graphics Programming with GDI+ & DirectX

LIMITED WARRANTY AND DISCLAIMER OF LIABILITY

A-LIST, LLC, AND/OR ANYONE WHO HAS BEEN INVOLVED IN THE WRITING, CREATION, OR PRODUCTION OF THE ACCOMPANYING CODE (ON THE CD-ROM) OR TEXTUAL MATERIAL IN THIS BOOK CANNOT AND DO NOT GUARANTEE THE PERFORMANCE OR RESULTS THAT MAY BE OBTAINED BY USING THE CODE OR CONTENTS OF THE BOOK. THE AUTHORS AND PUBLISHERS HAVE WORKED TO ENSURE THE ACCURACY AND FUNCTIONALITY OF THE TEXTUAL MATERIAL AND PROGRAMS CONTAINED HEREIN; HOWEVER, WE GIVE NO WARRANTY OF ANY KIND, EXPRESSED OR IMPLIED, REGARDING THE PERFORMANCE OF THESE PROGRAMS OR CONTENTS.

THE AUTHORS, PUBLISHER, DEVELOPERS OF THIRD-PARTY SOFTWARE, AND ANYONE INVOLVED IN THE PRODUCTION AND MANUFACTURING OF THIS WORK SHALL NOT BE LIABLE FOR ANY DAMAGES ARISING FROM THE USE OF (OR THE INABILITY TO USE) THE PROGRAMS, SOURCE CODE, OR TEXTUAL MATERIAL CONTAINED IN THIS PUBLICATION. THIS INCLUDES, BUT IS NOT LIMITED TO, LOSS OF REVENUE OR PROFIT, OR OTHER INCIDENTAL OR CONSEQUENTIAL DAMAGES ARISING FROM THE USE OF THE PRODUCT.

THE CD-ROM, WHICH ACCOMPANIES THE BOOK, MAY BE USED ON A SINGLE PC ONLY. THE LICENSE DOES NOT PERMIT ITS USE ON A NETWORK (OF ANY KIND). THIS LICENSE GRANTS YOU PERMISSION TO USE THE PRODUCTS CONTAINED HEREIN, BUT IT DOES NOT GIVE YOU RIGHT OF OWNERSHIP TO ANY OF THE SOURCE CODE OR PRODUCTS. YOU ARE SUBJECT TO LICENSING TERMS FOR THE CONTENT OR PRODUCT CONTAINED ON THIS CD-ROM. THE USE OF THIRD-PARTY SOFTWARE CONTAINED ON THIS CD-ROM IS LIMITED THE RESPECTIVE PRODUCTS.

THE USE OF "IMPLIED WARRANTY" AND CERTAIN "EXCLUSIONS" VARY FROM STATE TO STATE, AND MAY NOT APPLY TO THE PURCHASER OF THIS PRODUCT.

Graphics Programming with GDI+ & DirectX

Alex Polyakov
Vitaly Brusentsev

Copyright (c) 2005 by A-LIST, LLC

All rights reserved.

No part of this publication may be reproduced in any way, stored in a retrieval system of any type, or transmitted by any means or media, electronic or mechanical, including, but not limited to, photocopying, recording, or scanning, *without prior permission in writing* from the publisher.

A-LIST, LLC
295 East Swedesford Rd.
PMB #285
Wayne, PA 19087
702-977-5377 (FAX)
mail@alistpublishing.com
http://www.alistpublishing.com

This book is printed on acid-free paper.

All brand names and product names mentioned in this book are trademarks or service marks of their respective companies. Any omission or misuse (of any kind) of service marks or trademarks should not be regarded as intent to infringe on the property of others. The publisher recognizes and respects all marks used by companies, manufacturers, and developers as a means to distinguish their products.

Graphics Programming with GDI+ & DirectX
By Alex Polyakov and Vitaly Brusentsev

ISBN 1-931769-39-7

Printed in the United States of America

05 06 7 6 5 4 3 2 1

A-LIST, LLC, titles are available for site license or bulk purchase by institutions, user groups, corporations, etc.

Book Editor: Julie Laing

Contents

Introduction _____ 1
   The Book's Structure _____ 3
   Acknowledgments _____ 4
   Feedback _____ 4

PART I: MAIN CONCEPTS OF COMPUTER GRAPHICS AND OVERVIEW OF IMPLEMENTATION TOOLS _____ 5

Chapter 1: Programming Tools _____ 7
1.1. .NET Framework Environment _____ 8
   1.1.1. Common Language Runtime Environment _____ 9
   1.1.2. Metadata _____ 10
   1.1.3. .NET Framework Class Library _____ 13
   1.1.4. First Programs _____ 14
1.2. Introduction to GDI+ _____ 18
   1.2.1. What's New in GDI+? _____ 18
   1.2.2. Execution Environment Requirements _____ 20
   1.2.3. GDI+ Support for Windows 95 _____ 21
   1.2.4. Supported Development Technologies _____ 21
   1.2.5. GDI+ Class Hierarchy _____ 22
   1.2.6. Initialization and Termination _____ 24
1.3. Creating the First Application _____ 25
   1.3.1. Using GDI+ in WinAPI _____ 25
   1.3.2. Typical C++ Compiling and Linking Problems _____ 28
   1.3.3. Making Your Life Easier: Automatic Library Initialization Class ___ 30
   1.3.4. Example WinForms GDI+ Application _____ 33

PART II: VECTOR GRAPHICS PROGRAMMING — 35

Chapter 2: Using GDI+ To Construct Vector Images — 37
2.1. Graphics Objects — 37
   2.1.1. GDI Stateful Model — 38
   2.1.2. GDI+ Stateless Model — 39
   2.1.3. Used Brushes, Pens, Paints, and Other Garbage — 40
   2.1.4. Separating the Fill and Outline Methods — 42
   2.1.5. The Brush Family: A Set of Brushes to Anyone's Taste — 42
   2.1.6. The Pen is Mightier than the Sword — 45
2.2. Vector Primitives — 46
   2.2.1. GDI+ Clock Program — 47
   2.2.2. Splines — 51
   2.2.3. Bezier Curves — 54
2.3. Conclusion — 56

Chapter 3: Working with Output Devices and Using Metafiles — 57
3.1. Configuring an Output Device — 57
   3.1.1. Smoothing Rough Outlines — 58
   3.1.2. Transforming Coordinates in GDI+ — 59
   3.1.3. Regions and Paths — 63
3.2. Metafiles — 68
   3.2.1. Loading a Metafile — 69
   3.2.2. Playing Back a Metafile — 70
   3.2.3. Creating and Saving a New Metafile — 71
   3.2.4. Converting a Metafile into a Bitmap Image — 73
   3.2.5. Studying Metafile Commands — 73
   3.2.6. .NET-Specific Record Enumeration — 75

Chapter 4: Implementing 3D Transformations Using Software — 79
4.1. The Painter Program — 79
4.2. Creating a Class for Drawing 3D Shapes — 80
4.3. Drawing a 3D Surface — 91
   4.3.1. Constructing Level Lines on a Surface — 95
4.4. Notes — 104

PART III: BITMAP GRAPHICS _____ 107

Chapter 5: Operations with Bitmaps and Graphics Formats in GDI+ _____ 109
5.1. Basic Principles _____ 109
5.2. The Bitmap Class: A Container for Raster Images _____ 110
    5.2.1. Support for the Main Graphics Formats _____ 110
    5.2.2. Loading from Files and Streams (IStream) _____ 112
    5.2.3. Creating Bitmaps from Program Resources _____ 112
    5.2.4. More Complex Ways of Loading Images _____ 114
5.3. Graphics File Formats _____ 116
    5.3.1. Working with a Codec List _____ 116
    5.3.2. Saving Images _____ 118
5.4. Specific Capabilities of File Formats _____ 123
    5.4.1. Saving a GIF with Transparency _____ 123
    5.4.2. Loading and Saving Multiframe Files _____ 124
    5.4.3. Thumbnail Images _____ 125
    5.4.4. Working with Image Metadata _____ 128
5.5. Using Bitmaps When Working with Graphics Objects _____ 129
    5.5.1. Image Output and Geometric Transformations _____ 129
    5.5.2. Image Quality _____ 131
    5.5.3. Flicker Removal _____ 133
    5.5.4. Efficiency _____ 134
    5.5.5. Demonstration Applications _____ 137
5.6. Direct Work with Raster Data _____ 138
    5.6.1. The Color Class _____ 138
    5.6.2. Direct Pixel Access _____ 139
    5.6.3. Transparency Support _____ 141
    5.6.4. Raster Operations _____ 143

Chapter 6: Viewing and Editing Bitmap Images _____ 147
6.1. Creating an Application _____ 147
    6.1.1. The Document/View Architecture _____ 148
    6.1.2. Creating a Multidocument Application _____ 149
6.2. The Bitmap Class _____ 149
6.3. Attaching GDI+ and Modifying the Application Class _____ 150
6.4. Modifying the Document Class to Work with Images _____ 155
6.5. Using a Virtual Screen _____ 157

6.6. Modifying the View Class ... 158
6.7. Editing Images ... 168
    6.7.1. Image Brightness Histogram ... 170
    6.7.2. Software Procedure for Implementing Transformations
        and Graphics Filters ... 180
    6.7.3. Lookup Tables ... 187
    6.7.4. The Filter Class ... 188
    6.7.5. Using a Brightness Histogram and the Histogram Filter ... 195
    6.7.6. The Brightness/Contrast Filter ... 202
    6.7.7. The Color Inversion Filter ... 209
    6.7.8. The Emboss Filter ... 210
    6.7.9. The Blur Filter ... 212
    6.7.10. The Contour Filter ... 214
    6.7.11. The Sharpen Filter ... 216
    6.7.12. The Denoise Filter ... 218
    6.7.13. Using Filters ... 228
6.8. Printing Images ... 229
6.9. Saving Results ... 232
6.10. Conclusion ... 234

PART IV: USING THE DIRECTX 9 LIBRARY ... 235

Chapter 7: Using Direct3D Tools to Work with Graphics ... 237

7.1. Review of the DirectX 9.0 Library ... 237
7.2. The DirectX 9.0 SDK Package ... 238
7.3. The First Programs ... 241
    7.3.1. Writing the First Program in C++ ... 241
    7.3.2. Component Object Model: An Overview ... 252
    7.3.3. Managed DirectX and .NET Programming ... 257
7.4. Getting Started and Initializing Direct3D ... 262
    7.4.1. Initializing and Enumerating Graphics Devices Using C++ Tools ... 262
    7.4.2. Enumerating Devices and Video Modes for Managed Direct3D ... 264
    7.4.3. Initializing the Graphics Mode for C++ ... 266
    7.4.4. Initializing the Graphics Mode for C# ... 268
7.5. Removing Hidden Details ... 269
    7.5.1. The Visibility Pyramid ... 269
    7.5.2. The Z-Buffer ... 272
    7.5.3. Removing Back Faces ... 277
7.6. Conclusion ... 278

Chapter 8: Looking Closer at Direct3D — 279
8.1. Application of Geometric Transformations — 279
8.1.1. Direct3D Coordinate Transformation Matrices for C++ — 280
8.1.2. Transformation Matrices: The Managed DirectX Version — 283
8.1.3. Applying Transformations to the Output Device — 284
8.2. Working with Polygons — 284
8.2.1. Format of Vertices — 285
8.2.2. Creating and Filling a Vertex Buffer — 288
8.2.3. Outputting Primitives and Using the Index Buffer — 290
8.2.4. Using Mesh Objects — 294
8.3. Modeling Visual Effects — 296
8.3.1. Light Sources and Materials — 296
8.3.2. Fog Effects — 297
8.3.3. Applying Textures — 298
8.3.4. Sprites — 298
8.4. Shaders — 299
8.4.1. Vertex Shaders — 300
8.4.2. Pixel Shaders — 300
8.4.3. The Development Tools: Assembler and HLSL — 300
8.5. Conclusion — 303
8.5.1. Internet Resources — 303

APPENDIXES — 305

Appendix 1: Mathematical Fundamentals of Spline Construction — 307
A1.1. Definitions — 307
A1.2. Specifying Curves Parametrically — 310
A1.3. Spline Varieties — 311
A1.3.1. The Catmull-Rom Interpolation Spline — 311
A1.3.2. The Basic Beta-Spline — 312
A1.3.3. The Bezier Spline — 313

Appendix 2: Mathematical Fundamentals for Plane and 3D Transformations — 315
A2.1. Vectors — 315
A2.1.1. Vector Properties — 315

A2.1.2. The Vector Dot Product 317
A2.1.3. The Vector Cross Product 318
A2.2. Determinants 319
A2.2.1. Properties of Determinants 320
A2.3. Homogeneous Coordinates 322
A2.4. Using Homogeneous Coordinates 323
A2.5. Planar Transformations 324
A2.6. Matrix Notation for 2D Transformations 327
A2.7. Translation and Rotation in 3D Space 328
A2.8. Parallel Projection 330
A2.8.1. View Conversion 331
A2.8.2. Perspective Transformations 333
A2.9. Two Approaches to Removing Hidden Lines and Surfaces 334
A2.9.1. Algorithms for Culling Back Faces 335
A2.9.2. The Roberts Algorithm 335
A2.9.3. The Z-Buffer Algorithm 336
A2.9.4. Warnock's Algorithm 337
A2.9.5. The Line Scanning Algorithm 337

Appendix 3: General Information about Raster Graphics — 339
A3.1. Graphics Formats 339
A3.2. Graphics File Elements 341
A3.3. Format Conversion 342
A3.4. Pixels and Color 342
A3.5. Color Palettes 343
A3.6. Color and Color Models 344
A3.7. Data Compression 345
A3.8. Comparison of Popular Graphics Formats 346

References — 349
Internet Resources 351

CD Contents — 353

Index — 355

Introduction

Once upon a time, when computers went big...

This joke has been around for a couple of decades, but progress in computers is not showing any signs of abating. Computers are becoming more compact and powerful, and their software is becoming more complex.

Especially important is the evolution of the imaging capabilities of digital helpers. Scientists claim that the human visual system is topmost in the structural hierarchy of the human brain. We receive 70 to 90% of our information about the surrounding world visually.

It is no wonder, then, that computer graphics is constantly developing, based primarily on technological innovations. Judge for yourself: The main algorithms have remained practically unchanged over last decades; only their implementation and hardware support has been improved. Nevertheless, modern computer graphics does not cease to astonish us by its new, spectacular capabilities.

This book focuses on technologies. This means that it puts at your disposal information about the currently most advanced programming aids, such as the Visual Studio .NET 2003 development environment, GDI+, and DirectX 9.0.

GDI+ is a new generation library with significantly expanded capabilities that allow run-of-the-mill programmers to produce graphics of quality once obtainable only in products of the CorelDraw or Adobe Photoshop class. The following is a list of some benefits of the new library:

- *Support for popular graphics file formats*—A surprisingly pleasant innovation for all programmers dealing with different graphics formats. The BMP, GIF, TIFF, JPEG, Exif (TIFF and JPEG format for digital cameras), PNG, ICO, WMF, and EMF formats are supported. Decoders for individual formats are implemented with the format specifics taken into consideration; thus, you can, for example, display an animation GIF file or add a comment to a TIFF file. A loaded, created, or modified file can be saved to disk in a suitable format.

- *Bitmap operations*—Practically everything is possible now. Bitmaps can be drawn with an external alpha channel applied, and they can be scaled, stretched, sheared, and rotated. For all of these operations, individual pixel imaging modes can be specified, from simple translating to prefiltering (the best image quality). Texture-filled vector primitives can be drawn.
- *Gradient brushes*—This technology allows you to fill complex shapes with hues following different color distribution laws and to draw vector primitives (e.g., lines) that gradually change color.
- *Transparency support*—Transparent and semitransparent brushes and bitmaps can be created, regions can be filled with semitransparent colors, a color key can be assigned to a bitmap image, its alpha channel can be manipulated, and semitransparent vector primitives and text can be drawn.

The object-oriented interface and the new design of the graphics function objects make GDI+ easy and convenient to use.

DirectX is a program interface developed by Microsoft to enable convenient access to the multimedia and game capabilities of modern computers. If you are planning to write a captivating network game, a multimedia application, or a 3D graphics screensaver, you ought to start by considering the capabilities provided by DirectX.

This book considers the Graphics component of DirectX, which combines the capabilities of the DirectDraw and Direct3D graphics programming interfaces of the previous versions of DirectX.

The DirectX library is based on the COM architecture, which allows the easy modification of its components and the use of their versions for different programming languages. If you are not familiar with this technology, you can read introductory information about it in the DirectX materials.

The DirectX SDK installation package, which needs to be installed before you can use the library, contains header and library files, documentation, and numerous examples. It also contains wizards to help you create DirectX projects. But you will also learn how to create 3D images from scratch, without using the wizards.

Moreover, the DirectX 9 SDK contains the Managed interface that allows this library to be used in .NET applications. We give proper attention to this capability and provide Direct3D C# examples.

The Book's Structure

The presentation begins with a review of the new programming tools. In *Chapter 1*, you are introduced to the .NET Framework environment and the GDI+ library and learn how to create your first Visual C++ and Visual C# programs.

Chapters 2 and *3* consider in detail working with vector graphics using GDI+. In particular, the following subjects are considered: vector primitives and GDI+ geometry, graphics objects and their states, working with coordinates, regions and path, and using metafiles.

Chapter 4 describes how to construct vector images in 3D space. In this chapter, a program is developed that outputs to the screen an image of a 3D surface with level lines and allows this image to be viewed from different perspectives. The graphics output interface of this program uses MFC library classes, wrappers for Windows GDI functions. Modifying the program to use the GDI+ functions considered in the previous chapters will be a good exercise for you.

Chapter 5 is devoted to working with bitmap images using GDI+. It considers the `Bitmap` class, the support of the standard graphics formats, the bitmap screen output, and the creation of animation and special effects.

Chapter 6 considers creating and using graphics filters for correcting contrast and brightness, removing noise, determining image boundaries, and adding various effects to an image. A program is developed that allows various format bitmap images to be loaded, edited, and saved. An example illustrates using a multidocument interface, a multithread program operation method, and methods to directly access raster data of GDI+ objects.

Chapters 7 and *8* are devoted to DirectX 9.0. They describe using the capabilities of the DirectX Graphics and Direct3D components. The issues considered range from constructing objects using primitives to adding realistic special effects.

Mathematical principles for constructing splines, surface and 3D transformations, and general information about bitmap graphics are given separately in the appendixes.

Acknowledgments

Alex Polyakov:

I express my gratitude to my colleagues at Elecard for the creative and friendly atmosphere, for sharing their experience, and for overall support. Profound gratitude goes to my wife and son for their joy and happiness every day.

Vitaly Brusentsev:

I thank Pavel Bludov, my colleague in the RSDN.RU project, for the valuable comments regarding DirectX organization. I send my heartfelt thanks to my loved ones for the support and understanding they rendered me during my laboring on the book. I hope that now I will be able to devote more of my time to you.

Our joint thanks go to you, esteemed reader, for selecting our book from many other graphics books. We hope that it will be of good use to you in your work and study.

Feedback

Please send any questions, comments, requests, criticisms, or suggestions to **books@triaxes.com**. We will be glad to have you sharing your impressions about the book with us. Answers to FAQs will be published at the following address: **http://www.triaxes.com/books**.

PART I:
MAIN CONCEPTS OF COMPUTER GRAPHICS AND OVERVIEW OF IMPLEMENTATION TOOLS

Chapter 1: Programming Tools 7

Chapter 1: Programming Tools

In this chapter, the following subjects are considered:

- Fundamental concepts and function of the .NET Framework environment
- The Graphics Device Interface-plus (GDI+) library
- How to write your first programs in Visual C++ and Visual C#

Developers of graphics software are undoubtedly in the vanguard of the programmers' army. When a powerful processor or graphics video card is introduced, they try to obtain (and sometimes to develop) the newest versions of graphics tools packages and libraries that allow programmers to squeeze even more performance out of the desired megabytes and gigahertz.

In this chapter, we will introduce two such new technologies and you will learn the useful innovations they offer to programmers.

The *.NET Framework* platform was presented by Microsoft to general public in 2001. The debut of .NET and the rapid application development tools based on it can be considered a success. The C# (pronounced "see sharp") language, developed especially for the .NET environment, has become widely known. There are many sites and forums on the Internet devoted to C# programming and to helping programmers who work with the traditional environments such as Visual C++, Visual Basic, and Delphi migrate to this newer language.

The other innovation that undoubtedly has aroused the interest of graphics and multimedia programmers is the *GDI+ library*. It allows run-of-the-mill programmers to produce graphics of quality once obtainable only in products of the CorelDRAW or Adobe Photoshop class.

This chapter introduces these two technologies. We tried to make the material both easy enough to be understood by novice programmers and sufficiently challenging to keep experienced programmers interested.

The GDI+ library is the main graphics tool in the .NET environment; therefore, it will be easy to port demonstration examples that use GDI+, both C++ (for the Windows platform) and C# (for the .NET platform), to this environment.

For hands-on experimenting with these examples, it would be best to have the *Visual Studio 2003* package, which installs the Visual C++ 7.1 and C# 1.1 compilers on your machine. But this is not a prerequisite; the Visual C++ 6.0 compiler alone will do if you install additional software development kits (SDKs) described later in this chapter.

1.1. .NET Framework Environment

Developing complicated software complexes has always been a difficult task; doing this for the Internet and mobile technologies is even more so. In addition to putting algorithms and formulas into code, developers need to reuse previously written (possibly by others) code, to have access to diverse databases, and to interact with computer devices that may be located halfway around the world. Things are more difficult because the complexes being developed often contain separate software components written in different languages and are subject to ongoing modifications.

The .NET platform is an attempt by Microsoft to make solving these and related problems easier. Not a universal solution, it nevertheless has won developers' recognition as the most promising recent technological innovation in the programming area.

Moreover, the principles proclaimed by this environment are not new ones. To some extent, it has absorbed the best features of existing technologies, both rival ones (Java, EJB, CORBA, and Delphi) and those created by Microsoft itself (COM, ADO, etc.).

The Microsoft .NET Framework is presented as a new application development and execution environment with the Internet as its backbone. It makes information accessible from any device, relieving programmers from the need to tie themselves to specific hardware architecture (processor instruction set, machine word width, number of registers, etc.).

Software developed using the .NET Framework does not need the Internet to work. Nevertheless, this environment makes it easier to port existing desktop applications to a distributed environment, allowing software developers to concentrate purely on problem-solving tasks.

A brief overview of .NET platform components and features follows.

1.1.1. Common Language Runtime Environment

The heart of the .NET platform is its Common Language Runtime (CLR) environment. This is a collection of services stored in the mscoree.dll library that makes all of the environment's capabilities function. These capabilities include the following:

- Loading executable .NET modules (containing instructions coded in Microsoft intermediate language, or MSIL).
- Translating MSIL instructions into optimized machine code of the specific processor at the first launch, taking into account the platform's specifics.
- Checking the security of the executable instructions. .NET modules loaded from suspicious sources will not be able to gain access to the computer's vulnerable areas (e.g., the file system) without your prior agreement.
- Supporting managed code. *Managed code* is executed not by the operating system directly but by the CLR environment, which takes care of such code execution parameters as destruction of unused objects and proper method calls. It relieves the programmer of these tasks, so if, for example, some allocated dynamic memory has to be released, it will be done by the CLR's built-in garbage collector. The programmer will not need to remember to write a routine in the code to do this.
- Handling common (regardless of the programming language) program errors and exceptions.
- Allowing .NET modules to interact with the old-style, unmanaged code, particularly calling methods from dynamic link libraries (DLLs), and work with component object model (COM) objects.

One innovation is worth mentioning separately. Painstaking work was done during the .NET development to unify the data types and specificities of different languages under one execution system. As a result, *all* data types in .NET (even integer types and Boolean values) are classes derived from the common `System.Object` base class.

What does this mean in practical terms? First, an opportunity appears to develop code that can process input data of any type in the same way (e.g., mechanisms to save object states or to transfer objects over networks). Second, the interaction issues of different language components are resolved. A string for a Visual Basic.Net program means the same thing as a string for a C# program (and is represented identically in the memory[i]).

Moreover, the support for the CLR environment provides a previously unseen degree of interlanguage integration. For example, successor classes in C++ or Visual Basic.Net can be inherited from a base class created in C#. It gives a glimmer of hope that the wars that have been raging for decades among adherents of different programming languages will finally become things of the past.

Already numerous .NET development languages are supported. The *Visual Studio 7.1* distribution package includes compilers for C#, Visual Basic, C++, J#, and JScript as well as the MSIL assembler. Moreover, third parties are developing .NET compilers for other programming languages, including those widely used (Java, Smalltalk, Perl, Pascal, Cobol, and Fortran) and those less so (Python, Mercury, Oberon, and Eiffel). There are more than 20 languages on this list, and the number is growing rapidly.

As a separate note, it must be said that the importance of C++ language is not being depreciated by the .NET creators. The C++ compiler supplied with Visual Studio 7.1 is the only compiler capable of generating both x86 processor family machine code and MSIL instructions. Programmers can continue developing their Windows software and then port it to .NET by simply recompiling the source code.

To build GDI+ .NET examples, we selected C# because it is fairly easy to learn and popular: You will find plenty of instructional material on the Internet. To distinguish C++ source code listings (for the Windows platform) from C# listings (for the .NET platform), I indicate the language name in the listing headers.

1.1.2. Metadata

Writing even simple programs often involves more than just writing code and compiling it. Practically any programming environment requires you to specify supplementary, descriptive data to make the software being developed to function correctly.

---

[i] Programmers who have experience with C++ strings will understand the significance of this: this language alone has several incompatible classes supporting the string concept.

For example, for other programs to be able to use it, a C++ language DLL needs its entry points defined in a special definition (DEF) file. The COM technology also uses external data, in the form of the so-called type libraries, to describe interfaces and COM objects. As a result, the C++ programmer is forced to create the program itself (a collection of source files), create the supplementary data for it (files with the extensions DEF, IDL, RC, etc.), and ensure that they correspond.

Another typical problem is the necessity to constantly expand the list of supplementary information. Providing support for specific technologies (e.g., introducing nonstandard keywords of the `_export` type into the C++ language) does not solve the problem: tomorrow, a new concept may be described (e.g., a security level of the created class), for which there will be no keyword available.

Data describing other data (i.e., data about data) are customarily called *metadata*. Different programming technologies provide different levels of metadata support. For example, including the run-time type information mechanism in a C++ program allows the type of an object to be determined at run time. A Visual Basic program can use a COM object in a compiled OCX file because of the type library included in the same file.

The most impressive metadata support is implemented in the .NET Framework environment. Previously, only the compiler had access to complete information about the types, methods, variables, and similar data used in the program. Using this information, it built the machine code that operated not in types but in bytes, processor instructions, machine words, stack, and other low-level units. Now, each .NET environment program unit (*assembly*), in addition to the compiled MSIL code, includes metadata that describe it as a whole (*manifest*) and separately for each type it contains.

The programmer can easily reference any metadata using the *reflection* mechanism built into .NET (and into the programming languages supported by it). This mechanism provides huge capabilities; in particular, examining metadata allows a variable of any type—even of a compound class, consisting of many component fields—to be written to disk (e.g., in the eXtensible Markup Language, or XML, format) and then recreated (perhaps, on another computer). Such tools are available in .NET (*serialization* and *remoting*), and their operation is based on metadata.

Moreover, you are not limited to using only the existing collection of metadata. Using a language tool introduced in .NET, called *attributes*, new types of metadata can be created and analyzed by software in whatever way needed.

For example, assume that you are developing a component that represents all classes you have created (e.g., to build a class diagram). Suppose that you need to add to this diagram a capability to paint classes and methods different colors. You do not have to store this information separately from the code: it just needs to be embedded into the definition as attributes. To do this, the new `ColorAttribute` class, inherited from the `System.Attribute` class, is defined and all necessary program elements are marked (colored in this example) with the necessary attributes in square brackets.

A pseudocode fragment for such coloring is shown in Listing 1.1. It states in there that the color of the defined `MyClass` class is red and the color of its `MyMethod` method is blue.

Listing 1.1. Using attributes to expand class metadata [C#]

```
[Color("Red")]
class MyClass
{
   [Color("Blue")]
   public void MyMethod(int arg);
}
```

User attributes can be added to practically any program element (types, variables, methods, parameters, etc.); the extent of your imagination is the only limiting factor. Such auxiliary information allows methods to be differentiated by types of access and parameters to be specified for calling external libraries and passing objects across process boundaries—in short, metadata can be used in many ways.

Concluding the introduction to this vast subject, we give one example of metadata use directly connected to graphics programming.

The GDI+ library contains quite a few enumerations (sets of named constants) used to set parameters for some methods. In particular, as you will learn in *Chapter 3*, the `EmfPlusRecordType` enumeration comprises 253 items. What if you need to obtain an item's string name, which was assigned to it at compilation, from its numerical value? You will encounter this task when studying disk metafile commands.

In C++, you will have to add to your program a 253-element array containing, accordingly, names and values of each element of the enumeration.

In .NET, the solution to this problem is elementary because of the power of the reflection mechanism: Any element in any enumeration knows its string name. Calling the `Object.ToString()` method (as you should remember, in .NET all types are derived from the `System.Object` class) will return a string containing the element's name.

1.1.3. .NET Framework Class Library

Another attractive component of the .NET Framework environment is its rich collection of software components available for use by all programs written in all languages supported by the .NET environment, called the *.NET Framework Class Library*.

The library contains thousands of components forming complete subsystems (grouped for solving various problems). Even simply listing the namespaces of all of the library's classes would take too much space for this book. Because teaching you to work with all .NET components is not the purpose of this book, we will limit ourselves to giving only a partial (but impressive) list of the subsystems (their namespaces are shown in parentheses).

- *GDI+* (`System.Drawing` and `System.Imaging`)—The namespace you will most often encounter in this book. Implements the .NET GDI+ classes. Will be used in each C# program example.
- *Windows forms*, or *WinForms* (`System.Windows.Forms`)—Implements the graphical window interface. Comprises descriptions of windows (*forms*), visual components (*controls*), and hidden components. Will be also intensively used in the examples.
- *ASP.NET* (`System.Web`)—A system for creating web-applications using .NET and the Microsoft Internet Information Server. Allows programmers to create Internet versions of their desktop programs (because it is convenient to use and similar to windows forms).
- *Collections* (`System.Collections`)—Extensive sets of classes used for storing data sets (arrays, hash tables, and mixed collections) and performing typical operations on these data (searching, sorting, deleting, inserting, replacing, etc.).
- *Internet classes* (`System.Net`)—Components for working with the Internet protocols. Ready-made classes for using hypertext transfer and mail protocols as well as a collection of low-level classes for socket programming.
- *Text processing* (`System.Text`)—Various character data-processing tools, including those for text-encoding conversion and *regular expressions* (tools for narrowly defined text-processing tasks).
- *Reflection* (`System.Reflection`)—A rich collection of components for working with metadata. Contains tools not only for examining existing metadata but also for adding metadata to a program being executed (and even for modifying programs on the fly).

- *Security services* (`System.Security`)—.NET security classes. Include the access control tools and a collection of cryptographic classes for strong cryptography work.
- *ADO.NET* (`System.Data`)—Tools to access various data sources (including databases) and represent them in the XML form.
- *XML* (`System.Xml`)—Extensive means for processing XML. It can be said that XML is the library's native format and for working with it, this namespace contains dozens of auxiliary classes geared toward disassembling and creating XML files and toward saving (serializing) objects in XML format.

As previously noted, this list is far from complete. In these examples, we deal mostly with GDI+ components. To obtain reference information regarding other .NET classes, we strongly recommend that you read the Microsoft .NET Framework SDK documentation.

1.1.4. First Programs

The time has come to get a practical taste of the new development environment. For starters, you will write two simple programs in the new C# language. Of course, the Visual Studio 2003 environment is the most fitting for creating software for the .NET platform, but this is not a requirement. The only thing needed to build all C# examples in the book is the free .NET Framework SDK 1.1 package. It can be downloaded from the Microsoft Web site at this address:

http://www.microsoft.com/downloads/details.aspx?FamilyID=9b3a2ca6-3647-4070-9f41-a333c6b9181d&DisplayLang=en (108 MB).

Console Version of "Hello, World!"

Start with a trial version of a program everyone knows: "Hello, World!"

Open any text editor (the Notepad will be enough, but there is a decent freeware editor with a syntax highlighting feature for C#: SharpDevelop, http://www.icsharpcode.net/). Enter the text in Listing 1.2 into it.

Listing 1.2. A console program [C#]

```
using System;

class Hello
{
```

```
static void Main(string[] args)
{
  string name = "World";
  if(args.Length>0) name = args[0];
  Console.WriteLine("Hello, {0}!", name);
}
}
```

What does the first line mean? The `using` directive is similar to its C++ sister: It allows type names to be used from a namespace without explicitly specifying its name. In this case, the scope is specified to be the `System` namespace. Without using this directive, the statement `Console.WriteLine` would have to be written explicitly `System.Console.WriteLine` (because the `Console` class is defined in the `System` namespace).

Then the `Hello` class is defined, which contains all the code of the program. Recall that all data types in .NET inherit from the `System.Object` class (in the given case, the compiler declares inheritance implicitly).

Note that C# has no traditional functions; all code must be contained in class methods, which makes this language very similar to Java. Like in Java, the program entry point is customarily considered to be the static `Main` method of any class (although in Java this method is called `main`). This method can have a parameter: a string array. In such a case, the command line parameters of the launched program are passed to it. Note that arrays in C# are defined differently from those in C++: the square brackets immediately follow the type name and not the variable name.

In the body of the `Main` method, the parameters are analyzed and either the string `"Hello, World!"` or a greeting to the name specified in the command line is output to the console. In short, for C++ programmers, this portion of the code will be no mystery.

Compile this example. Save the file under the test.cs name. In the Visual Studio environment (or in SharpDevelop), select the compilation command in the menu. To compile from the command line, the following steps must be done:

1. Make sure that the folder with the .NET Framework executable files is on the executable files path list (the PATH variable). For example, it can look like this: C:\winnt\microsoft.net\framework\v1.1.4322\. If a Windows 9*x* operating system is used for the development, the needed path can be set in the autoexec.bat file. If an NT family operating system is used, the environment variables need to be set (right-click **My Computer**, select the menu item **Properties**,

and in the **Advanced** tab of the **System Properties** dialog window, press the **Environment Variables** button).
2. Execute the following command line:
   ```
   csc test.cs
   ```

Here, `csc` is the name of the C# compiler executable file and `test.cs` is the name of the source code file.

If no mistakes were made entering the code, the source file will compile without errors and a test.exe file of about 3 KB will be written to the disk. Try to execute it with a parameter. Enter the following:

```
>test Programmer
```

The program should reply with the following line:

```
Hello, Programmer!
```

Well, you can now consider yourself introduced to the .NET environment.

Using WinForms

The second program will be more illustrative: to create it, you will use the WinForms library. This library is the main tool for creating a window interface in .NET.

First, note that the main principle remains the same: at least one class with the static `Main` method needs to be created. In addition, an object of a class derived from the `System.Windows.Forms.Form` class needs to be created for the main window (or form). To keep the matters simple, we combined these two classes into one in Listing 1.3.

Listing 1.3. A program using WinForms [C#]

```
using System.Drawing;
using System.Windows.Forms;

class FirstForm: Form
{
  Label label;

  public static void Main()
  {
    FirstForm form = new FirstForm();
```

```
    form.ShowDialog();
}

public FirstForm()
{
  Text = "First form";
  Height = 100;

  label = new Label();
  label.AutoSize = TRUE;
  label.Text = "Example for WinForms";
  label.Location = new Point(3, 3);
  label.Font = new Font("Arial", 16);
  Controls.Add(label);
}
}
```

Because the static method Main is the program's entry point, when it starts executing no FirstForm object exists (accordingly, there is no form on the screen). Therefore, a new form object must be created in this method and output to the screen using the ShowDialog method.

In the constructor of the newly-created object, its parameters are set (the Text and Height properties) and the single child element is created (the Label string label).

As you can see, although the example is compact, it can create a full-fledged form. Try to compile and execute it on your own. You should get a window similar to the one shown in Fig. 1.1.

The only thing that could slightly discomfit C++ programmers is that the method of working with the dynamic memory is unfamiliar. There are no pointers in the conventional meaning of this term, and the new operator is used without subsequent memory release.

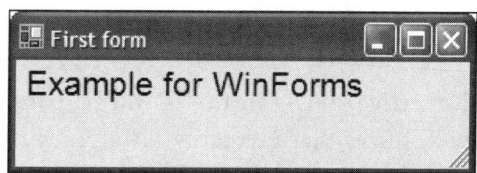

Fig. 1.1. WinForms program window

Welcome to the managed-code world! All C# classes are of the reference type, and ensuring their release is the responsibility of the .NET's built-in garbage collector. This subject will not be treated in detail in this book, so just rely on the execution environment to clean up after your program.

This concludes the brief introduction to the .NET Framework environment. The provided information is sufficient for understanding the .NET program examples presented in this book. If you are interested in learning more about this (undoubtedly promising) platform, we recommend that you start by studying the documentation supplied with the .NET Framework SDK.

But now, move on to the second subject of this chapter: the GDI+ library.

1.2. Introduction to GDI+

Another popular innovation from Microsoft is the GDI+ technology. This technology (rather, the new graphical interface based on it) is the face of the Microsoft new operating systems: Windows XP and Windows Server 2003.

So what is GDI+? The official documentation modestly calls it a class-based Application Program Interface (API). It is often called a library or a class library. In reality, the collection of classes made available by GDI+ is a thin shell over a multitude of usual functions implemented in one dynamic library, *gdiplus.dll* (about 1.5 MB). Keeping all this in mind, in general, we will simply call GDI+ a library.

So, GDI+ is a library called upon to replace the almost two-decades-old GDI, the graphics core of the previous Windows versions. It combines (or at least is intended to combine) all advantages of its predecessor with many new, powerful capabilities. Moreover, the least-painful application migration to 64-bit platforms was one of the starting goals of its development. Consequently, even though the existing GDI applications will execute under newer Windows operating systems, using GDI+ should be considered for new projects.

1.2.1. What's New in GDI+?

The specific (and effective) GDI+ features will be considered later on. For now, only the main new features that favorably distinguish this library from its predecessor will be described.

The advantages of the C++ implementation are the following:

- *Object-oriented interface*—Support of C++ compiler provides "free" control over types and over object lifetimes.
- *Transparent memory management*—GDI+ core objects are created in the heap using the library's own memory manager invisible to the programmer.
- *Using function name overloading*—Same-purpose functions differ only in their parameters.
- *Dedicated namespace*—All GDI+ types are defined in the `Gdiplus` namespace, which allows meaningful type names (`Rect`, `Pen`, `Matrix`, etc.) to be used without conflicts with other libraries.
- *Operator overloading*—This makes the handy + and − operations available to such types as `Point` and `Size`.

The library's architectural novelties are the following:

- *Hardware abstraction*—As already noted, this makes porting to 64-bit platforms easier.
- *New design of graphics function-objects*—Now you do not have to worry about deleting a brush while it is still selected in the context, a blunder typical for GDI!
- *Fill and draw methods are separated*—This provides greater drawing flexibility: For example, open shapes can be filled.
- *Enhanced support of paths and their interactions with regions*—Now paths are full-fledged objects that do not belong to the device context, as they did in GDI, and that can be easily transformed into regions.

New technologies and capabilities (hold your breath) include the following:

- *Gradient brushes*—This technology allows you to fill complex shapes with hues following different color distribution laws and drawing vector primitives (e.g., lines) that gradually change colors.
- *Transparency support*—Transparent and semitransparent brushes and bitmaps can be created, regions can be filled with semitransparent colors, a color key can be assigned to a bitmap image, its alpha channel can be manipulated, and semitransparent vector primitives and text can be drawn.
- *Enhanced imaging modes*—These allow a significantly improved perception of images by antialiasing and prefiltering (interpolation) of bitmap images.
- *Splines*—In addition to Bezier curves, which are already supported by GDI, new types of curves are supported—so-called splines—that imitate behavior of a bent taut steel strip. Splines are smooth curves.

- *Paths*—As previously mentioned, paths are now independent of the drawing context and are powerful tools for creating complex vector objects. Moreover, a capability to flatten paths has been introduced (i.e., to convert them into sequences of straight lines).
- *Coordinate transformations*—The `Matrix` object provides the capability of performing rotate, translation, scale, and reflection operations on GDI+ objects.
- *Regions*—Unlike in GDI, where regions are stored in device coordinates, regions in GDI+ are stored in world coordinates, which allows regions to undergo any transformation.
- *Bitmap operations*—Practically everything is possible now! Bitmaps can be drawn with an external alpha channel applied and can be scaled, stretched, sheared, and rotated. For all of these operations, individual pixel imaging modes can be specified, from simple translation to prefiltering (the best image quality). Texture-filled vector primitives can be drawn.
- Support for popular graphics file formats—A surprisingly pleasant innovation for all programmers dealing with different graphics formats. The BMP, GIF, TIFF, JPEG, Exif (TIFF and JPEG format for digital cameras), PNG, ICO, WMF, and EMF formats are supported. Decoders for individual formats are implemented with the format specifics taken into consideration; thus, you can, for example, display an animation Graphics Interchange Format (GIF) file or add a comment to a TIFF file. A loaded, created, or modified file can be saved to disk in a suitable format. A capability for creating custom decoders is also declared (but not implemented so far).
- *EMF+ format*—Of course, all of these riches could not fit into the tight confines of the old enhanced metafile. To define the new capabilities, a new metafile format was created: EMF+, which allows a sequence of graphics commands to be saved to disk then executed. A capability exists to write a dual metafile, readable by old GDI programs. New programs will read GDI+ information from such a file. Metafiles will be dealt with in more detail in *Chapter 3*.

1.2.2. Execution Environment Requirements

GDI+ support is built directly into the Windows XP and Windows Server 2003 operating systems. For applications using this library to execute under the previous Windows versions, the *gdiplus_dnld.exe* distribution package, about 1 MB, must be installed. It can be found on the Microsoft Web site at the following address:

http://www.microsoft.com/downloads/details.aspx?displaylang=en&FamilyID=BFC0B436-9015-43E2-81A3-54938B6F4614

It includes only the installation instructions and the previously mentioned gdiplus.dll, which must be copied into the system folder of the Windows 98, Windows Millennium Edition (ME), Windows NT SP6, or Windows 2000 operating systems. This library, however, will not make available the capabilities provided directly by the Windows XP kernel (in particular, the ClearType technology for quality font displays on liquid crystal display monitors).

Installing the .NET Framework environment or the Visual Studio.Net package on your system will also automatically install the GDI+ library.

1.2.3. GDI+ Support for Windows 95

As far as the technical aspects are concerned, experiments have shown that it is possible to install gdiplus.dll on Windows 95 systems and that GDI+ applications execute on such systems (i.e., with the library installed) without noticeable problems.

From the legal point of view, however, doing this is prohibited. Microsoft strictly states in the distribution package license agreement that this library can be installed only on the following operating systems: Windows 2000, Windows ME, Windows NT 4.0, and Windows 98. As previously noted, Windows XP has its own version of GDI+ included.

Why this restriction? Perhaps it is because a corporation from Redmond (WA) has ceased to support Windows 95 (see **http://www.microsoft.com/windows/lifecycleconsumer.asp**).

1.2.4. Supported Development Technologies

We will consider GDI+ interfaces implemented for WinAPI and for the CLR system, which is included in the Microsoft .NET Framework. Interfaces for other development environments (e.g., Delphi) have been created by devotees, but we will not describe those.

As you will remember, GDI+ (rather, its shell for CLR) is the main graphics tool in the .NET environment. However, it has substantial differences from the C++ implementation (not only architectural but also cosmetic ones, e.g., different names of some classes). We will be pointing them out as it becomes necessary.

What should you do if you do not have the latest Visual Studio version?

A collection of header files and the gdiplus.lib import library necessary for building C++ demonstration applications are included in the latest platform SDK package. If you have not yet updated the 1998 vintage platform SDK supplied with

Visual Studio 6.0, you can download it from the Microsoft Web site at the following address: **http://www.microsoft.com/msdownload/platformsdk/sdkupdate/**.

This package can be downloaded as a collection of installation files totaling 342 MB. At the time this material was written, the February 2003 platform SDK was available for download from the Microsoft Web site.

The demonstration examples for Windows will be written using mostly Windows API, which will allow you to concentrate on using GDI+. But you will have no problems linking this library to your Microsoft foundation classes (MFC) or Windows template library applications. Corresponding examples for the .NET platform will be written in C# for WinForms.

1.2.5. GDI+ Class Hierarchy

A typical C++ programmer's workplace, as a rule, includes a wall, on which proudly hangs in its entire splendor a class diagram (it makes no difference of what classes). Now, it will have to share that place with another diagram.

The hierarchy of the GDI+ classes is given in Fig. 1.2. To keep things manageable, 8 data structures and about 50 enumerations have been left out.

A first look at the diagram reveals that it bears a great resemblance, for example, to the part of the MFC library responsible for drawing but that it has many more classes: 40 versus 15 in MFC. This similarity should not be surprising because both of these libraries were developed by the same company. The main differences reflect the new capabilities introduced in GDI+. We will consider them in detail in subsequent chapters.

As can be seen, most objects have the `GdiPlusBase` class as their root base class. You will not need to create instances of this class because it contains only the memory management tools (the `new/new[]` and `delete/delete[]` operators, which use the GDI+ `GdipAlloc` and `GdipFree` functions, are overloaded for this class). All classes encapsulating operations with the GDI+ resources inherit from the `GdiPlusBase` class. This does not mean that their instances could not be created on the stack; on the contrary, this way their lifetimes would be even easier to control. But this type of inheritance architecture makes it possible, for example, to pass a pointer to a created GDI+ object to a module written using different development tools and to safely delete the object in this module. Moreover, this theoretically allows garbage collection to be organized for the objects chosen in this way, just as it is done in .NET.

Chapter 1: Programming Tools 23

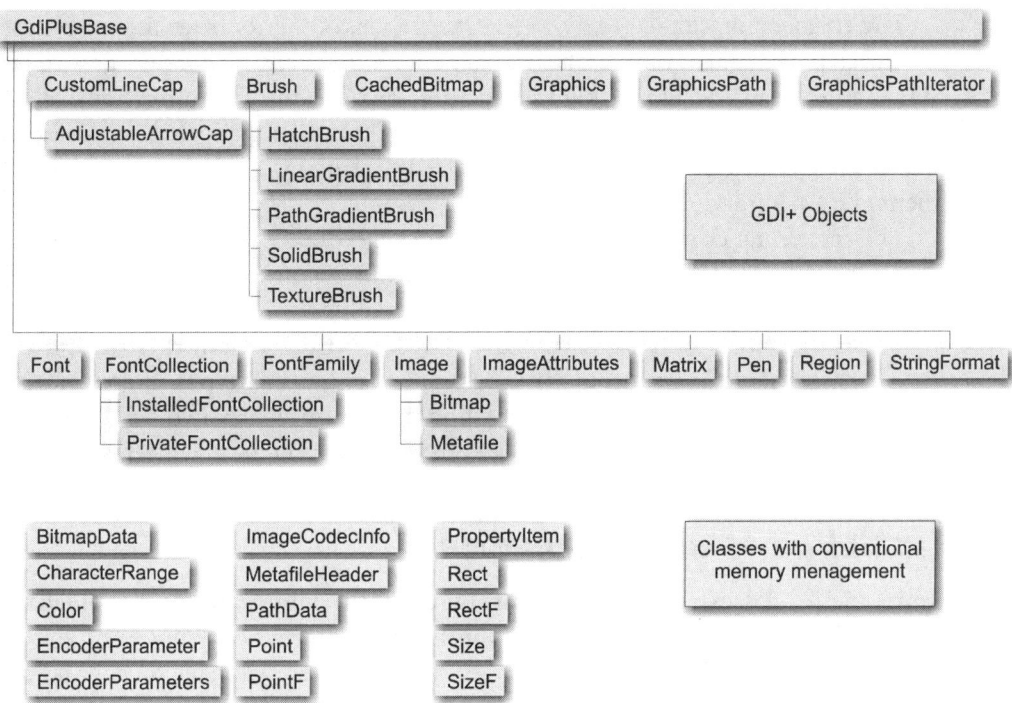

Fig. 1.2. GDI+ class hierarchy

 **NOTE** Do not confuse memory allocation management for instances of C++ wrapper classes, which is performed by the overloaded new/delete operators, with GDI+ resources management, which is hidden from developers deep in the innards of the corresponding functions (e.g., GdipCreateSolidFill).

The key class in GDI+ is the Graphics class (here, J++ programmers may give a start remembering the same name for a Microsoft Java virtual machine class). This class has almost 200 methods for drawing, clipping, and setting the output device parameters. A manifest analogy with the GDI device context suggests itself; indeed, these two concepts are closely connected. Out of the four Graphics constructors, two create this class from the handle to the device context (HDC). The main difference is the changed program model: now you do not work with the HDC but call the class methods. MFC programmers are familiar with this concept.

The further inheritance (e.g., `TextureBrush` class inherits from `Brush`) reflects the developers' goals (hiding the implementation details and reusing wrapper code) rather than the library's infrastructure, because the inline methods of the relative classes contain simple calls to various gdiplus.dll functions. You could say that Microsoft has projected the regular, flat C language API onto the object-oriented C++ library once again.

The remaining classes do not have a common parent and are intended to simplify work with the GDI+ data structures. You will become acquainted with them when we describe the bitmap and vector graphics tools.

The C++ implementation is not used in the .NET Framework environment, and all classes serve as wrappers for the low-level gdiplus.dll types. It appears that some differences in the class and method names in these two environments (e.g., `Rect` in C++ and `Rectangle` in .NET) have something to do with this.

1.2.6. Initialization and Termination

Before GDI+ classes and functions can be used, the library has to be initialized. In the .NET Framework environment, this is done automatically upon the start of a WinForms application; WinAPI programmers, however, will have to labor a little. For this, a call to the `GdiplusStartup` function must be placed somewhere in the beginning of the program:

```
Status GdiplusStartup( ULONG_PTR* token,
    const GdiplusStartupInput* input,
    GdiplusStartupOutput* output );
```

The fields of the `GdiplusStartupInput` structure control various aspects of the initialization; in particular, a function can be specified to be called on errors or to intercept all calls to GDI+ functions. We will not be considering these details in this book. Fortunately, the default constructor of the `GdiplusStartupInput` function performs initialization sufficient for most cases. The `output` parameter in this case can be specified as NULL.

The "magic number" pointed to by the output parameter `token` must be saved.

To finish working with the library, the `GdiplusShutdown` function is called as follows:

```
VOID GdiplusShutdown( ULONG_PTR token );
```

Here, the number returned by the `GdiplusStartup` function in its `token` parameter must be passed as the function's parameter.

NOTE The `GdiplusStartup` and `GdiplusShudown` functions can be called from different threads, but it must be ascertained that no references to GDI+ objects are made outside of these functions. In particular, be careful when declaring global instances of classes because their destructors are executed after `WinMain`. Moreover, as usual, initialization and cleanup functions cannot be called from `DllMain` because this may cause entrance to an endless loop or other unpleasantness.

1.3. Creating the First Application

But enough of dry theory! The time has come to put all this knowledge to practical use. For this, create two simple windows programs that do the same thing: Load an image from a GIF file, output it in a window as the background, then output a text line in a specified font and color gradation over this background. The first program will be written in C++ and the second in C#.

1.3.1. Using GDI+ in WinAPI

Launch Visual Studio and create a new Win32 application. Select the **A typical "Hello, World!" application** and press the **Finish** button. The obtained application will have to be prepared so that it can use GDI+. For this, in the stdafx.h file, after the following comment lines:

```
// TODO: Reference additional headers
// your program requires here
```

add the following code lines:

```
#include <gdiplus.h>
using namespace Gdiplus;
```

This will allow you to dispense with specifying the `Gdiplus::` prefix when using any of the library's names. As previously mentioned, all are located in the `Gdiplus` namespace.

At the end of the stdafx.cpp file, add the following line:

```
#pragma comment(lib, "gdiplus.lib")
```

In addition, in the stdafs.h file, the following line needs to be deleted or commented out:

```
#define WIN32_LEAN_AND_MEAN // Exclude rarely-used stuff
// From Windows headers
```

Otherwise, the compiler will issue a great deal of error messages about missing symbols: `MIDL_INTERFACE`, `PROPID`, `IStream`, etc.

If the resulting application source code builds without errors, you have done everything right and can move on.

In the generated main CPP file of your project, find the `WinMain` function and add the following initialization code at its beginning:

```
GdiplusStartupInput gdiplusStartupInput;
ULONG_PTR gdiplusToken;
GdiplusStartup(&gdiplusToken, &gdiplusStartupInput, NULL);
```

At its end, before the `return` statement, add the following cleanup code:

```
GdiplusShutdown(gdiplusToken);
```

Done. Finally you can draw something! In the body of the `WndProc` function, find the handler of the `WM_PAINT` message and replace it with the code in Listing 1.4.

Listing 1.4. Source code of the `WM_PAINT` window message handler [C++]

```
case WM_PAINT:
{
    RECT rc;
    GetClientRect(hWnd, &rc);
    hdc = BeginPaint(hWnd, &ps);
    // Calling the draw function
    OnPaint(hdc, rc);
    EndPaint(hWnd, &ps);
    break;
}
```

Now, somewhere before the `WndProc` function, create an `OnPaint` function containing the drawing code in Listing 1.5.

Listing 1.5. Drawing function [C++]

```
void OnPaint(HDC hdc, const RECT& rc)
{
    // All strings are in Unicode.
    WCHAR welcome[]=L"Welcome, GDI+ !";

    // Creating the drawing context and setting
```

```
    // the pixel coordinate system
    Graphics g(hdc);
    g.SetPageUnit(UnitPixel);
    RectF bounds(0, 0, float(rc.right), float(rc.bottom));

    // Loading the background image
    // and stretching it over the entire window
    Image bg(L"backgrnd.gif");
    g.DrawImage(&bg, bounds);

    // Creating a semitransparent brush
    // with a gradient over the entire window
    LinearGradientBrush brush(bounds,
        Color(130, 255, 0, 0), Color(255, 0, 0, 255),
        LinearGradientModeBackwardDiagonal);

    // Preparing font format and parameters
    StringFormat format;
    format.SetAlignment(StringAlignmentCenter);
    format.SetLineAlignment(StringAlignmentCenter);
    Font font(L"Arial", 48, FontStyleBold);

    // Outputting the greeting text; length -1 means
    // that the string ends in zero.
    g.DrawString(welcome, -1, &font, bounds, &format, &brush);
}
```

Fig. 1.3. Results of the program execution

The results of your labors should look like the image in Fig. 1.3.

NOTE

The presented example is intended only for familiarization purposes. In a real application, to draw a bitmap, it does not have to be loaded from a disk file.

The created program prototype will be used to create further demonstration applications. Only the pertinent code fragments will be given in the drawing examples. The full source code texts can be found on the accompanying CD-ROM.

1.3.2. Typical C++ Compiling and Linking Problems

In this section, we point out a few hidden dangers that can cause confusion when trying to compile and link a GDI+ project for the first time. Mostly, only problems encountered by the beginners (and constantly discussed in various forums) are dealt with.

Where Do I Obtain gdiplus.h?

As already mentioned, all header files, the import library, and its documentation are included in the latest platform SDK. They are not included in Visual C++ 6.0, Visual Studio 7.0, or their service packs. The fortunate owners of Visual Studio 2003 do not have to download anything: the header files are included in the distribution package of this development environment.

What Are These Strange Type Names?

Many novices are confused by the parameter types used in GDI+: `INT`, `REAL`, `ULONG_PTR`, etc. These are just synonyms of the types more familiar to C++ programmers: `int`, `float`, and `unsigned long`. Nevertheless, these synonyms are recommended: using them will make the source code of your programs more compatible with other companies' compilers and will help you port them to 64-bit platforms.

Why Do I Get the ULONG_PTR Type Error?

It looks like the compiler finds the old basetsd.h header file, for example, from the Visual C++ 6.0 package. Change the header file search paths so that it finds header files of the new platform SDK first.

Why Won't the Compiler Create a GDI+ Object Using new?

This behavior is possible when trying to compile an MFC application using GDI+ in the debug configuration.

Probably, the following code fragment is at the beginning of the program file:

```
#ifdef _DEBUG
#define new DEBUG_NEW
#undef THIS_FILE
static char THIS_FILE[] = __FILE__;
#endif
```

This code fragment overrides the standard memory distributor `new` and does not allow the `operator new` statement defined in the GDI+ header files to be used.

To solve this problem, you can either dispense with creating GDI+ objects using the `new` statement or dispense with performing dynamic memory checks in this file (by deleting the `#define` directive).

NOTE

An article on this subject was published on the Microsoft Web site in Knowledge Base—Q317799 PRB: Microsoft Foundation Classes DEBUG_NEW Does Not Work with GDI+ (http://support.microsoft.com/default.aspx?scid=kb;en-us;Q317799).

Don't Forget about the Gdiplus Namespace and Import Library

In the presented code examples, simple class names such as `Brush` or `Rect` are used. This is possible because the `using namespace Gdiplus;` directive was placed at the beginning of the header file.

If this solution cannot be used (e.g., there already are classes with such names in the project), then class names must be preceded with namespace prefixes, e.g., **Gdiplus**::Rect rect;.

Also, if for some reason the `#pragma comment(lib, "gdiplus.lib")` directive cannot be used, the gdiplus.lib import library must be explicitly specified in the linker options.

1.3.3. Making Your Life Easier: Automatic Library Initialization Class

All cited Microsoft Developer Network (MSDN) examples are geared toward static linking of the gdiplus.lib import library. In the course of GDI+ use, a rather interesting question has arisen: What if the system, on which a GDI+ application has been launched, does not support GDI+? How can you avoid a system error message and continue your work using GDI?

Usually, in such cases the programmer loads the necessary DLL using the `LoadLibrary` function and, if successful, obtains addresses of the needed functions using the `GetProcAddress` procedure. But here, this method cannot be used: Unlike most import libraries, the GDI+ innards are hidden behind the structure of the wrapper classes.

In this situation, you can get help from the relatively little-known Visual C++ capability for *delayed loading* of DLLs. When this linker option is used, the linker generates special pseudocode in place of each imported function. The application starts much faster, and library loading is delayed until the first call to any of the imported functions. Detailed information about this technique can be found in the December 1998 issue of the *Microsoft System Journal* (now *MSDN Magazine*) in two articles: *"Under the Hood"* by Matt Pietrek and *"Q&A Win32"* by Jeffrey Richter.

Here, we will only say that to use the delayed load linker option, the delayimp.lib library must be included in the project and the dynamic library must be linked with the `/delayload:module_name` linker switch (`module_name` is the name of the library).

The details of DLL use and GDI+ initialization can be hidden by placing the necessary code into methods of some class (e.g., `InitGdiPlus` in Listing 1.6). This will make the life of the programmer substantially easier: to initialize the graphics subsystem, only one instance of this class will need to be defined in the program.

Listing 1.6. Defining the `RSDN::InitGdiPlus` class [C++]

```
// initgdiplus.h
namespace RSDN
{
  class InitGdiPlus
  {
   public:
    InitGdiPlus();
    virtual ~InitGdiPlus();
```

Chapter 1: Programming Tools   31

```
// Was the initialization successful?
    bool Good(){ return present; }
  private:
    bool present;
    ULONG_PTR token;
  };
}
```

When examining the implementation of this class, some information must be taken into account.

First, an attempt to use any gdiplus.dll function in a system that does not have this library installed generates a structured exception. The class must handle this exception and inform the programmer about the failure. In the given case, we added a `Good()` method to the class to indicate success or failure of the GDI+ initialization.

Second, at least one development environment, Visual Studio 6.0 SP4/SP5, has a bug causing the linker to crash when linking the delayed load and debug modules. Therefore, the delayed loading of the debug class version will not execute (it makes no difference because for the debug version, GDI+ is installed on the system anyway).

Third, it is desirable to make class use simple to the maximum and keep the implementation details internal (in particular, it would be sensible to specify linker options as the `#pragma comment` directive, as shown in Listing 1.7).

NOTE

Unfortunately, the Visual C++ 7.1 compiler perceives the `#pragma` directive with the `/delayload` option specified as an error and issues a corresponding warning. Visual C++ 7.1 users will have to specify this option either in the compiler command line or in the project properties.

Listing 1.7. Implementing the `RSDN::InitGdiPlus` class [C++]

```
// initgdiplus.cpp
#define STRICT
#include <windows.h>
#include <gdiplus.h>
#include "initgdiplus.h"
```

```
#pragma comment(lib, "gdiplus.lib")

#ifndef _DEBUG
#pragma comment(lib, "delayimp.lib")
#pragma comment(linker, "/delayload:gdiplus.dll")
#endif

namespace RSDN
{
  InitGdiPlus::InitGdiPlus()
  {
    present = TRUE;
    Gdiplus::GdiplusStartupInput input;
    __try
    {
      Gdiplus::GdiplusStartup(&token, &input, 0);
    }
    __except(1)
    {
      present = FALSE;
    }
  }

  InitGdiPlus::~InitGdiPlus()
  {
    if(present) Gdiplus::GdiplusShutdown(token);
  }
}
```

Consequently, this class singly initializes and cleans up GDI+ and handles structured exceptions arising when the gdiplus.dll library is missing. Declaring an instance of this class is sufficient to initialize the library. Just don't forget that its lifetime must be longer than the lifetimes of the GDI+ objects created in your program; otherwise, their destructors will be executed after the GdiplusShutdown call.

NOTE

The DelayLoadDllExceptionFilter function described in the previously mentioned article by Richter can be employed for more detailed analyses of the exception arising in the constructor of the class.

1.3.4. Example WinForms GDI+ Application

To have an opportunity to compare the GDI+ implementation just considered with the one used in .NET, consider the complete source code of a corresponding application in C#.

For those new to the .NET world, the following circumstance will be of interest: Work with windowed Windows messages is completely hidden by the WinForms library. Instead of the programmer handling the message cycle, messaging is based on the paradigm of *events* (callback mechanism) and *delegates* (reactions to events, similar to the function pointers in C++).

As a rule, to draw in a WinForms window (or in a control element), a subscription to the `Paint` event must be made, as shown in Listing 1.8. To keep the matters simple, we took advantage of this event's generation in the body of the form's `OnPaint` virtual method and overrode it using the `override` keyword. For this chain of events to function correctly, the original `OnPaint` method must be called.

Listing 1.8. Source code for the WinForms program [C++]

```
using System;
using System.Drawing;
using System.Drawing.Drawing2D;
using System.Windows.Forms;

// Form class
public class GraphicsForm: Form
{
    // Execution starts from here.
    public static int Main()
    {
        Form fm = new GraphicsForm();
        fm.ShowDialog();
        return 0;
    }

    // Overriding the virtual paint method
    protected override void OnPaint(PaintEventArgs a)
    {
        DoPaint(a.Graphics, a.ClipRectangle);
        // Calling the inherited method (important!)
        base.OnPaint(a);
```

```
    }

    // Function with the painting code
    protected void DoPaint(Graphics g, Rectangle clipBox)
    {
        RectangleF bounds = clipBox;
        string welcome = "Welcome, GDI+ !";
        Bitmap bg = new Bitmap("backgrnd.gif");
        g.DrawImage(bg, bounds);
        LinearGradientBrush brush =
            new LinearGradientBrush(bounds,
                Color.FromArgb(130, 255, 0, 0),
                Color.FromArgb(255, 0, 0, 255),
                LinearGradientMode.BackwardDiagonal);
        StringFormat format = new StringFormat();
        format.Alignment = StringAlignment.Center;
        format.LineAlignment = StringAlignment.Center;
        Font font = new Font("Arial", 48, FontStyle.Bold);
        g.DrawString(welcome, font, brush, bounds, format);
    }
}
```

As you can see, principal differences exist in addition to the purely syntactic ones, for example, using properties in the CLR model as opposed to using Set methods in C++. Moreover, namespaces are actively used in .NET.

NOTE

The *full listing* of the program analogous in its capabilities to the one created in Listing 1.7 is given here. Compare the sizes of the source codes of these two examples (available on the accompanying CD-ROM). As can be seen, the .NET environment takes most of the routine work for creating a window class and handling window messages.

If you launch the presented example for execution, you will see that the text is drawn without the antialiasing characteristics of the previous example. This is because WinForms by default disables the enhanced font drawing mode because there already are enough performance-degrading factors. In *Chapter 3,* you will learn how antialiasing modes are managed.

Now, you have been introduced to the GDI+ library and have learned how to use it in your .NET and Windows API programs.

In *Chapter 2,* you will consider the extensive capabilities made available by GDI+ for vector image operations.

PART II:
VECTOR GRAPHICS PROGRAMMING

Chapter 2: Using GDI+ To Construct Vector Images 37

Chapter 3: Working with Output Devices and Using Metafiles 57

Chapter 4: Implementing 3D Transformations Using Software 79

Chapter 2: Using GDI+ To Construct Vector Images

This chapter is devoted to the following topics:

- Working with graphics objects
- Outputting vector primitives
- Outputting splines

2.1. Graphics Objects

To output *primitives* (the lowest-level computer graphics components that output devices can understand), certain parameters usually must be specified. For example, to draw curves, the color and width of the lines (*pen,* in the parlance) must be specified. When filling solid shapes, the brush parameters need to be indicated (a solid color, an image, a gradient color, etc.). Outputting text may require creating a font of a certain size and outline.

As a rule, various software graphics interfaces store such settings as their own data structures: *graphics objects.* Although this holds true for both GDI and GDI+, the ways, in which graphics objects are used, in each environment are different. We will consider these differences using a simple problem as an example: drawing a square.

2.1.1. GDI Stateful Model

GDI uses a programming model called the *stateful model*. The main principle of this model is that it saves the entered settings for the output device and has a notion of the current selected object. Before primitives are output, the necessary graphics object must be selected for the output device (using the `SelectObject` function). Having made such a setting—for example, setting the line width to three pixels—several segments that have this setting can be output (Listing 2.1).

Listing 2.1. Creating and using a graphics object in GDI [C++]

```
void OnPaint(HDC hDc)
{
  HPEN hPen = CreatePen(PS_SOLID, 3, RGB(0, 0, 128));
  HGDIOBJ hOldPen = SelectObject(hDc, hPen);
  MoveToEx(hDc, 10, 10, 0);
  LineTo(hDc, 10, 100);
  LineTo(hDc, 100, 100);
  LineTo(hDc, 100, 10);
  LineTo(hDc, 10, 10);
  SelectObject(hDc, hOldPen);
  DeleteObject(hPen);
}
```

This approach has its advantages: setting the selected pen once (`HPEN`) obviates the need to pass it to the output function every time it is called. This simplicity, however, often produces a serious problem: the notorious *resource leak*.

Take a look at the lines in bold. Why was it necessary to save and restore the old pen in the context if it was not used for drawing? What will happen if the bold code is commented out?

The problem is that the graphics object selected in the context *cannot be deleted*: this type of architecture just happened to be chosen when designing GDI. Consequently, without this code line, the `DeleteObject` call will fail and the created `hPen` pen will remain in the *GDI heap*, wasting resources needed for the system.

Because the window receives the `WM_PAINT` message frequently, this piece of code will execute over and over. In Windows 9*x* systems (in which the heap size is limited to 64 KB), this will rapidly exhaust system resources. When this happens, all programs will start acting strangely: they will fail to redraw some menu elements and icons, will print text in dubious fonts, etc. The NT systems will stay afloat somewhat longer because their graphics heap can expand as needed, but even there a limit is placed on the number of simultaneously existing graphics objects: 12,000 per user process and 16,000 for the entire system.

The other problem is that C++ programmers are accustomed to the automatic resource cleanup made possible by having classes with destructors and smart pointers available. These tools make it easy to forget about needing to explicitly delete something. However, the GDI wrapper class libraries (the MFC library in particular) cannot solve for the programmer the problem of deleting an object selected in a context. For these classes to be able to cleanup resources automatically, their code would have to contain constant checks for the current object being selected in the context, which would negatively affect the performance. But using automatic destructors would also result in a GDI resource leak.

2.1.2. GDI+ Stateless Model

A GDI+ feature that affects programmers is the changed output device operation software model. The concept of the graphics object currently selected in a device context has been discarded as less efficient and obsolete. Instead of the sequential setting of the context (`Graphics`) parameters, attributes are enumerated every time a graphics method is called. The output device has no state but receives the necessary information through parameters. This model is called the *stateless model*.

NOTE

This classification extends only so far. Some parameters (e.g., current antialiasing settings and the selected coordinate system) are saved in the `Graphics` class and its associated structures. But the *state of primitives* in GDI+ is not saved in the display context.

Now, each method that uses a graphics object for output requires this object to be explicitly specified as a parameter (Listing 2.2).

Listing 2.2. Working with graphics objects in GDI+ [C++]

```
using namespace Gdiplus;
void OnPaint(Graphics &g)
{
  Pen pen(Color::Blue, 3);
```

```
  Point points[] = {
    Point(10, 10), Point(100, 10), Point(100, 100),
    Point(10, 100), Point(10, 10)
  };
  // Using the specified Pen, output a set
  // of lines made up of an array of points
  g.DrawLines(&pen, points, sizeof points / sizeof points[0]);
}
```

This approach eliminates the previously-described resource-leak problem and allows all necessary resources to be released in the GDI+ C++ wrapper class destructors.

NOTE

If you are a novice to C++, you may be confused by a strange construction: `sizeof points / sizeof points[0]`. This is only a useful way to calculate the number of elements in a randomly sized array at the compilation stage. The size (in bytes) of the `points` array is divided by the size of its first element.

No such tricks are needed in C#: arrays in this language are objects and have the standard `Length` property.

2.1.3. Used Brushes, Pens, Paints, and Other Garbage

You have probably guessed from this section's title that we are now going to cover not the GDI+ proper but its interaction with the .NET framework. In this environment, objects are cleaned up not right after they leave the scope but later when the *garbage collector* (GC) is launched. With this method of resource cleanup, creating an object in the dynamic memory (heap) is a much more efficient operation than it is in traditional environments. Moreover, the object no longer needs to be tracked to be deleted: GC will take care of it when no references to the object remain. Such conditions push programmers to write code in the style shown in Listing 2.3.

Listing 2.3. Type of resource handling to be avoided in .NET [C#]

```
private void Form1_Paint(object sender, PaintEventArgs e)
{
  Graphics g = e.Graphics;
  Point[] points = {
```

```
      new Point(10, 10), new Point(10, 100),
      new Point(100, 100), new Point(100, 10), new Point(10, 10)
   };
   g.DrawLines(new Pen(Color.Blue, 3), points);
}
```

As you can see, two objects are dynamically created here: the `points` structure array and an instance of the `Pen` class (the `new Point` statement only calls the constructor of the `Point` structure and does not create it dynamically). But a distinct difference must be made between these two cases. We will give a brief treatment of this without going into the details of the .NET framework.

To create a regular object (e.g., an array of value types, as in the given example), only dynamic memory is needed. But many objects control resources: entities whose quantity by definition has a certain limit independent of the program. These include database connections, file descriptors, and GDI+ graphics objects. With such an approach, resources are released only when objects are destroyed. This is acceptable for demonstration programs but may lead to early system resource exhaustion in a serious application.

As strange as it sounds, systems with greater amounts of installed memory are most susceptible to this danger. The call to the GC (and, subsequently, the resource cleanup) is simply postponed until the system starts running short of dynamic memory, which may take time.

Fortunately, the developers of GDI+ for .NET were aware of this problem and implemented the `IDisposable` interface for all necessary classes. More detailed information about this interface can be found in the *MSDN 2003 .NET Framework Developer's Guide* in the *"Programming for Garbage Collection"* section. Here, we will only note that the `IDisposable.Dispose` method directs object to release resources associated with it. The necessary cleanup can be performed implicitly in C# by employing the `using` construction (Listing 2.4).

Listing 2.4. Correct use of graphical resources in .NET [C#]

```
private void Form1_Paint(object sender, PaintEventArgs e)
{
   Graphics g = e.Graphics;
   Point[] points = {
      new Point(10, 10), new Point(10, 100),
      new Point(100, 100), new Point(100, 10), new Point(10, 10)
```

```
};
using (Pen pen = new Pen(Color.Blue, 3))
    g.DrawLines(pen, points);
}
```

When the scope of `using` is exited, the compiler will generate a call to `pen.Dispose()`.

2.1.4. Separating the Fill and Outline Methods

The move to the stateless model necessitated a redesign of the main methods for drawing primitives. Before, the behavior of the `Rectangle` function, for example, was determined by what brush and what pen were selected in the display context. To draw, say, unfilled rectangles, the transparent `HOLLOW_BRUSH` had to be selected in the context.

As already said, in GDI+, the state of primitives is not saved in the output device (`Graphics`). Instead, practically all closed-shape drawing methods have two versions: `DrawXXXX` for drawing shape outlines (these methods require an instance of the `Pen` class as a parameter) and `FillXXXX` for filling (these methods are passed a class inherited from `Brush`).

2.1.5. The Brush Family: A Set of Brushes to Anyone's Taste

To fill solid areas, the corresponding library methods require that a `Brush` class object be specified. On its own, this class is practically useless because it cannot be used directly. But its five descendants provide extensive functionality. Consider them more closely.

SolidBrush

This is the simplest class of the `Brush` family. Its function is to fill areas with a solid color. The fill color can be specified either in the class constructor or later for the already constructed object:

```
// Creating a bright red brush
SolidBrush br(Color(255,0,0));
. . .
// Setting black color for the brush
br.SetColor(Color::Black);
```

The only (and important) difference between the `SolidBrush` class and the analogous GDI object is the support of semitransparency by the former. You will recall that in addition to the three color components red, green, and blue (RGB), the `Color` class allows the *alpha* value (opacity) to be specified (by default, alpha takes the value 255, rendering the color opaque).

The WinForms designers have prepared a pleasant surprise for .NET users. In addition to the `Color` class with its 141 standard color name constants, this environment has the `System.Drawing.Brushes` class, which also comprises 141 static properties: brushes already initialized with a certain color. For example, a red circle 100 units in diameter can be drawn by writing this short expression:

```
g.FillEllipse(Brushes.Red, 0, 0, 100, 100);
```

Just like the same name constants of the `Color` class, these static properties contain the value 255 in the alpha field.

HatchBrush

The `HatchBrush` class is a tool for a bicolor, bit-based pattern fill. The C++ constructor of this class looks as follows:

```
HatchBrush(
  HatchStyle hatchStyle,
  const Color& foreColor,
  const Color& backColor );
```

GDI+ has a ready-made collection of 53 patterns defined by the `HatchStyle` enumeration. (Compare this number with the 6 predefined styles in GDI). The `foreColor` and `backColor` parameters allow the colors of the pattern outline lines and of the background brush, respectively, to be specified.

The position of the pattern starting point relative to the drawing area can be controlled (by the `SetRenderingOrigin` method and the `RenderingOrigin` property in .NET).

TextureBrush

This class allows areas to be filled with a bitmap image, or *texture*. To initialize an object of the `TextureBrush` class, an image is necessary: an instance of the `Image` class. This image can be either a bitmap (work with which will be considered in *Chapter 5*) or a metafile (which you will get to know in *Chapter 3*). This circumstance gives programmers enormous capabilities: having painted an intricate pattern, it, in turn, can be used as a brush for an even more complex drawing. Listing 2.5 gives a short example for WinForms.

Listing 2.5. Using the `TextureBrush` class [C#]

```
// Reading the source image (metafile)
private Image img = Image.FromFile("mybrush.emf");

private void Form1_Paint(object sender, PaintEventArgs e)
{
  Graphics g = e.Graphics;

  // Filling the form with the created brush
  g.FillRectangle(new TextureBrush(img), ClientRectangle);
}
```

The class has several overloaded constructors (we will not present them here). In addition to the image (`Image` class), they can take as parameters the instances of the `WrapMode` and `ImageAttributes` classes. These classes control various aspects of image output (we will consider them when describing bitmaps).

It is important to add that, unlike the `HatchBrush` class, the `TextureBrush` class not only allows images with unlimited color selection to be used for filling but also submits to GDI+ coordinate transformations. The applied texture can be scaled, translated, or rotated in any way desired.

LinearGradientBrush and PathGradientBrush

These two classes will be considered together because they are very similar. Their function is to fill areas by gradient colors. We already used this technique in an example in *Chapter 1*: a diagonal color gradient brush was used to draw text. Recall this piece of code:

```
// Creating a semitransparent brush
// with a gradient over the entire window
LinearGradientBrush brush(bounds,
    Color(130, 255, 0, 0), Color(255, 0, 0, 255),
    LinearGradientModeBackwardDiagonal);
```

The first constructor parameter is of the `Rect` type (`Rectangle` for .NET) and holds the coordinates of the rectangular area, in which the transition between the start (the second parameter) and the end (the third parameter) colors takes place. As can be seen from the example, there is nothing to prevent one of the colors from being semitransparent (alpha = 130). If the output shape is larger than the specified rectangular area, a question arises: what color are the image areas outside of the rectangle to be filled? This behavior is defined by the `SetWrapMode` method (as with other types of nonuniform filling).

The last parameter is an element of the `LinearGradientMode` enumeration and defines the gradient direction, that is, the location of the polar colors points.

The `PathGradientBrush` differs from its twin in that it can use a gradient of several colors. The location of the necessary polar points is defined by an arbitrary shape *path*.

Both these classes also support GDI+ coordinate transformations. Moreover, their color transition distribution rules can be adjusted (see the `SetSigmaBellShape` method in .NET and the `SetBlendBellShape` method for the C++ version).

2.1.6. The Pen is Mightier than the Sword

The function of the `Pen` class (`System.Drawing.Pen` for .NET) is to adjust parameters of various output lines: line sections, curve segments, ellipses, splines, and Bezier curves. In addition to the regular pen properties, such as line color and width, it contains a gamut of supplementary settings. First, a `Brush` type class can be specified as the source when creating an instance of the `Pen` class, meaning all possible gradient fills, textures, and pattern fills are available for drawing lines.

In C++, a `Pen` class constructor from a `Brush` class instance looks as follows:

```
Pen( const Brush* brush, REAL width = 1.0 );
```

In C#, the following would be used:

```
public Pen( Brush brush );
public Pen( Brush brush, float width );
```

Second, when specifying color, as is usual in GDI+, the level of alpha can be set, allowing the creation of semitransparent lines.

In C++, a `Pen` class constructor from a solid `Color` class instance looks as follows:

```
Pen( const Color& color, REAL width = 1.0);
```

In C#, the same result can be achieved using the following:

```
public Pen( Color color );
public Pen( Color color, float width );
```

As it does for the `Brush` class, the .NET Framework provides an easier way of creating standard (named) color pens. The `System.Drawing.Pens` class has 141 standard color name static properties available. Here is a short example of using one:

```
g.DrawEllipse(Pens.Red, 0, 0, 100, 100);
```

Finally, to specify geometric line characteristics, the interface of the `Pen` class has many settings. They are listed in Table 2.1 with short descriptions.

Table 2.1. Methods of Setting Pen Styles

Method	Description
`SetAlignment`	Defines the location of the pen points relative to the geometric line when drawing polygons: inside a polygon or at the center of its contour.
`SetCompoundArray`	Allows a line to be composed from a set of different-width parallel lines. See Listing 2.6 for more details.

`SetDashCap`
`SetDashOffset`
`SetDashPattern`
`SetDashStyle`
	Allow one of five standard line styles or a custom dotted line style to be specified.

`SetStartCap`
`SetEndCap`
`SetLineCap`
	Define the geometry and style (solid or dotted) of the line caps. Allow any of the eight standard caps to be set for each end of the line.

`SetCustomStartCap` `SetCustomEndCap`	Set custom-shape line caps based on path. Requires an object of a class derived from the `CustomLineCap` as a parameter. A ready-made `AdjustableArrowCap` exists for drawing more complex arrow-like line-end caps.
`SetLineJoin`	Sets the join type for polygon side lines: rounded, extending past the join, or clipped.
`SetMiterLimit`	Sets the miter limit for line segments connected at sharp angle (`Miter Join`).

As usual, all enumerated `Set` methods have their `Get` counterparts. In .NET, access to the pen setting is obtained by using properties (without `Get` or `Set` prefixes).

2.2. Vector Primitives

In this section, we briefly consider GDI+ tools for outputting traditional vector primitives. Programmers already familiar with GDI will have no difficulties using them. The new goodies (such as splines) will be given special attention.

2.2.1. GDI+ Clock Program

As a tutorial, a GDI+ Clock program created in C# for WinForms is presented in Listing 2.6.

It employs numerous primitives: rectangles, ellipses, and line segments. Their coordinates are calculated using not geometric GDI+ transformations (which will be considered in *Chapter 3*), but simple calculations. In particular, the created `RadialPoint` method of the `frmClock` form class returns the coordinates of the endpoints of the second hand with the radius of `radius` for the values of seconds (`seconds`).

To implement a constant redrawing of the clock, the `Time` component is used, which allows periodic generation of the `Tick` event. The rate, at which the event is generated, is set by the `Interval` property (in milliseconds). Initialize the necessary timer properties in the form constructor as shown in Listing 2.6.

Listing 2.6. Source code of the GDI+ Clock program [C#]

```
using System;
using System.Drawing;
using System.Drawing.Drawing2D;
using System.Windows.Forms;

namespace GDIPlusClock
{
  public class frmClock: Form
  {
    private Timer clkTimer;

    public frmClock()
    {
      clkTimer = new Timer();
      clkTimer.Enabled = TRUE;
      clkTimer.Interval = 1000;
      clkTimer.Tick += new EventHandler(clkTimer_Tick);
      Load += new EventHandler(frmClock_Load);
      Paint += new PaintEventHandler(frmClock_Paint);
    }

    static void Main()
```

```
{
  Application.Run(new frmClock());
}

private Point RadialPoint(int radius, int seconds)
{
  Point ptCenter = new Point(this.ClientRectangle.Width/2,
    this.ClientRectangle.Height/2);
  double angle = -((seconds-15)%60)*Math.PI/30;
  Point ret = new Point(
    ptCenter.X + (int)(radius*Math.Cos(angle)),
    ptCenter.Y - (int)(radius*Math.Sin(angle)));
  return ret;
}

private void frmClock_Paint(object sender, PaintEventArgs e)
{
  DateTime dt = DateTime.Now;
  Graphics g = e.Graphics;
  g.SmoothingMode = SmoothingMode.HighQuality;
  Point ptCenter = new Point(this.ClientRectangle.Width/2,
    this.ClientRectangle.Height/2);
  int radius = Math.Min(this.ClientRectangle.Width,
    this.ClientRectangle.Height)/2;
  using (LinearGradientBrush br = new LinearGradientBrush(
        this.ClientRectangle, Color.White, Color.DarkGray,
        LinearGradientMode.BackwardDiagonal))
  {
    g.FillEllipse(br, ptCenter.X - radius, ptCenter.Y - radius,
      radius*2, radius*2);
  }
  using (Pen pen = new Pen(Color.Black))
    g.DrawEllipse(pen, ptCenter.X - radius, ptCenter.Y - radius,
      radius*2, radius*2);

  // Drawing the minute marks
  for(int minute=0; minute<60; minute++)
  {
    Point pt = RadialPoint(radius-10, minute);
    using (SolidBrush br = new SolidBrush(Color.Black))
```

Chapter 2: Using GDI+ To Construct Vector Images

```csharp
    {
      if((minute%5) == 0)
        g.FillRectangle(br, pt.X - 3, pt.Y - 3, 6, 6);
      else
        g.FillRectangle(br, pt.X - 1, pt.Y - 1, 2, 2);
    }
}
// Refreshing the hour hand
using Pen pen = new Pen(Color.Black, 8))
{
  pen.StartCap = LineCap.Flat;
  pen.EndCap = LineCap.DiamondAnchor;
  float[] compVals = new float[]{0.0f, 0.2f, 0.5f,
    0.7f, 0.9f, 1.0f};
  pen.CompoundArray = compVals;
  g.DrawLine(pen, RadialPoint(15, 30 + dt.Hour*5 + dt.Minute/12),
    RadialPoint((int)(radius*0.75), dt.Hour*5 + dt.Minute/12));
}
// Refreshing the minute hand

using (Pen pen = new Pen(Color.FromArgb(100, 0, 0, 0), 6))
{
  pen.StartCap = LineCap.RoundAnchor;
  pen.EndCap = LineCap.Round;
  g.DrawLine(pen, RadialPoint(15, 30 + dt.Minute),
    RadialPoint((int)(radius*0.8), dt.Minute));
}

// Refreshing the second hand
using (Pen pen = new Pen(Color.FromArgb(80, 20, 70, 30), 4))
{
  pen.CustomEndCap = new AdjustableArrowCap(4, 6, TRUE);
  g.DrawLine(pen, RadialPoint(20, dt.Second + 30),
    RadialPoint(radius-2, dt.Second));
}
using (SolidBrush br = new SolidBrush(
  Color.FromArgb(100, Color.Wheat)))
  g.FillEllipse(br, ptCenter.X - 5, ptCenter.Y - 5, 10, 10);
}
```

```
private void clkTimer_Tick(object sender, EventArgs e)
{
  Text = DateTime.Now.ToLongTimeString()+" - GDI+ Clock";
  Invalidate();
}

private void frmClock_Load(object sender, EventArgs e)
{
  // Setting form styles for double buffering
  SetStyle(ControlStyles.AllPaintingInWmPaint, TRUE);
  SetStyle(ControlStyles.DoubleBuffer, TRUE);
  SetStyle(ControlStyles.UserPaint, TRUE);
}
}
}
```

Fig. 2.1. Execution results of the **GDI+ Clock** program

The program shows the current time on a stylized analog clock face (Fig. 2.1).

The way clock hands are displayed is worthy of notice. Each hand is drawn by *only one* call to the DrawLine method. As you see, GDI+ allows complex images to be created by simple means. You can find the program on the accompanying CD-ROM and experiment with setting different characteristics of the output lines.

2.2.2. Splines

One of the meanings of the word *spline* is a drawing curve (i.e., a wooden or metal tool for drawing curves). These drawing tools used to be made from a metal strip anchored at specified points to draw a curve. The strip bent around the anchor points produced a smooth curve. Using strips with different bending tension, a variety of curves could be obtained for a given set of points. Later this' dependency between the strip flexibility and the nature of curves was expressed in mathematical formulas describing *cubic splines*. These formulas are widely used in engineering calculations, for example, for approximating experiment results. You do not have to know these formulas to draw splines in GDI+. All you need to do is to call a function of the DrawCurve family.

Listing 2.7. Overload versions of the DrawCurve method [C#]

```
Status DrawCurve( const Pen* pen, const Point* points,
  INT count );
Status DrawCurve( const Pen* pen, const PointF* points,
  INT count );
Status DrawCurve( const Pen* pen, const Point* points,
  INT count, INT offset,
  INT numberOfSegments, REAL tension );
Status DrawCurve( const Pen* pen, const PointF* points,
  INT count, INT offset,
  INT numberOfSegments, REAL tension );
Status DrawCurve( const Pen* pen, const Point* points,
  INT count, REAL tension );
Status DrawCurve( const Pen* pen, const PointF* points,
  INT count, REAL tension );
```

The points pointer must point to the first element of the Point array of structures (for integer coordinates) or PointF (for floating-point coordinates).

NOTE

Implementation of these GDI+ methods in .NET differs only in that the number of the points array elements does not need to be specified.

As can be seen, there are a variety of methods taking the tension parameter, a floating-point number. This parameter, as can be seen from its name, is the one that specifies the bending tension of the imaginary strip. In methods not specifying this parameter, it is assumed to be 0.5.

A characteristic feature of splines is that the constructed curve passes through each point of the specified set. Moreover, to calculate spline endpoint coordinates, initial conditions must be specified. These conditions can be approximated but can also be set explicitly. This is done by calling a version of the DrawCurve method with the offset and numberOfSegments parameters and passing to this method an array with a number of points larger than necessary. The offset parameter defines the index (starting from zero) of the array point, from which the drawing of curve segments will start, and the numberOfSegments parameter specifies the number of the segments. The "invisible" points will be used for the calculations.

You can experiment with these supplementary parameters in the demonstration application by modifying the code of the method given in Listing 2.8.

Listing 2.8. The DrawSpline method of the demonstration application [C++]

```
void CCurveDlg::DrawSpline(Gdiplus::Graphics &g)
{
  using namespace Gdiplus;
  g.SetSmoothingMode(SmoothingModeHighQuality);
  g.DrawCurve(&Pen(Color::Blue, 3), points,
    sizeof points/sizeof points[0]);
}
```

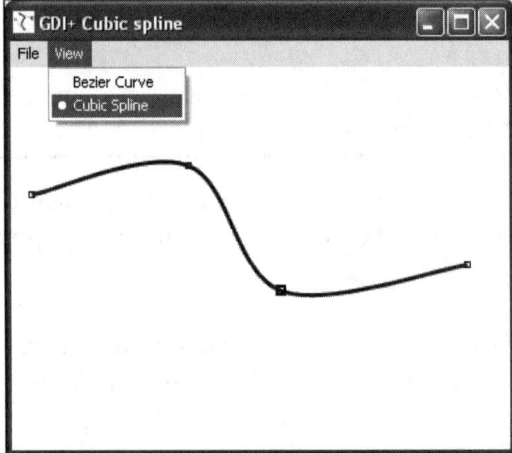

Fig. 2.2. Drawing splines using the **Curves** program

An example of the produced curve (the anchor points can be moved) is shown in Fig. 2.2. Completing the short introduction to splines, we will note that the `Graphics` class also has a `DrawClosedCurve` family of methods that allows you to draw closed curves for a specified set of points (Listing 2.9).

Listing 2.9. The `DrawClosedCurve` family of methods [C++]

```
Status DrawClosedCurve( const Pen* pen,
  const Point* points, INT count );
Status DrawClosedCurve( const Pen* pen,
  const PointF* points, INT count );
Status DrawClosedCurve( const Pen* pen,
  const Point* points, INT count, REAL tension );
Status DrawClosedCurve( const Pen* pen,
  const PointF* points, INT count, REAL tension );
```

These methods also use splines but with somewhat different ratios for the endpoints. Moreover, like all "decent" closed figures supported by GDI+, they have `Fill` counterparts (Listing 2.10).

Listing 2.10. The `FillClosedCurve` family of methods [C++]

```
Status FillClosedCurve( const Brush* brush, const Point* points,
  INT count );
Status FillClosedCurve( const Brush* brush, const PointF* points,
  INT count );
Status FillClosedCurve( const Brush* brush, const Point* points,
  INT count, FillMode fillMode, REAL tension );
Status FillClosedCurve(const Brush* brush, const PointF* points,
  INT count, FillMode fillMode, REAL tension );
```

The difference between these methods and the previous one is that these have the `Brush` parameter (to set the fill style) and an ability to specify the `FillMode` enumeration element. The latter is used to determine whether internal areas (created by the self-intersecting line) will be filled. By default, this parameter takes on the `FillModeAlternate` value, meaning that the internal areas created under the intersection parity rule do not have to be filled. When the `FillModeWinding` parameter is set, the entire shape created by the external contour of the curve will be filled.

In the GDI+ implementation for .NET, a funny blunder was discovered: For an unknown reason, an undocumented version of the `DrawClosedCurve` method accepting the `FillMode` parameter was implemented in it. Of course, setting this parameter does not affect the function behavior (which is not geared for filling areas); moreover, it is ignored in its body.

2.2.3. Bezier Curves

Bezier curves have been known to programmers for a long time. They are used in PostScript to describe fonts and to draw any type of curve, including elliptical. The Windows GDI also supports Bezier curve drawing, for example, using the `PolyBezierTo` and `PolyDraw` functions (the latter is unavailable in the Windows 9*x* operating systems).

There was no way such an important tool could be ignored in the GDI+ library. The library not only supports Bezier curves for drawing but also actively uses them, in particular when saving paths in metafiles.

Bezier curves owe their name to their inventor, Pierre Etienne Bézier (1910–1999). While working in Renault on the UNISURF CAD system, he invented a tool to describe complex curves that common designers found simple and understandable. Since then, they have been widely used in design systems.

To construct a Bezier curve, four points need to be specified: two endpoints and two control points (Fig. 2.3). Under common agreement, the first and the fourth points are the endpoints, and the second and the third points are the control points. The latter generally do not lie on the curve but define its shape.

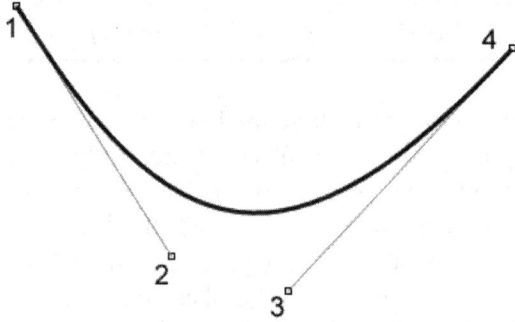

Fig. 2.3. Bezier curve with control points and endpoints

Chapter 2: Using GDI+ To Construct Vector Images

The methods in Listing 2.11 allow two endpoints to be connected with a two-control-point Bezier curve.

Listing 2.11. The `DrawBezier` family of methods [C++]

```
Status DrawBezier( const Pen* pen, const Point& pt1,
   const Point& pt2, const Point& pt3, const Point& pt4 );
Status DrawBezier( const Pen* pen, const PointF& pt1,
   const PointF& pt2, const PointF& pt3, const PointF& pt4 );
Status DrawBezier( const Pen* pen, INT x1, INT y1,
   INT x2, INT y2, INT x3, INT y3, INT x4, INT y4 );
Status DrawBezier( const Pen* pen, REAL x1, REAL y1,
   REAL x2, REAL y2, REAL x3, REAL y3, REAL x4, REAL y4 );
```

Listing 2.12 shows a fragment of the Curves demonstration application producing a Bezier curve segment in this way.

Listing 2.12. The `DrawBezier` method of the demonstration application [C++]

```
void CCurveDlg::DrawBezier(Gdiplus::Graphics &g)
{
  using namespace Gdiplus;
  g.SetSmoothingMode(SmoothingModeHighQuality);

  // Drawing two lines toward the control points
  g.DrawLine(&Pen(Color::Gray, 1), points[0], points[1]);
  g.DrawLine(&Pen(Color::Gray, 1), points[2], points[3]);

  // Drawing the curve
  g.DrawBezier(&Pen(Color::Blue, 3), points[0], points[1],
    points[2], points[3]);
}
```

You can experiment with the program, moving the control points and making the curve take on intricate shapes—all with just one call of the `DrawBesier` method.

There are `DrawBezier` methods that allow you to pass the `points` array of points to construct several curve segments at once.

```
Status DrawBeziers(
   const Pen* pen, const Point* points, INT count
```

```
);

Status DrawBeziers(
  const Pen* pen, const PointF* points, INT count
);
```

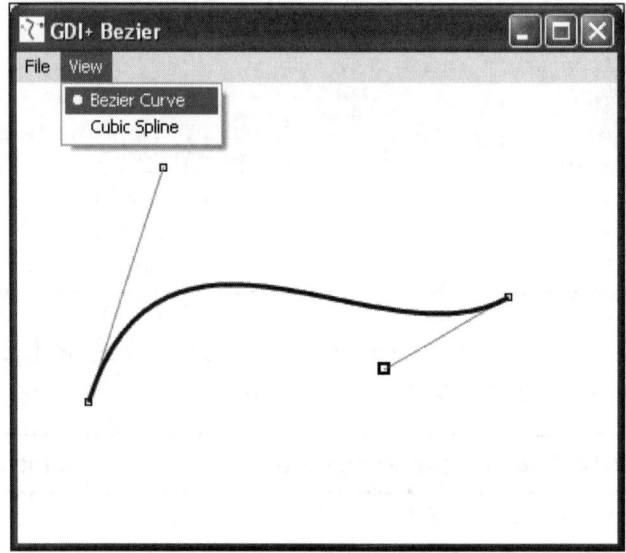

Fig. 2.4. Drawing Bezier curves using the **Curves** program

The `count` variable must contain the number of the `points` array elements. To build *N* curve segments, an array of exactly *3N + 1* points must be passed; otherwise, the function call will fail.

2.3. Conclusion

Having been introduced to implementing basic concepts of vector graphics as GDI+ primitives, you can start learning how to use them to construct complex vector images and metafiles. This will be explained in *Chapter 3*.

Chapter 3: Working with Output Devices and Using Metafiles

This chapter continues to explore the vector graphics capabilities of the GDI+ library. It deals with the following subjects:

- Using GDI+ regions and paths
- Configuring graphics devices
- Transforming coordinates
- Creating and studying metafiles

3.1. Configuring an Output Device

There are several parameters in GDI+ that change the characteristics of the graphics device. In particular, these are the following:

- The selected origin and scale of the coordinate system
- Geometric transformations applied to the output primitives
- The device clipping area (region)
- Adjustments to the quality of output primitives

Some of the device bitmap characteristics were described in the previous chapters. In this section, we describe parameters that mostly affect the output of vector primitives.

3.1.1. Smoothing Rough Outlines

As a rule, the human eye perceives tooth-edged, mosaic-like images negatively; this is especially true of low-resolution display graphics. For example, a human reads text on a screen, on average, 30 percent slower than on paper. To fight this, many smoothing technologies have been invented, ranging from the ClearType for liquid crystal display monitors to full screen antialiasing for modern graphics accelerators.

As mentioned in *Chapter 2*, the GDI+ library has its own set of tools for improving the visual perception of output graphics. Bitmaps are processed using *interpolation*, the calculation of the transitional colors of the output pixels; vector images may be processed using *antialiasing*, the elimination of the rough outline edges using color gradations.

When using antialiasing in constructing, for example, a straight line, the integer algorithms are not used; instead, their floating-point modifications are applied. The degree of transparence of each pixel of the physical output line is calculated depending on the given pixel's distance from the center of the geometric output line.

Antialiasing is managed by calling `Graphics::SetSmoothingMode` (by setting the `SmoothingMode` property in .NET). The `SmoothingMode` enumeration element is used as a parameter (Listing 3.1).

Listing 3.1. The `SmoothingMode` enumeration [C++]

```
enum SmoothingMode{
    SmoothingModeInvalid     = QualityModeInvalid,
    SmoothingModeDefault     = QualityModeDefault,
    SmoothingModeHighSpeed   = QualityModeLow,
    SmoothingModeHighQuality = QualityModeHigh,
    SmoothingModeNone,
    SmoothingModeAntialias
};
```

In the current GDI+ implementation, there practically is no difference among the `SmoothingModeDefault`, `SmoothingModeHighSpeed`, and `SmoothingModeNone` modes: they all disable antialiasing of primitives, rendering images with the usual staircase edges (Fig. 3.1).

The SmoothingModeHighQuality or SmoothingModeAntialias constants are used to enable the antialiasing mode (Fig. 3.2).

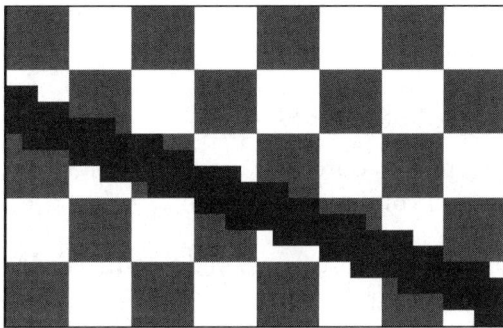

Fig. 3.1. Magnified fragment of a line output without antialiasing

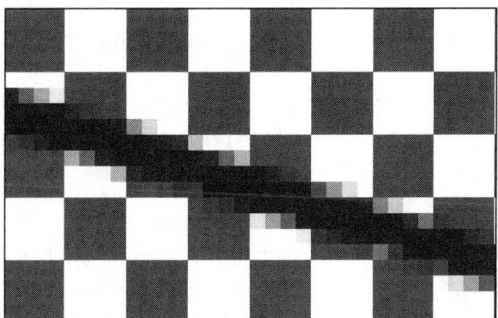

Fig. 3.2. Same line output with antialiasing enabled

Setting the SmoothingModeInvalid mode makes no sense because it will return an execution error (i.e., generate an exception in the .NET environment).

3.1.2. Transforming Coordinates in GDI+

You will now get acquainted with the GDI+ tools that can help you to implement planar coordinate transformations.

When working with the GDI+ coordinate system, you must realize that the library (at least its 1.0 version) is not based on integer mechanisms. The GDI+ processes coordinates as the float type: single-precision floating-point numbers.

On one hand, this circumstance allows great flexibility: for example, GDI+ programmers are no longer limited by the 16-bit coordinate limit when working with Windows 9x/ME. On the other hand, performing real number calculations places a great load on the central processing unit. Even with "heavy" effects such as antialiasing disabled, GDI+ noticeably loses to GDI when it comes to outputting simple vector primitives. The situation may change with an upcoming library version supporting graphics accelerators.

Types of Coordinate Systems

GDI+ uses three types of coordinate systems: world, page, and device. The following is a typical scenario of their interaction:

1. User output commands are issued in the world coordinate system.
2. The world transformations defined in the Graphics class are applied to the coordinates of the output primitive.
3. The obtained coordinates are scaled as necessary, depending on the selected characteristics of the page coordinate system.
4. The primitive is output in the device coordinates.

As you can see, when a simple command is executed (e.g., draw a line), the GDI+ graphics subsystem can perform intensive calculations. Primitives are output most rapidly when the world and page transformations are not used.

NOTE

In Windows GDI, a fourth coordinate system is defined: physical. As a rule, coordinates in the physical system are calculated by the driver or the controller of the output device. The hardware interaction layer is undocumented in GDI+; the only known things are that a software device control interface is employed and that the device coordinate system is assumed to be identical to the physical coordinate system.

The Matrix Class and Support for World Transformations

The Graphics class makes convenient tools available to the user for performing the most common world coordinate system transformations: rotation, scaling, and translation. These transformations are performed by the RotateTransform, ScaleTransform, and TranslateTransform methods, respectively.

```
Status RotateTransform( REAL angle, MatrixOrder order );
Status ScaleTransform( REAL sx, REAL sy, MatrixOrder order );
Status TranslateTransform( REAL dx, REAL dy, MatrixOrder order );
```

Chapter 3: Working with Output Devices and Using Metafiles 61

Note that the `angle` rotation angle is specified in degrees and not in radians, the unit used with the parameters for `sin`, `cos`, and similar functions.

Even when these methods are used inside the `Graphics` class, transformations are still carried out using matrix algebra. The `MatrixOrder` enumeration specifies, which operand (an existing or a new transformation matrix) will be on the left side during multiplication. By default, the `order` parameter takes on the `MatrixOrderPrepend` value.

For explicit preparation of transformations, the library makes available the `Matrix` class containing a 3 × 3 coefficient matrix. Its methods allow both the individual coordinate transformation coefficient values to be set and a ready-made set of coefficients for the most commonly performed transformations to be specified.

The `Graphics::SetTransform` method allows the setting of a prepared transformation matrix in the output device. The program fragments in Listings 3.2 and 3.3 produce identical results.

Listing 3.2. Using the `Graphics::RotateTransform` method [C++]

```
Graphics graphics(hdc);
graphics.RotateTransform(45.0f);
```

Listing 3.3. Using the `Matrix` class [C++]

```
Graphics graphics(hdc);
Matrix transformMatrix;
transformMatrix.Rotate(45.0f);
graphics.SetTransform(&transformMatrix);
```

You can also use the `Matrix` class independently of the other GDI+ classes: the `TransformPoints` and `TransformVectors` methods allow you to perform transformations for random points and vectors without directly drawing them.

NOTE

The order, in which separate transformations are performed, affects the final result. Performing a rotation first and then a translation will produce a different result than if the transformation order was reversed.

Page Transformations

By allowing a logical coordinate system to be selected, in which to produce output, graphical interfaces usually make it possible to abstract from the device's physical characteristics.

Of course, world transformations can also be used for solving these problems. In the end, everything comes down to the regular scaling operations. But it is preferable to dedicate a separate layer to handle this type of logic. In GDI+, the role of this separate layer is played by the page coordinate system.

The SetPageUnit method is used for setting a predetermined coordinate system (the PageUnit property in .NET). Its parameter defines the size of the output device's logical units.

Listing 3.4. The Unit enumeration [C++, C#]

```
enum Unit
{
    UnitWorld = 0,         // World units (undocumented)
    UnitDisplay = 1,       // Display units (pixels for monitors)
    UnitPixel = 2,         // Pixels
    UnitPoint = 3,         // 1 unit equals 1/72 of an inch
    UnitInch = 4,          // 1 unit equals 1 inch
    UnitDocument = 5,      // 1 unit equals 1/300 of an inch
    UnitMillimeter = 6     // 1 unit equals 1 mm
};
```

Moreover, the logical coordinate scaling coefficient can be specified (the same in both axes) by the SetPageScale method of the Graphics class (the PageScale property in .NET). In the following example, the logical coordinate system unit will be set to 1 cm regardless of the device, to which the output is made:

```
Graphics graphics(hdc);
// Selecting millimeters as logical units
graphics.SetPageUnit(UnitMillimeter);
// Setting logical unit scaling
graphics.SetPageScale(10.0f);
```

3.1.3. Regions and Paths

The concept of *regions* has been familiar to graphics programmers for a long time. In short, a region is a method to describe a complex area. In Windows, API regions are used to check for a point belonging to an area, to optimize redrawing of partially overlapping windows, to fill solid shapes, and to create nonrectangular windows.

We mention regions in this section mainly because of their powerful clipping functions: the Graphics output device uses regions to support the setting of complex clipping areas (by calling the SetClip method). You can easily create a complex shape and then draw "through" it, producing interesting effects.

Regions have been traditionally tied to the resolution of the output device, for which they were created. With the arrival of GDI+, this tradition was broken: now regions are created in the world coordinate system and submit to all the coordinate transformations described earlier. Moreover, it has become possible to apply the same region to several output devices.

Remember that using regions to clip output primitives leads to allocating great amounts of memory (for storing the scan lines of the clipped shape) and rectangular clipping areas are used as often as possible.

A set of overloaded constructors for creating regions from various sources is available (Listing 3.5).

Listing 3.5. The Region class constructors [C++]

```
Region(Rect&);
Region();
Region(BYTE*, INT);
Region(HRGN);
Region(RectF&);
Region(GraphicsPath*);
```

The most interesting item in this list is the last constructor; it allows regions to be created from areas delimited by *paths*.

A path is a more recent computer graphics concept, first implemented in GDI with Windows 95. A path can be defined as an ordered sequence of line and curve segments. These segments can be either connected by common points or not: it depends on the graphics commands included in the path.

The Graphics object supports the setting of a clipping area delimited by either a path or a region — the object, which is most convenient at the moment, can be used for clipping.

If you worked with paths in Windows GDI, you know that a path object is unavailable to user applications in this program interface. There, the construction of a path starts with the switching of the device context into the special mode by a call to the `BeginPath` function. Then, instead of being executed directly, graphics commands are saved in the context, forming the path outline. This process is terminated by a call to the `EndPath` command, which restores the device's initial mode, completes construction of the current path, and makes it available for use.

The `GraphicsPath` object, which provides path tools in GDI+, is more flexible. It is not tied to the output device and has its own set of methods for constructing paths. These methods are similar to the `Graphics` class methods for constructing the same primitives. The similar methods of these two classes are listed in Table 3.1. In practice, each method has numerous overloaded versions differing in parameter types.

Table 3.1. Comparison of the `GraphicsPath` and `Graphics` Methods

`GraphicsPath` Method	Analogous `Graphics` Method	Primitive Output or Action Performed
AddArc	DrawArc	An elliptical arc
AddBezier	DrawBezier	A Bezier curve
AddBeziers	DrawBeziers	A chain of connected Bezier curves
AddClosedCurve	DrawClosedCurve	A closed curve (cubic spline)
AddCurve	DrawCurve	An open curve (cubic spline)
AddEllipse	DrawEllipse	An ellipse
AddLine	DrawLine	A line segment
AddLines	DrawLines	A chain of separate line segments
AddPath	DrawPath	An existing path
AddPie	DrawPie	Outputting a circle sector (pie)
AddPolygon	DrawPolygon	A chain of connected line segments
AddRectangle	DrawRectangle	A rectangle
AddRectangles	DrawRectangles	A set of unconnected rectangles
AddString	DrawString	A text line
StartFigure	n/a	Starting a new geometric figure (without closing the previous figure)
CloseFigure	n/a	Closing the current figure
CloseAllFigures	n/a	Closing all open figures

Chapter 3: Working with Output Devices and Using Metafiles 65

NOTE

Like in Windows GDI, only straight lines and Bezier curves are used to store path segments. Elliptical curves (circular and elliptical arcs) are converted into Bezier curves when stored in the `GraphicsPath` object. This introduces some inaccuracy into the images, noticeable if the coordinates of the path-forming pixels are magnified many times.

Once a path object has been built, it can be reused as many times as needed. Paths in the `Graphics` class are output by the `DrawPath` (outlining the path's contours) and the `FillPath` (filling the path's closed areas) methods.

Listing 3.6. The `Graphics` class methods for drawing paths [C#]

```
Status DrawPath( const Pen *pen, const GraphicsPath *path );
Status FillPath( const Brush *brush, const GraphicsPath *path );
```

You will learn how to use these methods in the next section.

Using Paths: The RoundRect Class

One of the questions asked by beginners learning GDI+ is the following: "Why isn't there a `RoundRect` function?" Well, even though there is no method for drawing rounded rectangles in the `Graphics` class, nothing can stop you from obtaining a more practical functionality. For this, create a class (`GraphicsPath`) that returns a rounded rectangle path in one of its methods. The rest of this class' methods will draw the path and fill the area it encloses. The source code for such a class is given in Listing 3.7.

Listing 3.7. Implementing the `RoundRect` class [C#]

```
using System;
using System.Drawing;
using System.Drawing.Drawing2D;

namespace RSDN
{
  class RoundRect
  {
    public static GraphicsPath Create(float X, float Y,
```

```
                                      float Width, float Height,
                                      float Radius)
{
  GraphicsPath gp = new GraphicsPath();
  gp.AddLine(X + Radius, Y, X + Width - Radius, Y);
  gp.AddArc(X + Width - Radius, Y, Radius, Radius, 270, 90);
  gp.AddLine(X + Width, Y + Radius, X + Width, Y + Height - Radius);
  gp.AddArc(X + Width - Radius, Y + Height - Radius, Radius, Radius,
     0 , 90);
  gp.AddLine(X + Width - Radius, Y + Height, X + Radius, Y + Height);
  gp.AddArc(X, Y + Height - Radius, Radius, Radius, 90, 90);
  gp.AddLine(X, Y + Height - Radius, X, Y + Radius);
  gp.AddArc(X, Y, Radius, Radius, 180, 90);
  gp.CloseFigure();
  return gp;
}

public static void Draw(Graphics g, Pen p,
                        float X, float Y,
                        float Width, float Height, float Radius)
{
  using (GraphicsPath gp = Create(X, Y, Width, Height, Radius))
  {
    g.DrawPath(p, gp);
  }
}

public static void Fill(Graphics g, Brush br,
                        float X, float Y,
                        float Width, float Height, float Radius)
{
  using (GraphicsPath gp = Create(X, Y, Width, Height, Radius))
  {
    g.FillPath(br, gp);
  }
}

public static void DrawFilled(Graphics g, Pen p, Brush br,
```

```
                                    float X, float Y,
                                    float Width, float Height,
                                    float Radius)
  {
    using (GraphicsPath gp = Create(X, Y, Width, Height, Radius))
    {
      g.FillPath(br, gp);
      g.DrawPath(p, gp);
    }
  }
 }
}
```

The `RSDN::RoundRect` class makes drawing, for example, a rounded, 3D button an easy task (Listing 3.8).

Listing 3.8. Using the `RoundRect` class [C#]

```
protected override void OnPaint(PaintEventArgs e)
{
  base.OnPaint(e);
// Creating a path containing a rounded rectangle
  GraphicsPath path = RSDN.RoundRect.Create(10, 10,
    ClientRectangle.Width-20, ClientRectangle.Height-20, 6);
  e.Graphics.SmoothingMode = SmoothingMode.HighQuality;

  // Preparing a gradient brush for filling the enclosed area
  LinearGradientBrush br = new LinearGradientBrush(
    new Rectangle(0, 0, ClientRectangle.Width-10,
      ClientRectangle.Height-10),
    Color.DarkGray, Color.White, 90f);

  // Filling the enclosed area
  e.Graphics.FillPath(br, path);

  // Outlining it with a line 1 logic unit wide
  e.Graphics.DrawPath(Pens.Black, path);
}
```

3.2. Metafiles

From the first version, Windows has supported the concept of a *metafile:* a stored sequence of graphics commands. This sequence can be saved to disk as a file and then played back at any time, just like a tape recording. The saved metafile is composed of a collection of records corresponding to the executed GDI commands.

Unlike bitmaps, metafiles are not tied to the resolution of the output device, for which they were created. Because coordinates in GDI commands are easily scalable, image quality is not affected by magnification. Of course, this is not true of bitmap commands, which can also be saved in metafiles.

The first Windows versions supported a limited metafile format called the Windows Metafile. Metafiles in this format supported only the 16-bit coordinate system, did not include information about the resolution of the output device for which they were created, and did not allow all existing GDI commands to be written to them. These metafiles are stored to disk in files with the WMF extension.

A new format, the Enhanced Metafile (EMF), free of the shortcomings of its predecessor, was created for Windows 95. The format is truly independent of the output device and supports all GDI commands. It turned out to be so successful that it started to be used for Windows' own needs, in particular for preparing print manager files. Enhanced Metafiles are stored to disk in files with the EMF extension.

The GDI+ library has brought in a new set of graphics commands and necessitated the expansion of the original set of EMF records to store them. This expanded format was called, who would have guessed, EMF+. However, if so desired, traditional EMFs can also be created in GDI+. In this case, all GDI+ calls will be translated into a set of GDI commands. Of course, commands specific to GDI+ (such as setting the antialiasing mode) cannot be stored in EMF.

Moreover, the Dual EMF+ format is also available and contains both EMF and EMF+ records. Files in this format will open in both environments.

Be careful when creating traditional EMFs with the help of GDI+. Practice has shown that the code to store them has errors and does not execute properly on Windows 9x systems, producing metafiles that may have some commands missing. Moreover, problems with the code page of the texts stored to the metafiles and indications of system graphics resource leaks have been observed. The same actions executed on the Windows NT/2000/XP/2003 system produced correct metafiles.

For working with metafiles, the GDI+ hierarchy has the `Metafile` class. In the following section, some questions that may arise when using it will be considered.

3.2.1. Loading a Metafile

The `Metafile` class inherits from the `Image` class, in which two loading methods are defined: from files (specifying the name) and from `IStream` streams. A short C++ example is shown in Listing 3.9.

Listing 3.9. Loading a metafile [C++]

```
// Loading from a file
Metafile mf1(L"sample1.emf");
Metafile *mf2 = (Metafile*) Image::FromFile(L"sample2.emf");

// Loading from a stream
LPSTREAM pIS;
...
Metafile * mf3 = (Metafile*) Image::FromStream(pIS);
...
delete mf2;
delete mf3;
```

Realize that both the constructor and the `FromFile` method require as the file name a Unicode string that needs to be prefixed with the `L` character. In .NET, when specifying paths containing subfolders, a C# innovation called *verbatim strings* (string constants, in which escape sequences do not matter) is handy. Such string constants are prefixed with the @ symbol.

```
Image img = Image.FromFile(@"C:\rsdn\gdiplus\3\sample.emf");
```

When verbatim strings are used, the folder separator symbol (\) does not have to be doubled.

The `Image::FromFile` and `Image::FromStream` methods return a pointer to the `Image` class. If you are certain that a metafile and not a bitmap will be loaded, the pointer can be forced to the necessary `Metafile*` type. Otherwise, the `GetRawFormat` method (the `RawFormat` property in .NET) can be used to ascertain the type of the loaded image by returning the globally unique identifier of the codec used to load the image. For loaded EMF and EMF+ metafiles, the method returns a constant of the `ImageFormatEMF` type (the property will take on the `ImageFormat.EMF` value for .NET).

Moreover, all the might of the *reflection* mechanism works for programmers in the .NET environment. A call to the standard `GetType` method can be made in an `Image` object created with the help of `Image.FromFile()` method, which will return the information about the object type. In particular, the `Text == img.GetType().FullName;` call will assign the `System.Drawing.Imaging.Metafile` string to the form header.

3.2.2. Playing Back a Metafile

To play the contents of a loaded metafile back into the device context, the `Graphics:DrawImage` method is used. It has numerous overloaded versions available (16 for C++ and 30 for .NET). The following is a short illustration of how to use this method in a WinForms application:

```
Image img;

private void Form1_Paint(object sender, PaintEventArgs e)
{
  if(img != null)
  {
    e.Graphics.DrawImage(img, 0, 0);
  }
}
```

This method of metafile playback supports coordinate transformations and geometric distortions of the source image. Moreover, there are techniques for color correction and changing output attributes; these will be considered in detail in *Chapter 5*.

When versions of the `DrawImage` method are used with a limiting rectangle specified, only those records will be reproduced that correspond to the commands falling into the output area. The reproduction criteria are defined by both the commands' coordinates and their specific character: in particular, a call to the `DrawLine` method will not be let through if the endpoints of the segment lie outside of the specified area but the segment crosses it.

Moreover, the `Graphics` class implementation for the .NET framework has a useless `DrawImageUnscaled` method, which simply calls the `DrawImage` method with the parameters it receives (sometimes ignoring some of them). This can be easily verified by examining a disassembled listing of any of the overloaded `DrawImageUnscaled` method versions.

3.2.3. Creating and Saving a New Metafile

Having learned that loading and reproducing metafiles is simple, you may conclude that saving them to disk is a symmetrical operation. This is not so.

Instead, special metafile saving constructors need to be used. They are easily recognized by the mandatory two parameters: a string with the file name and the `referenceHdc` parameter, which must contain the context of the display device.

```
Metafile( const WCHAR* FileName, HDC referenceHdc,
    EmfType type, const WCHAR* description );
```

The created metafile will contain information about the resolution of this context. The `description` parameter allows you to specify the string description that will be stored in the metafile. The `type` parameter defines the format of the created metafile (in particular, this allows it to be stored in the already mentioned Dual EMF+):

```
enum EmfType{
    EmfTypeEmfOnly      = MetafileTypeEmf,
    EmfTypeEmfPlusOnly  = MetafileTypeEmfPlusOnly,
    EmfTypeEmfPlusDual  = MetafileTypeEmfPlusDual
};
```

Having to specify `referenceHdc` presents a problem for .NET programmers. It can be easily solved by creating a temporary `Graphics` object whose resolution characteristics are close to those of the device, for which the metafile is created. It is assumed in Listing 3.10 that the metafile is created to be output to the screen; consequently, the `CreateGraphics` method of the `Control` class is used.

Listing 3.10. Creating a metafile with screen resolution in .NET [C#]

```
RectangleF bounds = new RectangleF(0, 0, 40, 40);
using(Graphics grfxVideo = CreateGraphics())
{
  IntPtr ipHdc = grfxVideo.GetHdc();
  using(Metafile mf = new Metafile(FileName,
    ipHdc, bounds,
    MetafileFrameUnit.Millimeter,
    EmfType.EmfOnly))
  {
    grfxVideo.ReleaseHdc(ipHdc);
    Graphics g = Graphics.FromImage(mf);
```

```
    // Configuring measurement units
    g.PageUnit = GraphicsUnit.Millimeter;
    ...
    // Commands to draw to a metafile here
  }
}
```

The `grfxVideo` object in the presented example is used only to obtain the HDC of the display device; the output commands are sent to another `Graphics` object.

Writing to a metafile is done by simply constructing a `Graphics` object on it. Writing is considered complete when the display context is deleted.

We need a working example to illustrate the writing to a metafile process. For this, we will slightly modify the C++ program from *Listing 1.5*. Now, instead of outputting the greeting text into a window, the program writes it to a metafile (Listing 3.11).

Listing 3.11. Creating an EMF+ metafile and filling it with records [C++]

```
using namespace Gdiplus;
// All strings are in Unicode.
WCHAR welcome[] = L"Welcome, EMF+ !";
RectF bounds(0, 0, 400, 300);
Metafile metafile(L"sample.emf", GetDC(0));
Graphics g(&metafile);

// Creating a semitransparent brush with
// a gradient over the entire window
LinearGradientBrush brush(bounds, Color(130, 255, 0, 0),
   Color(255, 0, 0, 255),
   LinearGradientModeBackwardDiagonal);

// Preparing the format and parameters of the font
StringFormat format;
format.SetAlignment(StringAlignmentCenter);
format.SetLineAlignment(StringAlignmentCenter);
Font font(L"Arial", 48, FontStyleBold);

// Outputting the greeting text; the length of -1 means
// that the string ends in zero
g.DrawString(welcome, -1, &font, bounds, &format, &brush);
```

3.2.4. Converting a Metafile into a Bitmap Image

What if the created or loaded-from-disk metafile needs to be converted into a bitmap image and saved, for example, in portable network graphics (PNG) format? A possible solution would be to create a bitmap image (Bitmap) in memory, prepare a Graphics object for output to this bitmap, and draw into the obtained context the source metafile. This technique (called a *shadow buffer*) will be considered in detail in *Chapter 5* when we describe flicker.

Nevertheless, the GDI+ library, as usual, provides an easier way to skin this cat. A bitmap is created by simply using a Bitmap constructor, taking a pointer to Image as a parameter (an instance of the Image class in .NET). That's it! The result is a full-fledged bitmap that can be saved to disk.

```
Bitmap bm = new Bitmap(img);
bm.Save(@"C:\rsdn\gdiplus\3\sample.png", ImageFormat.Png);
```

The only limitation to using this method is that the created bitmap will have the screen resolution. Note that the saved image will contain correct transparency information (i.e., areas not affected by the output commands will remain transparent).

3.2.5. Studying Metafile Commands

The format of metafile records is documented. To analyze contents of a metafile, a program can be easily written that will read the metafile data structure and interpret its contents depending on the record type. But why do this? This work is already done by the GDI+ library when displaying metafiles, and developers can use it in their applications. The EnumerateMetafile method of the Image class is intended for these purposes. Because it has many overloaded versions, we will consider only two definitions for illustration purposes, one for C++ (the GDI+ library for Windows, as shown in Listing 3.12) and the other for C# (WinForms, shown in Listing 3.13).

Listing 3.12. Defining the EnumerateMetafile method [C++]

```
Status EnumerateMetafile(
  const Metafile* metafile,
  const Point& destPoint,
  EnumerateMetafileProc callback,
  VOID* callbackData,
  ImageAttributes* imageAttributes
);
```

Listing 3.13. Defining the `EnumerateMetafile` method [C#]

```
[ComVisible(FALSE)]
public void EnumerateMetafile(
   Metafile metafile,
   Point destPoint,
   Graphics.EnumerateMetafileProc callback,
   IntPtr callbackData,
   ImageAttributes imageAttr
);
```

As you can see, this method is very similar to `DrawImage`. The same as for the `DrawImage` method, the displayed metafile and the initial coordinates for drawing (`destPoint`) must be passed to the `EnumerateMetafile` method. The geometry and attributes of the output image can also be changed. The only unique parameters are the `callback` and `callbackData` parameters. The former is a pointer (a delegate in .NET) to the procedure that will be successively called by the library for each record it encounters in the metafile. The latter is useful if additional parameters are needed for the procedure's operation. A suggested definition of such a procedure for C++ and C# is given in Listings 3.14 and 3.15, respectively.

Listing 3.14. The syntax of the callback procedure [C++]

```
BOOL CALLBACK metaCallback( EmfPlusRecordType recordType,
   unsigned int flags, unsigned int dataSize,
   const unsigned char* recordData, void* callbackData );
```

Listing 3.15. The syntax of the callback procedure [C#]

```
public bool metaCallback( EmfPlusRecordType recordType, int flags,
   int dataSize, IntPtr recordData, PlayRecordCallback callbackData );
```

Using the `callbackData` parameter, for example, a pointer to the metafile whose records are being enumerated can be passed to the `metaCallback` procedure (C++ version). Then, the `Metafile::PlayRecord` method can be used for executing the graphics commands.

Listing 3.16. Drawing metafile records without `DrawImage` [C++]

```cpp
BOOL CALLBACK metaCallback( EmfPlusRecordType recordType,
  unsigned int flags, unsigned int dataSize,
  const unsigned char* recordData, void* callbackData)
{
  // Implicitly type casting the pointer type to Metafile*
  ((Metafile*)callbackData)->PlayRecord(
     recordType, flags, dataSize, recordData);
  return TRUE;
}
```

At every call of the callback procedure, the `recordType` parameter takes a value from the `EmfPlusRecordType` enumeration, which contains whole 253 elements (the largest GDI+ enumeration). All these elements either directly correspond to GDI/GDI+ commands or identify the metafile service records. When calling `PlayRecord`, you can replace this parameter with your own values to execute different GDI+ commands in this method. For this, however, you must have solid knowledge of the corresponding undocumented `recordData` and `dataSize` parameters (and pass the changed values to them).

3.2.6. .NET-Specific Record Enumeration

The WinForms documentation states that the .NET environment provides its own version of the delegate to execute the corresponding metafile commands in the body of the callback handler. This version is passed to the handler in the `callbackData` parameter. Calling the received delegate is sufficient to execute a command. Listing 3.17 shows a corresponding example from the .NET framework documentation.

Listing 3.17. Metafile command execution in .NET [C#]

```csharp
// Defining the callback method
private bool MetafileCallback(
            EmfPlusRecordType recordType,
            int flags,
            int dataSize,
            IntPtr data,
            PlayRecordCallback callbackData)
```

```
{
  // Playing only EmfPlusRecordType.FillEllipse records
  if (recordType == EmfPlusRecordType.FillEllipse)
  {
    // Playing the metafile
    callbackData(recordType, flags, dataSize, data);
  }
  return TRUE;
}
```

IMPORTANT

This is an obvious .NET Framework documentation error. The presented example will compile, but trying to execute it will produce something you will not like. The same thing is said in the book by Charles Petzold [4].

Experiments have shown that the 0 value is always passed in the `callbackData` parameter, regardless what phase the moon may be in. Calling such a "delegate" will terminate in the `NullReferenceException`.

Nevertheless, it is possible to create a working version of the `EnumerateMetafile` method for .NET. For this, you just have to tinker with the `Metafile.PlayRecord` method, taking advantage of the fact that this method accepts an array of bytes as the `data` parameter:

```
public void PlayRecord( EmfPlusRecordType recordType,
    int flags, int dataSize, byte[] data );
```

However, only the unmanaged `IntPtr recordData` pointer is available in the body of the callback method (see the delegate declaration). To copy the necessary data to a managed .NET array, the `System.Runtime.InteropServices.Marshal` class can be employed.

Listing 3.18. Enumerating metafile records [C#]

```
public bool DrawRecordsCallback(
  EmfPlusRecordType recordType, int flags,
  int dataSize, IntPtr recordData,
  PlayRecordCallback callbackData)
{
  // This will not work:
  // callbackData(recordType, flags, dataSize, recordData);
```

Chapter 3: Working with Output Devices and Using Metafiles 77

```
    byte[] arr = new byte[dataSize];

    // See the note following this listing.
    if(recordData != IntPtr.Zero)
      Marshal.Copy(recordData, arr, 0, dataSize);

    // Calling only the commands selected by the user
    if(frmItems.lbRecords.GetItemChecked(curRecord++))
      mfImage.PlayRecord(recordType, flags, dataSize, arr);

    return TRUE;
}
```

As you can see, the Copy method makes it possible to move data to a managed heap, which is exactly what was needed.

NOTE
In the book by Charles Petzold [4], a similar example of calling PlayRecord using Marshal.Copy is described. However, this example has a serious defect.

The Petzold version always calls the Copy method. When 0 is passed in the recordData parameter, this method attempts to reference a nonexisting memory area. The book's author admits that his program for some reason cannot display metafiles created by WinForms but works with GDI EMFs. This error is corrected by simply adding to the program a check for this condition, which is done in Listing 3.18.

To reach the cherished goal of analyzing metafile records in WinForms, you have to work a little. But all the difficulties are compensated with interest by another great .NET feature: the reflection. Any enumeration element (even of such a giant as EmfPlusRecordType enumeration) "knows" its string name, which makes it possible to easily create an application enumerating the records of the selected metafile by name. Listing 3.19 is a fragment of a demonstration program doing this.

Listing 3.19. Code for populating the record list [C#]

```
public bool EnlistRecordsCallback(
  EmfPlusRecordType recordType, int flags,
  int dataSize, IntPtr recordData,
  PlayRecordCallback callbackData)
```

```
{
    frmItems.lbRecords.Items.Add(recordType.ToString(), TRUE);
    return TRUE;
}
```

Simple, isn't it? The `ToString` method returns string names of enumeration elements, relieving the programmer of the tedious task of coding 253 string constants. The results produced by this method are shown in Fig. 3.3.

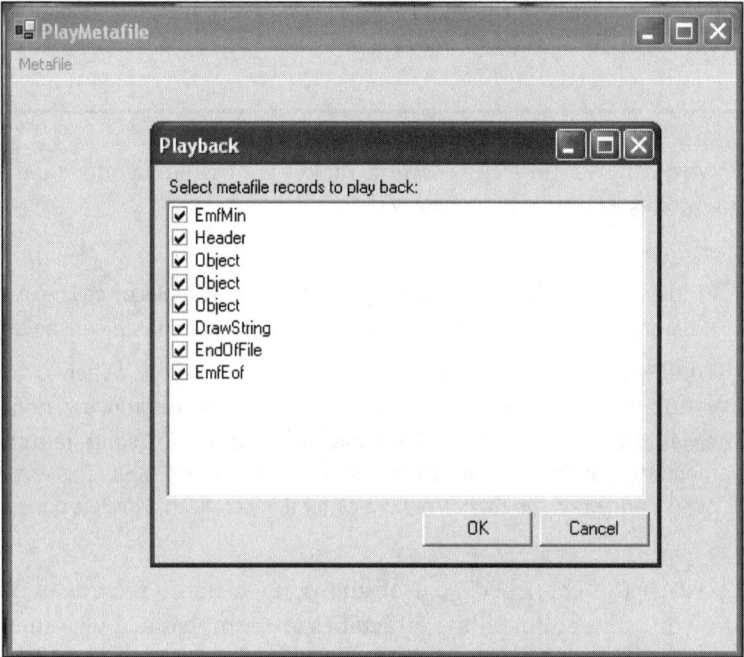

Fig. 3.3. Results of enumerating metafile records

The complete source code of the application (it allows the execution of only the metafile commands selected by the user) is on the accompanying CD-ROM. There also is the compiled version, which can be used for examining the contents of various metafiles (e.g., those included in the Microsoft Visual Studio distribution package).

Chapter 4: Implementing 3D Transformations Using Software

The following subjects are considered in this chapter:

- The *Painter* program
- Creating a class for drawing 3D shapes
- Constructing a $z = f(x, y)$ 3D surface
- Constructing level lines on a 3D surface

4.1. The Painter Program

The subjects covered in this chapter require some knowledge of 3D-shape construction theory (a mathematical foundation). If you are not familiar with it, we advise you to master the material in *Appendix 2* to better understand the material in this chapter.

To demonstrate the construction of 3D figures, we need a framework program for experiments. We use for this purpose the Painter program (the details on how to construct it are given in a book by David F. Rogers et al. [11]) and supplement its functions with capabilities to create 3D figures.

Painter is based on the Document/View (see *Section 6.1.1*) architecture application framework generated by AppWizard and a single document interface.

The program already has capabilities to construct various simple shapes—circles, rectangles, and polygons—and to save and load images. Each shape is implemented by its class, which has methods for displaying it on the screen and performing other operations on it. The class interface and the implementation are defined in the shapes.h and shapes.cpp files, respectively. The class hierarchy is shown in Fig. 4.1.

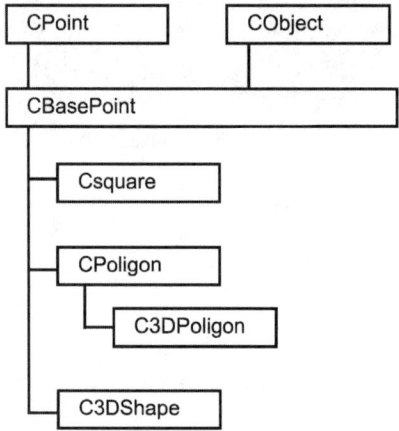

Fig. 4.1. Hierarchy of the classes implementing shape imaging in the Painter program

We will add the `C3DPolygon` and `C3DShape` classes for constructing 3D shapes. In Painter, drawing is implemented by the Windows GDI functions. We will not change the tools employed for displaying images because this is unimportant in the case. Should you desire, the program can be easily converted to use the GDI+ methods considered in *Chapter 3*. Let this task be an exercise to carry out on your own. The complete source code of the program is on the accompanying CD-ROM in the sources\painter folder. In the following section, only those code fragments relative to the subject of this chapter will be considered. In this chapter, all examples are written in C++.

4.2. Creating a Class for Drawing 3D Shapes

So then, add 3D-image creation and manipulation capabilities to the Painter project.

To specify a point in 3D space and the observer point and projection construction parameters, define `POINT3D` and `Perspective` data structures, respectively (Listing 4.1).

Chapter 4: Implementing 3D Transformations Using Software

Listing 4.1. Data structures for working with 3D shapes [shapes.h]

```
struct POINT3D
{
   double x, y, z;
};

// 3D-scene parameters
struct  Perspective
{
   POINT3D O;                // The pivot point
   double rho, theta, phi,   // Polar coordinates of the observer point (E)
                  d; // Distance from E to the screen
// 1 — Enable perspective transformations; 0 — Disable them
   WORD with_perspective;
   LONG dx, dy; // Screen projection offset

};
```

3D shapes will be represented as wireframes, each wire of which is a polygon in 3D space: a `C3DPolygon` class object. The `C3DPolygon` class is derived from the `CPolygon` class (Listing 4.2). To store the shape's 3D coordinates, define an `m_3DPointsArray` array of points in the `C3DPolygon` class. The new class will inherit the 2D `m_PointsArray` array of points and the methods to work with it from the `CPolygon` class. The shape screen coordinates will be stored in this array—that is, coordinates of the points from the `m_3DPointsArray` projection to the screen. To calculate screen coordinates, introduce a `MakeProjection()` method. Shapes will be displayed on the screen by the inherited `CPolygon::Show()` method.

Listing 4.2. The `C3DPolygon` class interface [shapes.h]

```
class C3DPolygon: public CPolygon
{
   DECLARE_SERIAL(C3DPolygon)
 protected:    // Serialization method

   void Serialize(CArchive& ar);
 public:
   // Constructors
```

```
    C3DPolygon(){};
    ~C3DPolygon(){};
// Data
    // Dynamic array of the apex points in world coordinates
    CArray <POINT3D, POINT3D> m_3DPointsArray;
// Methods
    // Adding a point
    void AddPoint(POINT3D point) {m_3DPointsArray.Add(point);};
    // Calculating screen coordinates
    void MakeProjection(Perspective P);
};
```

To assemble all wires, all class `C3DPolygon` objects, into one figure, define a `C3DShape` class, in which pointers to the 3D polygons will be stored (Listing 4.3).

Listing 4.3. The `C3DShape` class interface [shapes.h]

```
class C3DShape: public CBasePoint
{
    DECLARE_SERIAL(C3DShape)
 protected: // Virtual serialization method

    void Serialize(CArchive& ar);
 public:
    // Constructors
    C3DShape();
    ~C3DShape();
// Data
    Perspective m_Perspective; // Viewing parameters

    // List of the polygon pointers
    CTypedPtrList<CObList, C3DPolygon*> m_PtrPolygonList;
// Methods
    // Calculating the projection
    void MakeProjection();
    // Displaying the shape on the screen
    void Show(CDC *pDC);
    // Capturing region information
    void GetRegion(CRgn &Rgn);
```

Chapter 4: Implementing 3D Transformations Using Software 83

```
   // Adding a polygon
   void AddPolygon(C3DPolygon *pPolygon);
   // Reacting to a key pressed
   BOOL OnKeyDown(UINT nChar, UINT nRepCnt, UINT nFlags, UINT nMyFlags);
};
```

In addition to the list of 3D polygons, the figure-viewing parameters—the `m_Perspective` variable—are defined in the `C3DShape` class. Based on these parameters, the `MakeProjection()` method calculates the screen coordinates of each polygon from the `m_PtrPolygonList`. Consequently, if a drawing has several 3D shapes, each of them can be viewed differently. If this is not desired, common parameters for viewing the entire drawing (a 3D scene) can be defined and then passed as the parameters to the `C3DShape::MakeProjection()` method for each 3D shape in the scene.

Consider now how the methods for the new classes are implemented.

All that needed to be done in the 3D-polygon saving and loading `C3DPolygon::Serialize()` function was to call a method of the base `CPolygon` class (Listing 4.4).

Listing 4.4. The `C3DPolygon::Serialize()` method [shapes.cpp]

```
IMPLEMENT_SERIAL(C3DPolygon, CPolygon, -1)
void C3DPolygon::Serialize(CArchive &ar)
{
   CPolygon::Serialize(ar);
   if(ar.IsStoring())
   {  }
   else
   {  }
   m_3DPointsArray.Serialize(ar);
};
```

Screen coordinates are calculated in the `C3DPolygon::MakeProjection()` method in the following way: First, the transformation matrix coefficients are calculated (see Fig. A2.35). Next, screen projections are determined for all points in the `m_3DPointsArray` array. Finally, the perspective transformation performed (Listing 4.5).

Listing 4.5. The `C3DPolygon::Serialize()` **method [shapes.cpp]**

```cpp
void C3DPolygon::MakeProjection(Perspective P)
{
  // Converting into radians
  P.theta = P.theta*atan(1.0)/45.0; P.phi = P.phi*atan(1.0)/45.0;
  // Calculating coefficients of the transformation matrix
  // If the MM_TEXT mapping mode is set (which has
  // the coordinate origin in the upper left corner),
  // all that needs to be done is that the sign of
  // the coefficients in the second matrix column needs to be
  // reversed (the Y-axis needs to be turned upside down).

  double st = sin(P.theta), ct = cos(P.theta), sp = sin(P.phi), cp = cos(P.phi),
         v11 = -st,     v12 = -cp*ct,    v13 = -sp*ct,
         v21 = ct,      v22 = -cp*st,    v23 = -sp*st,
                        v32 = sp,        v33 = -cp,
         v41 = P.dx,    v42 = P.dy,      v43 = P.rho;
  double x, y, z;
  double TempZ = 0;
  // Calculating the points' view coordinates
  m_PointsArray.SetSize(m_3DPointsArray.GetSize());
  for(int i = 0; i<m_3DPointsArray.GetSize(); i++)
  {
      x = m_3DPointsArray[i].x - P.O.x;
      y = m_3DPointsArray[i].y - P.O.y;
      z = m_3DPointsArray[i].z - P.O.z;
      TempZ = v13*x + v23*y + v33*z + v43;
      m_PointsArray[i].x = (LONG)(v11*x + v21*y + v41 + 0.5);
      m_PointsArray[i].y = (LONG)(v12*x + v22*y + v32*z + v42 + 0.5);
      // Perspective transformations
      if(P.with_perspective)
      {
         m_PointsArray[i].x = (LONG)(P.d*m_PointsArray[i].x/TempZ + 0.5);
         m_PointsArray[i].y = (LONG)(P.d*m_PointsArray[i].y/TempZ + 0.5);
      }
      m_PointsArray[i].x += (LONG)(P.O.x + 0.5);
      m_PointsArray[i].y += (LONG)(P.O.y + 0.5);
  }
};
```

Chapter 4: Implementing 3D Transformations Using Software 85

The location of the viewing point and the screen distance are defined in the 3D object constructor (see Figs. A2.14 and A2.20); the memory taken by the figure is released in the destructor (Listing 4.6).

Listing 4.6. The C3DShape class constructor [shapes.cpp]

```
C3DShape::C3DShape(): CBasePoint()
{
   m_Perspective.O.x = 0;
   m_Perspective.O.y = 0;
   m_Perspective.O.z = 0;
   m_Perspective.rho = 50000; // 50 cm in the MM_HIMETRIC mode

   m_Perspective.theta = 30;
   m_Perspective.phi = 30;
   m_Perspective.d = 25000; // 25 cm in the MM_HIMETRIC mode

   m_Perspective.with_perspective = TRUE;
   m_Perspective.dx = 0;
   m_Perspective.dy = 0;
}

C3DShape::~C3DShape()
{
   while(m_PtrPolygonList.GetCount()>0)
       delete m_PtrPolygonList.RemoveHead();
};
```

The C3DShape::Serialize() 3D-figure method (Listing 4.7) saves and loads viewing parameters and calls the Serialize() method for the 3D-polygon list object.

Listing 4.7. The C3DShape::Serialize() method [shapes.cpp]

```
IMPLEMENT_SERIAL(C3DShape, CBasePoint, -1)
void C3DShape::Serialize(CArchive &ar)
{
   if(ar.IsStoring())
   {
       ar << m_Perspective.O.x;
```

```
        ar << m_Perspective.O.y;
        ar << m_Perspective.O.z;
        ar << m_Perspective.rho;
        ar << m_Perspective.theta;
        ar << m_Perspective.phi;
        ar << m_Perspective.d;
        ar << m_Perspective.with_perspective;
        ar << m_Perspective.dx;
        ar << m_Perspective.dy;
    }
    else
    {
        ar >> m_Perspective.O.x;
        ar >> m_Perspective.O.y;
        ar >> m_Perspective.O.z;
        ar >> m_Perspective.rho;
        ar >> m_Perspective.theta;
        ar >> m_Perspective.phi;
        ar >> m_Perspective.d;
        ar >> m_Perspective.with_perspective;
        ar >> m_Perspective.dx;
        ar >> m_Perspective.dy;
    }
    m_PtrPolygonList.Serialize(ar);
};
```

The `C3Dshape::Show()` 3D-shape method (Listing 4.8) calls the same name method for all polygons forming the shape.

Listing 4.8. The `C3Dshape::Show()` method [shapes.cpp]

```
void C3DShape::Show(CDC *pDC)
{
    // Outputting all polygons
    POSITION Pos = NULL;
    if(m_PtrPolygonList.GetCount()>0)
        Pos = m_PtrPolygonList.GetHeadPosition();
    while(Pos != NULL)
        m_PtrPolygonList.GetNext(Pos)->Show(pDC);
};
```

Chapter 4: Implementing 3D Transformations Using Software 87

The `C3DShape::GetRegion()` 3D-shape method (Listing 4.9) constructs a rectangular region encompassing the shape screen projection.

Listing 4.9. The `C3DShape::GetRegion()` method [shapes.cpp]

```
void C3DShape::GetRegion(CRgn &Rgn)
{
    // Constructing the rectangular C3DShape capture area
    // that encompasses the shape screen image

    CRect Frame; // The encompassing rectangle

    POSITION Pos = NULL;
    int i=0;
    CPolygon *pPolygon = NULL;
    if(m_PtrPolygonList.GetCount()>0)
        Pos = m_PtrPolygonList.GetHeadPosition();
    // Initializing the rectangle with the values
    // of the first point of the first polygon

    if(Pos != NULL && (pPolygon = m_PtrPolygonList.GetAt(Pos)) != NULL &&
       pPolygon->m_PointsArray.GetSize()>0)
    {
        Frame.left = Frame.right = pPolygon->m_PointsArray[0].x;
        Frame.top = Frame.bottom = pPolygon->m_PointsArray[0].y;
    }
    else return;
    // Obtaining the shape's dimensions
    while(Pos != NULL)
    {
        pPolygon = m_PtrPolygonList.GetNext(Pos);
        for(i=0; i < pPolygon->m_PointsArray.GetSize(); i++)
        {
            if(pPolygon->m_PointsArray[i].x < Frame.left)
                Frame.left = pPolygon->m_PointsArray[i].x;
            if(pPolygon->m_PointsArray[i].x > Frame.right)
                Frame.right = pPolygon->m_PointsArray[i].x;
            if(pPolygon->m_PointsArray[i].y > Frame.bottom)
                Frame.bottom = pPolygon->m_PointsArray[i].y;
            if(pPolygon->m_PointsArray[i].y < Frame.top)
```

```
                Frame.top = pPolygon->m_PointsArray[i].y;
        };
    }
    // Creating the region
    Rgn.CreateRectRgn(Frame.left, Frame.top, Frame.right, Frame.bottom);
}
```

The `C3DShape::AddPolygon()` method is used to add new 3D-shape-forming wires to the `m_PtrPolygonList` polygon list. This method also calculates the shape's center point, around which the 3D transformations will be performed (Listing 4.10).

Listing 4.10. The `C3DShape::AddPolygon()` method [shapes.cpp]

```
void C3DShape::AddPolygon(C3DPolygon *pPolygon)
{
    m_PtrPolygonList.AddTail(pPolygon); // Added to the list
    // Calculating the center point
    POSITION Pos = NULL;
    C3DPolygon* pCurPolygon = NULL;
    WORD Count = 0, i=0;
    if(m_PtrPolygonList.GetCount()>0)
        Pos = m_PtrPolygonList.GetHeadPosition();
    while(Pos != NULL)
    {
        pCurPolygon = (C3DPolygon*)m_PtrPolygonList.GetNext(Pos);
        for(i = 0; i<pCurPolygon->m_3DPointsArray.GetSize(); i++)
        {
            m_Perspective.O.x += pCurPolygon->m_3DPointsArray[i].x;
            m_Perspective.O.y += pCurPolygon->m_3DPointsArray[i].y;
            m_Perspective.O.z += pCurPolygon->m_3DPointsArray[i].z;
        }
        Count += i;
    }
    m_Perspective.O.x /= Count;
    m_Perspective.O.y /= Count;
    m_Perspective.O.z /= Count;
};
```

Chapter 4: Implementing 3D Transformations Using Software 89

The `C3DShape:MakeProjection()` method is simple; the only things it does are call the same name method for each 3D polygon and pass the shape-viewing parameters (Listing 4.11) to it. This method needs to be called every time a shape is created (before its first screen display) and every time the shape-viewing parameters change.

Listing 4.11. The `C3DShape::MakeProjection()` method [shapes.cpp]

```
void C3DShape::MakeProjection()
{
    POSITION Pos = NULL;
    if(m_PtrPolygonList.GetCount()>0)
    Pos = m_PtrPolygonList.GetHeadPosition();
    while(Pos != NULL)
        ((C3DPolygon*)m_PtrPolygonList.GetNext(Pos))->
                                        MakeProjection(m_Perspective);
};
```

The `OnKeyDown()` method was redefined in the `C3DShape` class to have a capability to change the shape-viewing parameters (Listing 4.12). The method checks the status of the <Ctrl> key: If it is pressed, the distance to the screen, onto which the shape is projected, can be changed using the <↑> and <↓> keys.

Listing 4.12. The `C3DShape::OnKeyDown()` method [shapes.cpp]

```
BOOL C3DShape::OnKeyDown(UINT nChar, UINT nRepCnt, UINT nFlags, UINT nMyFlags)
{
    BOOL res = TRUE;
    if(nMyFlags & SHIFT_HOLD)
    switch(nChar)
    {
        // Up — Moving the viewing point up
        case 38: m_Perspective.phi -= ROTATE_STEP; break;
        // Down — Moving the viewing point down
        case 40: m_Perspective.phi += ROTATE_STEP; break;
        // Left — Moving the viewing point to the left
        case 37: m_Perspective.theta -= ROTATE_STEP; break;
```

```
                // Right - Moving the viewing point to the right
            case 39: m_Perspective.theta += ROTATE_STEP; break;
            default: res = FALSE;
        }
    else
      if(nMyFlags & CTRL_HOLD)
         switch(nChar)
         {
            case 38: m_Perspective.d += MOVE_STEP; break;
                            // Up - Moving the screen away
            case 40: m_Perspective.d -= MOVE_STEP; break;
                            // Down - Moving the screen closer
            default: res = FALSE;
         }
    else // Moving the projection:
    {
        switch(nChar)
        {
            case 38: m_Perspective.dy += MOVE_STEP; break; // Up
            case 40: m_Perspective.dy -= MOVE_STEP; break; // Down
            case 37: m_Perspective.dx -= MOVE_STEP; break; // Left
            case 39: m_Perspective.dx += MOVE_STEP; break; // Right
    // The <P> key enables and disables perspective transformations
            case 80:
              m_Perspective.with_perspective = !m_Perspective.with_perspective;
                break;
            default:res = FALSE;
        }
    }
    if(res)
      // Projection calculation
       MakeProjection();
    return res;
};
```

4.3. Drawing a 3D Surface

All that is left to be done is to add a command to draw some 3D shape to the Painter program interface. Overall, this process is no different from embedding commands to draw the previously-considered shapes; therefore, we will not dwell on it. The difference lies in that a 3D shape needs to be constructed from individual polygons. Of course, special classes could be constructed to create specific shapes (e.g., a cube or a sphere). However, adding a special function (Listing 4.13) to the CPainterView class will suffice for the illustration purposes. This draws a 3D surface; consequently, the function will be called AddSurface(). This function is called from the CPainterView::AddShape() method (Listing 4.14) and takes a point and size as parameters. The surface is calculated as the ZFunction() function on the grid made of _GRID_DENSITY*_GRID_DENSITY nodes in a square with the size*2 side, with the center in the first_point point. The ZFunction is defined in the global.cpp file (Listing 4.15). The surface is built from polygon wires parallel to the X- and Y-axes. On the screen, the surface is displayed with the viewing parameters set in the 3DShape constructor taken into account.

Listing 4.13. The CPainterView::AddSurface() method [painterview.cpp]

```
const int _GRID_DENSITY = 30;
CBasePoint* CPainterView::AddSurface(CPoint first_point, int size)
{
   C3DShape *pShape = NULL;
   pShape = new C3DShape();
  // Calculating the surface in the specified area
   double dx = (double)size*2/_GRID_DENSITY,
      dy = (double)size*2/_GRID_DENSITY;
   // Creating a 3D-surface object as an aggregate of 3D polygons
   POINT3D point3d;
   C3DPolygon *p3Dpolygon = NULL;
   for(int i=0, j=0; i < _GRID_DENSITY; i++)
      {
      p3Dpolygon = new C3DPolygon();
      for(j=0; j<_GRID_DENSITY; j++)
         {
         point3d.x = first_point.x + dx*i - size;
         point3d.y = first_point.y + dy*j - size;
         point3d.z = ZFunction(fabs(first_point.x - point3d.x),
                       fabs(first_point.y - point3d.y));
         p3DPolygon->AddPoint(point3d);
```

```
        }
        pShape->AddPolygon(p3DPolygon);
    }

    for(j=0; j<_GRID_DENSITY; j++)
    {
        p3Dpolygon = new C3DPolygon();
        for(i=0; i < _GRID_DENSITY; i++)
        {
            point3d.x = first_point.x + dx*i — size;
            point3d.y = first_point.y + dy*j — size;
            point3d.z = ZFunction(fabs(first_point.x - point3d.x),
                        fabs(first_point.y - point3d.y));
            p3DPolygon->AddPoint(point3d);
        }
        pShape->AddPolygon(p3DPolygon);
    }
    pShape->MakeProjection();
    return pShape;
};
```

Listing 4.14. The `CPainterView::AddShape()` method [painterview.cpp]

```
void CPainterView::AddShape(int shape, CPoint first_point, CPoint second_point)
{
    CPainterDoc *pDoc = GetDocument();
    CBasePoint *pShape = NULL;
    // Size calculation
    int size = 0;
    size = (int) floor( sqrt((second_point.x - first_point.x)*
                             (second_point.x - first_point.x) +
                             (second_point.y - first_point.y)*
                             (second_point.y - first_point.y)) + 0.5);
    switch(shape)
    {
        case OP_LINE:
            break;
        case OP_POINT:
            // Creating a point object
            pShape = new CBasePoint(second_point.x, second_point.y, 100);
            // Light-gray filling
            pShape->SetBrush(RGB(200, 200, 200));
            break;
```

```
        case OP_CIRCLE:
           // Creating a circle object
           pShape = new CBasePoint(first_point.x, first_point.y, size);
           // A black 2-mm-wide line
           pShape->SetPen(RGB(0, 0, 0), 200, PS_GEOMETRIC);
           // Dark-gray filling
           pShape->SetBrush(RGB(100, 100, 100));
           break;
        case OP_SQUARE:
           // Creating a square object
           pShape = new CSquare(first_point.x, first_point.y, size*2);
            // A red 1-mm-wide line
           pShape->SetPen(RGB(200, 0, 0), 100, PS_GEOMETRIC);
            // Dark-gray diagonal hatching
           pShape->SetBrush(RGB(100, 100, 100), 0, HS_DIAGCROSS);
           break;
        case OP_SURFACE:
            // Creating a surface object
           pShape = AddSurface(first_point, size);
           break;
    }
    if(pShape != NULL) // A shape has been created
    {
        // Adding it to the end of the list
        pDoc->m_ShapesList.AddTail(pShape);
        // The last shape becomes active
        pDoc->m_pSelShape = pShape;
        // Indicating that the document has been modified
        pDoc->SetModifiedFlag();
    }
}
```

Listing 4.15. The `ZFunction()` function [global.cpp]

```
double ZFunction(double x, double y)
{
   return (x*x + y*y)/10000;
};
```

Results of the surface drawing function program are shown in Fig. 4.2.

To illustrate the perspective effect, Figs. 4.3 and 4.4 show two 3D planes ($z = 10,000$) with the perspective transformation calculation modes enabled and disabled, respectively.

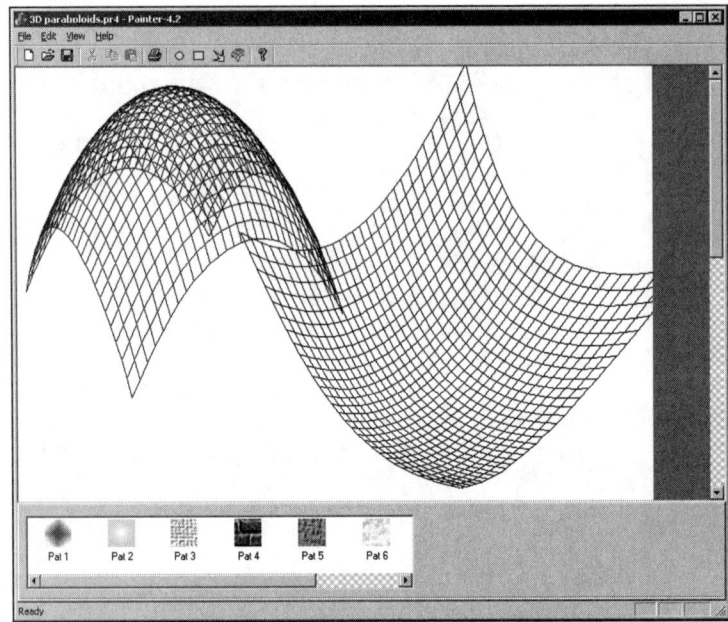

Fig. 4.2. Drawings of 3D surfaces

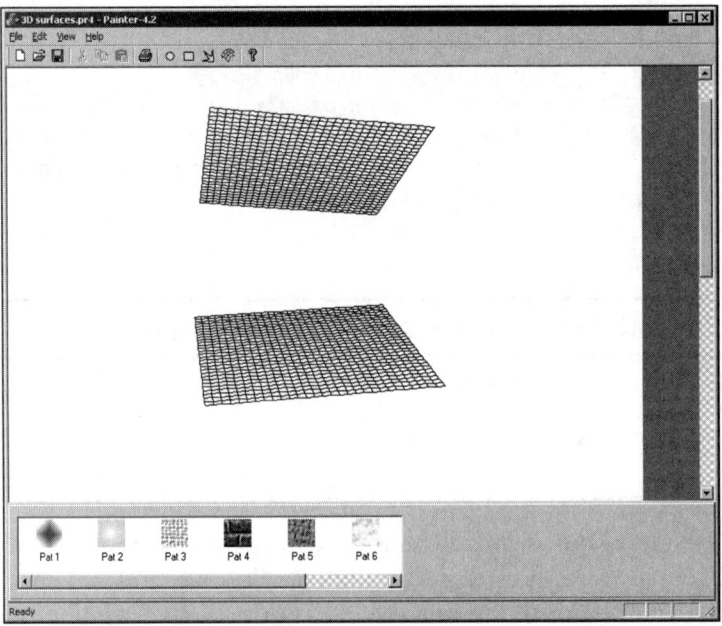

Fig. 4.3. Planes drawn with the perspective transformation calculation mode enabled

Chapter 4: Implementing 3D Transformations Using Software

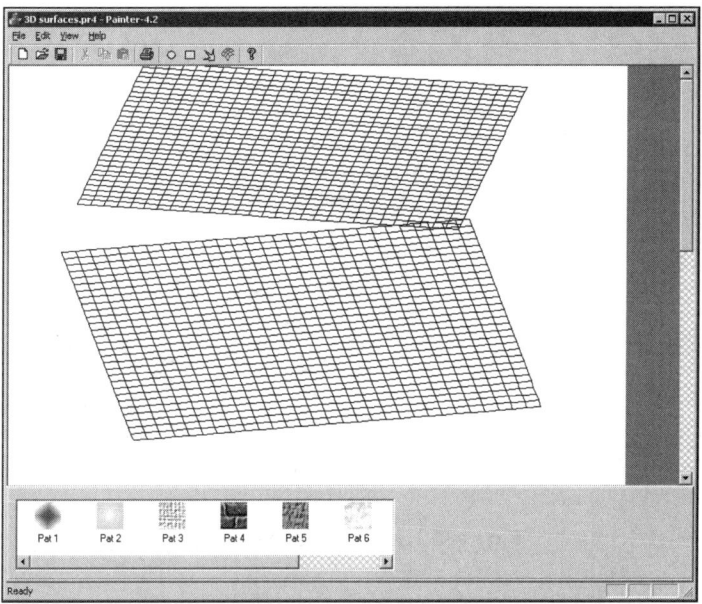

Fig. 4.4. Planes drawn with the perspective transformation calculation mode disabled

To disable perspective transformations, use the <Insert> key to switch to the *select* mode, select a shape, and press the <P> key.

4.3.1. Constructing Level Lines on a Surface

The problem of constructing level lines on surfaces is often encountered when visualizing experimental or calculated data. In particular, you should be familiar with level lines from topographic maps, where they are used to indicate an area's elevation above sea level.

You can also solve this problem by using the 3D-shape class. All that you need to do is define a few more functions and modify the `CPainterView::AddSurface()` method.

Let the surface of a $z = f(x, y)$ function be given by an array of the values $z(x, y)$ calculated on the $x = (X_{min}, ..., X_{max})$, $y = (Y_{min}, ..., Y_{max})$ grid (Fig. 4.5). To find the L level line, the intersection of the $z = f(x, y)$ surface with the $z = L$ plane needs to be determined.

In this case, the general approach to constructing level lines consists of the following:

1. The surface is triangulated, with each grid cell divided into two triangles (Fig. 4.6).
2. Each triangle's intersection with the L plane is found (Fig. 4.7).

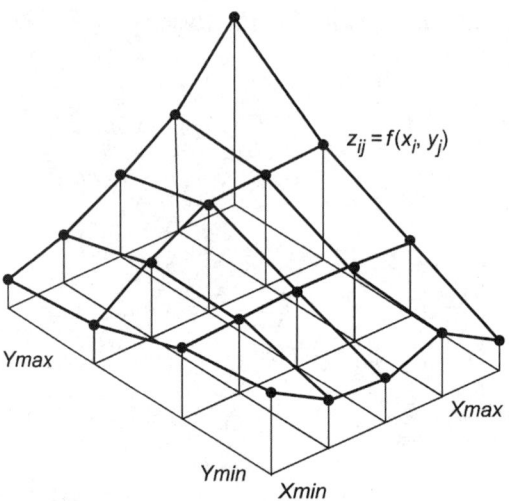

Fig. 4.5. Surface defined by $z = f(x, y)$

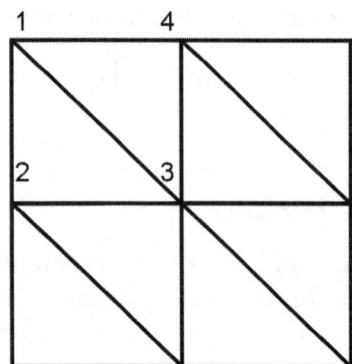

Fig. 4.6. Triangulating the surface

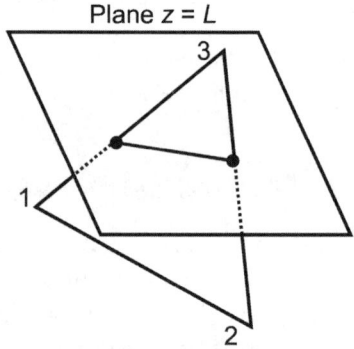

Fig. 4.7. Intersection of a triangle with the $z = L$ plane

This method is simple and allows you to obtain a quality level-line image. It must be noted that the level line may have breaks in it. We will call the individual line parts *segments*. A general flowchart for level line construction is shown in Fig. 4.8.

Chapter 4: Implementing 3D Transformations Using Software

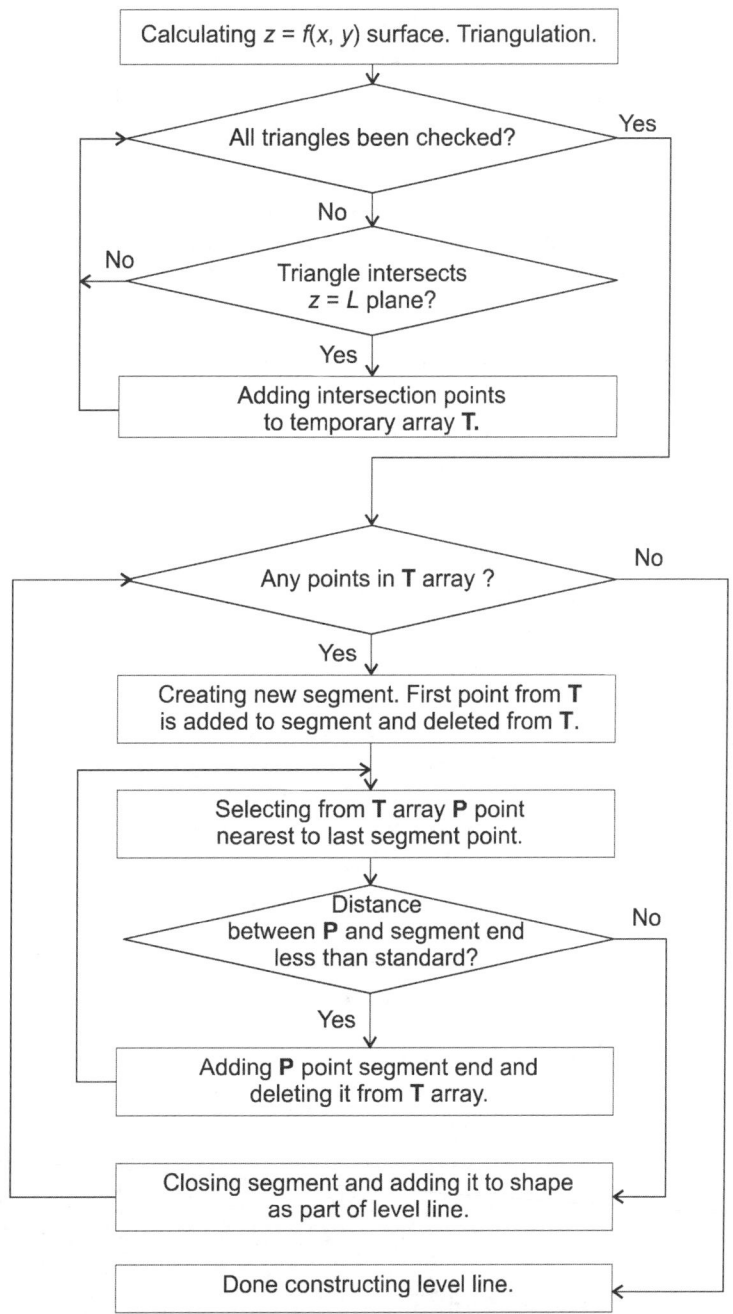

Fig. 4.8. Flowchart for constructing level lines

Part II: Vector Graphics Programming

To implement the described approach, slightly modify the `CpaintView::AddSurface()` method so that the values of the grid nodes are saved in an array that will be used to construct the surface (Listing 4.16). In addition, the minimum and maximum *z* values will be determined; these will be used to calculate several intermediate levels.

Listing 4.16. The modified `CPainterView::AddSurface()` method [painterview.cpp]

```
const int _GRID_DENSITY = 30;
const int _LEVELS_DENSITY = 5;
CBasePoint* CPainterView::AddSurface(CPoint first_point, int size)
{
    C3DShape *pShape = NULL;
    pShape = new C3DShape();


    // Calculating the surface of the given area
    // dx, dy — Grid step

    double dx = (double)size*2/_GRID_DENSITY,
           dy = (double)size*2/_GRID_DENSITY;
    // The array of surface points is used for temporary storage.
    POINT3D point3d[_GRID_DENSITY*_GRID_DENSITY];
    // Creating a 3D-surface object as a collection of 3D polygons
    C3DPolygon *p3Dpolygon = NULL;
    // Adding wires along the Y-axis
    for(int i=0, j=0; i < _GRID_DENSITY; i++)
    {
        p3Dpolygon = new C3DPolygon();
        for(j=0; j < _GRID_DENSITY; j++)
        {
            point3d[j*_GRID_DENSITY+i].x = first_point.x + dx*i — size;
            point3d[j*_GRID_DENSITY+i].y = first_point.y + dy*j — size;
            point3d[j*_GRID_DENSITY+i].z = ZFunction
                    (fabs(first_point.x - point3d[j*_GRID_DENSITY + i].x),
                     fabs(first_point.y - point3d[j*_GRID_DENSITY + i].y));
            p3DPolygon->AddPoint(point3d[j*_GRID_DENSITY + i]);
        }
        pShape->AddPolygon(p3DPolygon);
    }
```

```
    double minz = point3d[0].z, maxz = point3d[0].z;
    // Adding wires along the X-axis
    for(j=0; j < _GRID_DENSITY; j++)
    {
        p3Dpolygon = new C3DPolygon();
        for(i=0; i < _GRID_DENSITY; i++)
        {
            p3DPolygon->AddPoint(point3d[j*_GRID_DENSITY + i]);
            // Determining the limits of z change
            if(point3d[j*_GRID_DENSITY + i].z < minz)
                minz = point3d[j*_GRID_DENSITY + i].z;
            if(point3d[j*_GRID_DENSITY + i].z > maxz)
                maxz = point3d[j*_GRID_DENSITY + i].z;
        }
        pShape->AddPolygon(p3DPolygon);
    }
    // Constructing level lines
    double l_step = (maxz - minz)/_LEVELS_DENSITY;
    int color_step = 200/_LEVELS_DENSITY; // Color change
    for(i=0; i < _LEVELS_DENSITY; i++)
    AddRsection(pShape, point3d, _GRID_DENSITY, _GRID_DENSITY,
        minz + l_step/2 + l_step*i, RGB(0, 0, 55 + color_step*i));
    // Calculating the screen projection
    pShape->MakeProjection();
    return pShape;
};
```

In the `CPainterView::AddSurface()` method, the `AddRsection()` function is called. Each call to this function adds the specified level line to the `C3DShape` class object. The following are passed to the function as arguments: a pointer to the object, to which the level line will be added, the array of the grid nodes defining the surface, the number of grid nodes, and the level and color values. For each triangle, the function calculates its intersection with the $z = L$ plane. All triangle–plane intersection points are added to the common temporary array. This array is then sorted, and one or several polygons (because the level line can be broken), the `C3DPolygon` class objects, are formed from its data. The source code for the `AddRsection()` function, the `AddTriangleSection()` function (finding the triangle–plane intersection), the `CutCross()` function (calculating the segment–plane intersection coordinates), and the `Dist()` function (calculating the distance between two points) is shown in Listing 4.17. These functions are global; their prototypes are defined in the shapes.h file.

Listing 4.17. Functions to build level lines [shapes.cpp]

```
int AddRsection(C3DShape *pShape, POINT3D *pSur, int x_size, int y_size,
    double level, COLORREF color)
{
  if(x_size<2 || y_size<2) return 0;
  // Polygon for temporary storage of the level line points
  C3DPolygon *pTempPolygon = new C3DPolygon();
  if(pTempPolygon == NULL) return 0;
  // The surface is broken into triangles and an attempt is made
  // to determine the intersection of each triangle with the
  // level plane. The intersection points are added to PTempPolygon.
  for(int x=0, y=0; y < y_size - 1; y++)
     for(int x=0;  x < x_size - 1; x++)
     {
         AddTriangleSection(pTempPolygon, &pSur[y*x_size + x],
             &pSur[(y + 1)*x_size + x + 1], &pSur[y*x_size + x + 1], level);
         AddTriangleSection(pTempPolygon, &pSur[y*x_size + x],
             &pSur[(y + 1)*x_size + x], &pSur[(y + 1)*x_size + x + 1], level);
     }

  // From the obtained set of points, neat little polygons are created.
  // To make working with points easier, obtain a reference to the data.
  // Of course, this is not the best illustration of
  // the object-oriented programming principles, but it is convenient.
  CArray <POINT3D, POINT3D> &TempPointsArray =
                            pTempPolygon->m_3DPointsArray;
  int pos = 0, posmin = 0;
  POINT3D EndSegPoint;
  double D = 0, dcur = 0, dmin = 0;    // Distance between points
  C3DPolygon *pSeg;
  BOOL fContinueSeg = TRUE;      // The "extend the current segment" flag
  // The standard distance between points is calculated.
  // The standard distance is assumed to be a grid plane diagonal.
  POINT3D P1 = pSur[0], P2 = pSur[x_size+1];      P1.z = P2.z = 0;
  D = Dist(&P1, &P2);
```

Chapter 4: Implementing 3D Transformations Using Software 101

```cpp
// While at least one pair of points remains in the temporary
// array, keep creating section segments from the array.
while(TempPointsArray.GetSize()-1 > 0)
{
    // A new segment/polygon
    pSeg = new C3DPolygon(); fContinueSeg = TRUE;
    if(pSeg == NULL) return 0;
    // Setting the color
    pSeg->SetPen(color);
    // The first point — The segment's beginning and end
    pSeg->AddPoint(TempPointsArray[0]);
    EndSegPoint = TempPointsArray[0];
    // Deleting a point from the array of the common points
    TempPointsArray.RemoveAt(0);
    // Continuing to draw the polygon
    while(fContinueSeg )
    {
       posmin = 0;
       dmin = D*2;
       // Starting from the beginning of the array,
       // select the point nearest the end of the segment.
       for(pos = 0; pos < TempPointsArray.GetSize(); pos++)
       {
           dcur = Dist(&EndSegPoint, &TempPointsArray[pos]);
           if(dcur<dmin) // Save the position (number) of the
                         // nearest point.
               {dmin = dcur; posmin = pos;}
       }
       if(dmin <= D) // The distance to the nearest point
                     // is less than the standard, but the point
       {             // still does not coincide with the end of the
                     // segment; therefore, add it to the segment.
           if(dmin > D/1000)
           {
               // Adding the nearest point to the segment
               pSeg->AddPoint(TempPointsArray[posmin]);
               // The new point becomes the end of the segment.
               EndSegPoint = TempPointsArray[posmin];
           }
```

```
                // Deleting this point
            TempPointsArray.RemoveAt(posmin);
        }
        else   // No point nearest to the end found.

                pSeg->AddPoint(TempPointsArray[posmin]);
                    // The new point becomes the end of the segment.
                EndSegPoint = TempPointsArray[posmin];
        }
                // Closing the segment
            fContinueSeg = FALSE;
    };
    // Checking whether the segment needs to be closed
    if(pSeg->m_3DPointsArray.GetSize()>2)
        if(Dist(&pSeg->m_3DPointsArray[0],
           &pSeg->m_3DPointsArray[pSeg->m_3DPointsArray.GetSize()-1]) < D)
            pSeg->AddPoint(pSeg->m_3DPointsArray[0]);

    // Adding the polygon to the shape
    pShape->AddPolygon(pSeg);
    }
    // The temporary polygon is no longer needed.
    delete pTempPolygon;
    return 1;
}

void AddTriangleSection(C3DPolygon *p3DPolygon, POINT3D *pP1,
                        POINT3D *pP2, POINT3D *pP3, double level)
{
    int    f1, f2, f3;
    double x1, x2, x3, y1, y2, y3;
    POINT3D P1, P2;
    if(!((pP1->z == level) && (pP2->z == level) && (pP3->z == level)) &&
       !((pP1->z >  level) && (pP2->z >  level) && (pP3->z >  level)) &&
       !((pP1->z <  level) && (pP2->z <  level) && (pP3->z <  level)) )
    if((pP1->z == level) && (pP2->z == level))  // The side is in the plane.
                                                // Add its points to the polygon.
    {
        p3DPolygon->AddPoint(*pP1);
        p3DPolygon->AddPoint(*pP2);
```

```
        }
        else
        if((pP2->z == level) && (pP3->z == level))  // The side is in the plane.
                                                    // Add its points to the polygon.
        {
            p3DPolygon->AddPoint(*pP2);
            p3DPolygon->AddPoint(*pP3);
        }
        else
        if((pP3->z == level) && (pP1->z == level))  // The side is in the plane.
                                                    // Add its points to the polygon.
        {
            p3DPolygon->AddPoint(*pP3);
            p3DPolygon->AddPoint(*pP1);
        }
        else
        {
            // Finding the intersection of each triangle side with the plane
            f1 = CutCross(level, pP1, pP2, x1, y1);
            f2 = CutCross(level, pP2, pP3, x2, y2);
            f3 = CutCross(level, pP3, pP1, x3, y3);
            if(f1 && f2)
            {
                P1.x = x1; P1.y = y1; P1.z = level;
                P2.x = x2; P2.y = y2; P2.z = level;
                p3DPolygon->AddPoint(P1);
                p3DPolygon->AddPoint(P2);
            }
            if(f2&&f3)
            {
                P1.x = x2; P1.y = y2; P1.z = level;
                P2.x = x3; P2.y = y3; P2.z = level;
                p3DPolygon->AddPoint(P1);
                p3DPolygon->AddPoint(P2);
            }
            if(f1&&f3)
            {
                P1.x = x1; P1.y = y1; P1.z = level;
                P2.x = x3; P2.y = y3; P2.z = level;
                p3DPolygon->AddPoint(P1);
```

```
                    p3DPolygon->AddPoint(P2);
            }
        } // Else
}

int CutCross(double level, POINT3D *pP1, POINT3D *pP2,
             double &x, double &y)
{
    if( (pP1->z < level && pP2->z < level) ||   // The segment is under the
                                                // level plane.
        (pP1->z > level && pP2->z > level) ||   // The segment is over the
                                                // level plane.
        (pP1->z == pP2->z)   )                  // The segment is in the
                                                // level plane.
        {x = pP1->x; y = pP1->y; return 0;}
    else
    {
        x = pP2->x - (pP1->x - pP2->x)*(level - pP2->z)/(pP2->z - pP1->z);
        y = pP2->y - (pP1->y - pP2->y)*(level - pP2->z)/(pP2->z - pP1->z);
        return 1;
    }
}

double Dist(POINT3D *pP1, POINT3D* pP2)
{
    if(pP1 == NULL || pP2 == NULL) return 0;
    return sqrt(pow(pP1->x - pP2->x, 2) +
                pow(pP1->y - pP2->y, 2) +
                pow(pP1->z - pP2->z, 2));
};
```

4.4. Notes

The complete source code listing of the program is on the accompanying CD-ROM in the sources\painter folder.

Surfaces drawings can be found on the same CD-ROM in the pics\painter folder in the files *surface sketches.pr4, level line surfaces.pr4*, etc. These drawings can be viewed and changed with the help of the Painter program.

It must be noted that the presented way of constructing surfaces is far from optimal. It doubles every surface node, which, accordingly, doubles all calculations and the memory used. Therefore, if constructing surfaces is an important part of your application, a more efficient implementation is advisable. You could start by constructing your own class for working with surfaces and making the global functions that handle the construction of level-lines members of this class. You could also add level-value captions to the level lines. The outcome will be a tool for visualizing results of digital simulation (Fig. 4.9).

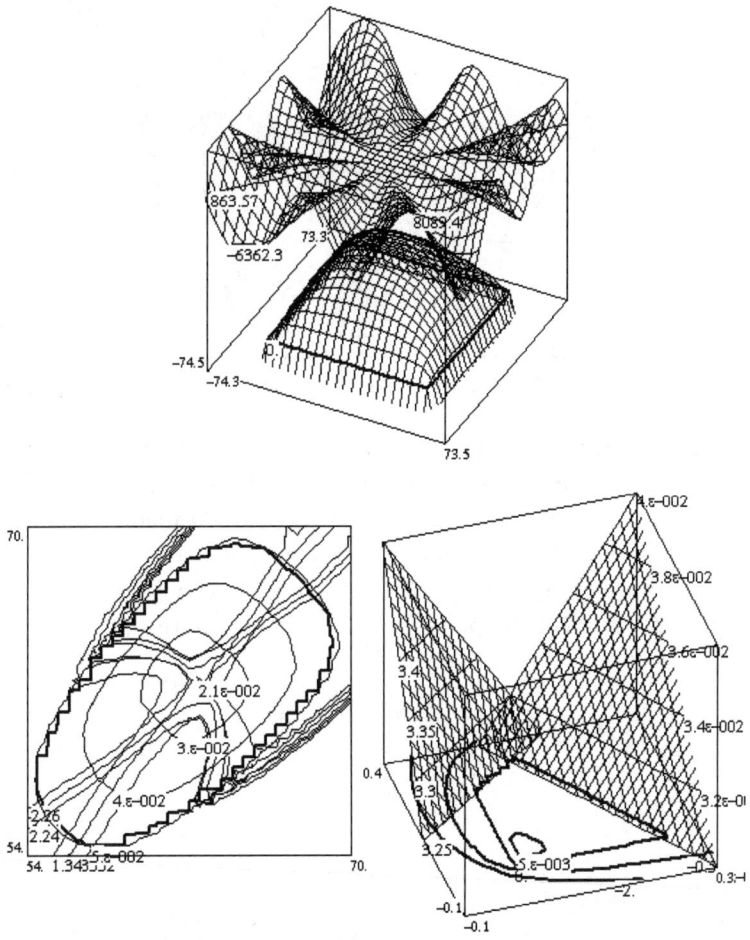

Fig. 4.9. Using surfaces and level lines to visualize the design data of the technical device design program

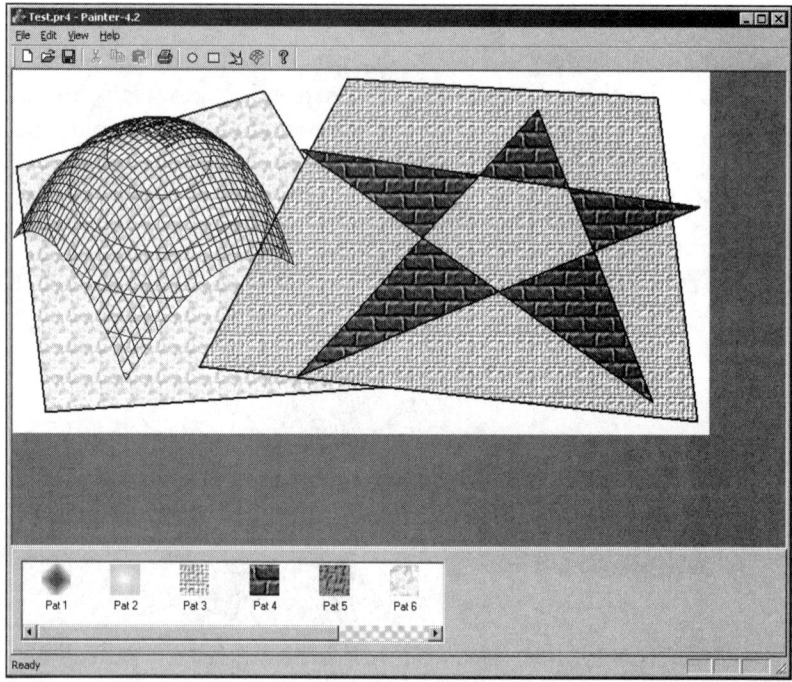

Fig. 4.10. Masterpiece created by the Painter program

Experiment with various $z = f(x, y)$ functions: You may find it interesting. It is helpful that methods to save and load 3D objects are already implemented in the program, which makes the Painter program capable of storing surface drawings. One such masterpiece is shown in Fig. 4.10.

In addition, the book by Feng Yuan [10] can be recommended for further study of the subject. In of that book, several interesting data visualization algorithms are given.

PART III:
BITMAP GRAPHICS

Chapter 5: Operations with Bitmaps and Graphics Formats in GDI+ 109

Chapter 6: Viewing and Editing Bitmap Images 147

Chapter 5: Operations with Bitmaps and Graphics Formats in GDI+

The following subjects are considered in this chapter:

- ❑ GDI+ library classes for saving and outputting bitmaps
- ❑ Operations with standard graphics file formats
- ❑ Controlling bitmap output
- ❑ Direct access to GDI+ bitmap data

5.1. Basic Principles

Raster graphics deals with individual image dots or pixels. The built-in raster operation tools of GDI+ make this library an extremely powerful tool. Before explaining their use, some terminology needs to be introduced:

- ❑ *Source*—A bitmap image used for output.
- ❑ *Destination*—The bitmap (or graphics device), into which pixels of the source are output.
- ❑ *Transparency*—A property of some the source pixels not to be displayed, leaving the destination pixels they overlie visible.

- *Color key*—A conventional color (or an index in the color table) used to indicate transparent pixels.
- *Alpha blending*—The interaction of the source and destination pixels in a way that the final color is determined by the weighted sum of their color components. Thus, the source becomes semitransparent.
- *Alpha coefficient* (or *alpha value*)—The weight coefficient used in alpha blending. Alpha coefficients in GDI+ have integer values ranging from 0 (complete transparency) to 255 (complete opacity).
- *Alpha channel*—A bitmap data aggregate containing alpha coefficient values for each pixel (by analogy with the RGB channel mechanism)
- *Antialiasing*—A system of smoothing vector images to remove outline jaggedness.

More detailed information on raster graphics can be found in *Appendix 3*. But now you will start your study of the Bitmap class.

5.2. The Bitmap Class: A Container for Raster Images

Images in the GDI+ library are stored in the Image class. Its descendants, the Bitmap and Metafile classes, implement the functionality of raster and vector image operations, respectively. The .NET Framework documentation states that the Icon class also is a descendant of the Image class, but this is not correct: it inherits from the System.MarshalByRefObject class. There is no Icon class in the GDI+ C++ class hierarchy (all the tools needed for icon operations are provided by Bitmap).

Thus, in this chapter, we will try to thoroughly teach you the Bitmap class and the specifics of working with it. Such attention to only one class is well founded because it provides many capabilities. For example, if a bitmap brush (TextureBrush) or a graphics context (Graphics) is created in the memory, an instance of the Bitmap class is needed to initialize them.

5.2.1. Support for the Main Graphics Formats

This GDI+ library property is one of its most attractive characteristics. For example, the plain and modest graphics editor Paint in Windows XP obtained the capability to load and save not only BMP but also JPEG, TIFF, GIF, and PNG images,

Chapter 5: Operations with Bitmaps and Graphics Formats in GDI+ 111

which made it a tool an order more powerful than its old version. It acquired this useful feature because of GDI+.

In trade parlance, the GDI+ graphic format operation modules are called *codecs* (a combination of the terms *compressor* and *decompressor*). This is the name we use in this book.

The `Bitmap` class has a set of overloaded constructors to create and load images. When file contents are loaded, their format (not the extension) is analyzed and a corresponding codec is automatically used. The `Image::GetRawFormat()` method can be used to determine the codec used to load the file and thus to determine the file's format.

Listing 5.1. Loading JPEG format graphics files [C++]

```
Bitmap bm(L"Picture.dat");   // Notice the file extension.
GUID guidFileFormat;
bm.GetRawFormat(&guidFileFormat);
// Checking whether the file really contained a JPEG image
if(guidFileFormat == ImageFormatJPEG)
   MessageBox(0, "This is JPEG!", 0, MB_OK);
```

The format constants (`ImageFormatXxx`, where `Xxx` is the format) are defined in the GDI+ header files. But be careful not to confuse them with the codec identifiers, which will be described later. In .NET, formats are defined using the property `public ImageFormat RawFormat {get;}`.

In addition to constructors, bitmap images can be created using the `FromXxx` static family methods of the `Bitmap` class. They return a pointer to the object, which has to be deleted using the `delete` operator at the end of work.

In the Microsoft .NET Framework environment, the `System.Drawing.Bitmap` class also has the corresponding static methods. Of course, in .NET, instead of `delete`, `Dispose` should be used (or even better, the C# `using` operator):

```
using(Bitmap bm = Bitmap.FromFile("photo.jpg"))
{
  // Using the picture,
} // bm will be released here
```

Every codec tries to take into account the specific properties of its format as often as possible: for example, a GIF loader will correctly recognize transparency, which the `OleLoadPicturePath` function sorely lacked.

There also is a capability to save created bitmaps in different graphics file formats. Work with codecs will be considered in greater detail later; for now, consider some specifics of loading and displaying bitmaps.

5.2.2. Loading from Files and Streams (IStream)

The image is loaded from a file using the following constructor:

```
Bitmap(const WCHAR* filename, BOOL useIcm);
```

The `filename` parameter must contain a name of an existing file. All string parameters of GDI+ methods require Unicode strings; therefore, when passing a string constant in a C++ program, it must be prefixed with the L character.

The `useIcm` parameter determines whether image color management (ICM) API will be used when loading the bitmap; by default, its value is FALSE. If it is necessary to use ICM, the graphics file must contain all the necessary information—for example, color profiles of the specific devices.

```
Bitmap(IStream* stream, BOOL useIcm);
```

More flexible loading options are secreted in the `Bitmap(IStream* stream, BOOL useIcm);` Bitmap constructor. It can be used for reading images from any source that supports the `IStream` interface. This makes it possible to load images from databases, structured storage, memory blocks, etc. During the load process, the data format is analyzed and the necessary codec is used to unpack the image.

5.2.3. Creating Bitmaps from Program Resources

The `Bitmap(HINSTANCE hInstance, const WCHAR* bitmapName);` Bitmap constructor allows bitmaps to be loaded from resources.

However, other resources cannot be loaded this way. This constructor is intended specifically for loading *bitmap* resources and does not support, for example, GIF loading. Perhaps, these are limitations of just the current implementation. Fortunately, they can be easily bypassed: simply make the `IStream` interface and the necessary data available to the loader. This can be done with the help of, for example, the Windows API `CreateStreamOnHGlobal` function (Listing 5.2).

Listing 5.2. Loading bitmaps from Windows program resources [C++]

```
Bitmap* BitmapFromResource(HINSTANCE hInstance,
  LPCTSTR szResName, LPCTSTR szResType)
{
```

```
HRSRC hrsrc = FindResource(hInstance, szResName, szResType);
if(!hrsrc) return 0;
// Dummy HGLOBAL — See the description of LoadResource in MSDN.
HGLOBAL hgTemp = LoadResource(hInstance, hrsrc);
DWORD sz = SizeofResource(hInstance, hrsrc);
void* ptrRes = LockResource(hgTemp);
HGLOBAL hgRes = GlobalAlloc(GMEM_MOVEABLE, sz);
if(!hgRes) return 0;
void* ptrMem = GlobalLock(hgRes);
// Copying bitmap data
CopyMemory(ptrMem, ptrRes, sz);
GlobalUnlock(hgRes);
IStream *pStream;
// TRUE means that memory is to be released at the final Release.
HRESULT hr = CreateStreamOnHGlobal(hgRes, TRUE, &pStream);
if(FAILED(hr))
{
  GlobalFree(hgRes);
  return 0;
}
// Loading from IStream
Bitmap *image = Bitmap::FromStream(pStream);
pStream->Release();
return image;
}
```

NOTE Calling `Release` in Listing 5.2 will not immediately destroy the `IStream` stream. When loaded from files and streams, `Bitmap` objects retain the data source for the duration of their lifetime and release it only in the destructor. If you forget this circumstance, you will spend a long time wondering why a graphics file cannot be accessed after it has been read into `Bitmap`.

In a .NET application, graphics resources can be loaded from a `System.IO.Stream` object. An instance of the `Stream` class can be obtained from a resource with the following method of the `System.Reflection.Assembly` class:

```
public virtual Stream GetManifestResourceStream(string name);
```

Here, `name` is the name, under which the resource is stored in the assembly.
In this case, loading the image from resources will look as is shown in Listing 5.3.

Listing 5.3. Loading bitmaps from the resources of a .NET program [C#]

```
Bitmap bmp = new Bitmap(
  Assembly.GetExecutingAssembly().
  GetManifestResourceStream("demo.mypicture.jpg"));
```

IMPORTANT

Beginners are often nonplussed by the need to place some file into the resources of an executable .NET application. Visual Studio.NET makes this a trivial task: simply add the file to the application project, activate the **Properties** panel, and change the value of the file's **Build Action** property to **Embedded Resource**.

By adding a file to the application resources in this way, the resource is given a name consisting of the file name and the namespace prefix (Demo in this case). If a resource is placed into the module with the help of the command line utilities, you can specify the name, under which it will be stored in the program.

5.2.4. More Complex Ways of Loading Images

In addition to loading standard format bitmap images from files and streams, images can be created on the fly or converted from other formats, for example, from GDI objects or DirectDraw surfaces. Here are the corresponding constructors:

```
Bitmap(const BITMAPINFO* gdiBitmapInfo, VOID* gdiBitmapData);
Bitmap(HBITMAP hbm, HPALETTE hpal);
Bitmap(HICON hicon);
Bitmap(IDirectDrawSurface7 * surface);
```

It is important to understand that all these constructors create a copy of the bitmap data. If you modify the Bitmap object in any way (e.g., draw it into the Graphics object created on its base), the data source will remain unchanged. Moreover, carrying the modifications back into the initial GDI object is often accompanied by difficulties: for example, you may have to handle palettes and bit arrays yourself. Some recommendations in this respect can be found in *Section 5.6*.

In our opinion, great attention was given in GDI+ to the issue of backward compatibility. At the same time, this compatibility to a great extent is implemented in the read-only mode. Thus, for example, the library will correctly read from memory a bitmap image with the BITMAPV4HEADER header containing the alpha channel information; however, when saving images with transparency into the BMP format using GDI+, only the BITMAPINFOHEADER header will be generated; all transparency information will be lost.

Chapter 5: Operations with Bitmaps and Graphics Formats in GDI+   115

NOTE

You should not mix the GDI+ codec functionality and the Windows 98/2000 JPEG capabilities: they are independent. At first, this may lead to confusion. In particular, you will not succeed in creating a `Bitmap` object from the `BITMAPINFO` structure, in which the `bmiHeader.biCompression` field holds the `BI_JPEG` value, because the GDI+ bitmap data loader supports only simple formats (such as `BI_RGB` or `BI_BITFIELDS`). To load JPEG images, simply create `IStream` on a JPEG data block and call the proper `Bitmap` class constructor.

As for saving bitmap images with transparency, you have TIFF, PNG, and GIF at your service (we explain this later in the chapter).

There also are constructors that allow the format of the created bitmap image to be specified:

```
Bitmap(INT width, INT height, PixelFormat format);
```

The `PixelFormat` enumeration has a large number of constants that define bitmap formats. The default value of the format parameter is `PixelFormat32bppARGB`. The format providing the most rapid output, however, is the `PixelFormat32bppPARGB` format. In it, the color component of each pixel is already multiplied by the alpha value of the same pixel, which eliminates the need to do this multiplication (for each pixel) when overlaying the image.

A buffer for the created bitmap image can be allocated manually. Here is the corresponding constructor:

```
Bitmap(INT width, INT height, INT stride, PixelFormat format, BYTE* scan0 );
```

Here, `stride` is the offset value (in bytes) between the end of one bitmap string and the start of the next one and `scan0` is the pointer to the byte array holding the bitmap data. Regardless of the format, the `stride` value must be divisible by 4 without a remainder (and, naturally, be sufficiently large to store a string of the necessary length). It may also be negative (for creating bitmap images with the reversed string order).

The idea of such complex manipulations is that specifying the `stride` value allows you to work with a rectangular fragment of a large bitmap image as if it were a separate resource (Fig. 5.1).

After such a `Bitmap` object is destroyed, the allocated buffer is not deleted and the programmer is responsible for its release.

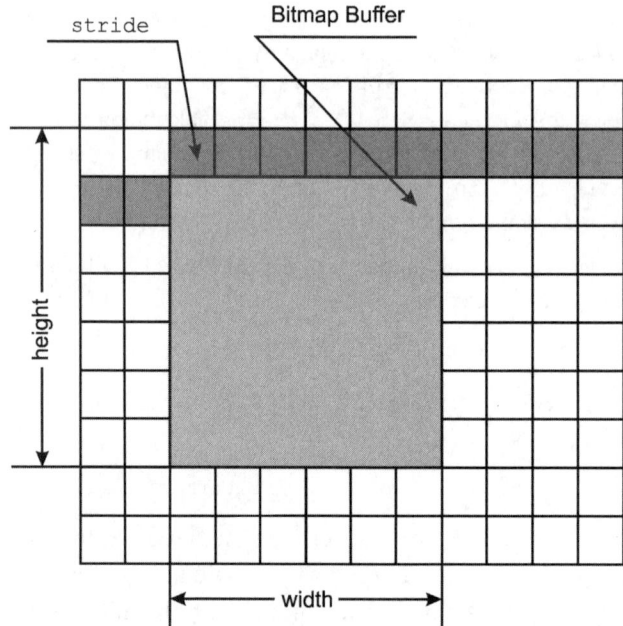

Fig. 5.1. Loading a rectangular fragment of a bitmap image using the `stride` value

5.3. Graphics File Formats

As already stated, the GDI+ library supports operations with several graphics file formats, which allows it to be used for loading, storing, and other specific operations. Consider how the support of these formats is organized.

5.3.1. Working with a Codec List

Like COM objects, each GDI+ codec has its unique class identifier (CLSID). The list of available codecs can be obtained by calling the `GetImageDecoders()` function (which returns a list of the import filters) and the `GetImageEncoders` function (which returns the list of the export filters). These functions fill the buffer, whose size is specified by the `size` variable that was passed to them with the `ImageCodecInfo` structure array (Listing 5.4).

Listing 5.4. The `ImageCodecInfo` class [C++]

```cpp
class ImageCodecInfo
{
public:
  CLSID  Clsid;
  GUID   FormatID;
  const WCHAR* CodecName;
  const WCHAR* DllName;
  const WCHAR* FormatDescription;
  const WCHAR* FilenameExtension;
  const WCHAR* MimeType;
  DWORD  Flags;
  DWORD  Version;
  DWORD  SigCount;
  DWORD  SigSize;
  const BYTE* SigPattern;
  const BYTE* SigMask;
};
```

To view the properties of the GDI+ codecs installed in the system, we created a C++ utility using MFC. Its source and object codes can be found on the CD-ROM accompanying this book.

The codecs.zip file is the source code project, and the codecs_exe.zip file is the compiled application.

The program shows the list of the codecs available in GDI+ and allows you to view the properties of each codec; for the export codecs, the supported parameters can also be viewed.

Running the program for the first time produced interesting results. For example, although the two lists are separate—one for loading and one for storing—they enumerate the same codecs (simply comparing their CLSID will show this). This is, of course, an implementation quirk, which may be rectified in future GDI+ versions.

A question immediately arises: Is it possible to add your own codecs to this list to be able to load files of other formats with the help of GDI+? For example, the `Flags` field has the `Builtin` bit, which, judging from its name, is supposed to indicate whether the particular codec is built in. Alas, there is no documented way of doing this: in GDI+ 1.0, codecs are not ActiveX objects but are built into the library code. Microsoft promises to add external codec support in the next version.

5.3.2. Saving Images

When saving an image, the format codec to be used must be specified. The `Image::Save` function takes the `filename` Unicode string and the `clsidEncoder` pointer to the Globally Unique IDentifier (GUID) codec as parameters:

```
Status Save(
    const WCHAR* filename,
    const CLSID* clsidEncoder,
    const EncoderParameters* encoderParams
);
```

The last parameter, `encoderParams`, is a pointer to the `EncoderParameters` structure containing various settings for saving codecs: compression ratio, color depth, etc.

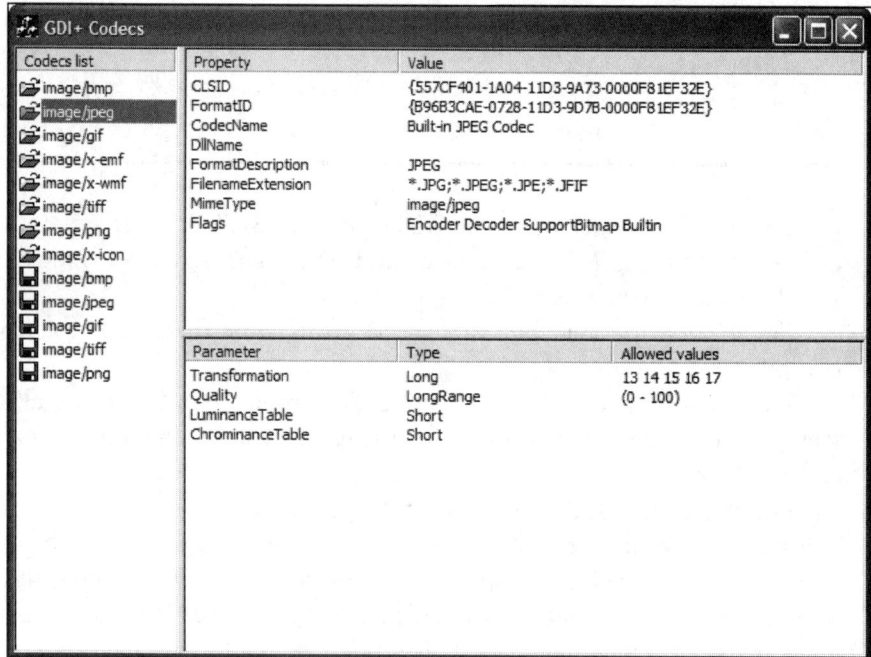

Fig. 5.2. **Codecs** utility output window

The platform SDK documentation describes in detail settings for working with various codecs. To rapidly master the permissible setting values for a specific installed codec, you can avail yourself of the **Codecs** utility mentioned with Fig. 5.2.

Chapter 5: Operations with Bitmaps and Graphics Formats in GDI+ 119

For example, according to this program, the `Transformation` parameter can take on the following values for the JPEG codec: 13, 14, 15, 16, or 17.

```
EncoderValueTransformRotate90,
EncoderValueTransformRotate180,
EncoderValueTransformRotate270,
EncoderValueTransformFlipHorizontal,
EncoderValueTransformFlipVertical
```

These constants describe the allowable geometric transformations when saving JPEG format files. By the way, GDI+ implements a useful feature: if a JPEG file is loaded with the size that is a multiple of 16, then there will be no additional quality loss when saving it with one of the enumerated transformations described previously.

Where can the CLSID value for the selected codec be obtained? Of course, a constant taken, for example, from the window of the Codecs program can be hardwired into the code. But this approach is justified only if the application will be distributed with the exact GDI+ library version; otherwise, the codecs' GUIDs may change. Microsoft recommends a more flexible approach.

Usually, to obtain the CLSID for, say, a JPEG codec, a string `image/jpeg` is formed and the list is searched for a codec that has the same string in the `MimeType` field. GDI+ documentation describes how to implement this approach: Its section titled *"Retrieving the Class Identifier for an Encoder"* gives the source code for the `GetEncoderClsid` function.

If the codec has to be selected several times, then another method will be preferable. In this method, an associative container (e.g., `std::map`) is filled with a list of codecs; then the codec is sought using the graphics format GUID (the `FormatID` field), which you are already familiar with from the description of the `GetRawFormat` method.

Listing 5.5. Preparing a fast codec search [C++]

```cpp
// Type of the associative array, in which
// the FormatID-CLSID codec pairs are stored
typedef std::map<GUID, GUID> CodecsList;

// Defining the < operator to compare the GUIDs
bool operator<(REFGUID g1, REFGUID g2)
{
   return memcmp(&g1, &g2, sizeof(GUID))<0;
}
```

```
// Function for reading the codec list;
// the Encoders parameter indicates, which
// codec list is needed: for saving or for loading
CodecsList ReadCodecsList(bool Encoders)
{
  using namespace Gdiplus;
  UINT  num, size;
  if(Encoders)
    GetImageEncodersSize(&num, &size);
  else
    GetImageDecodersSize(&num, &size);

  // Buffer size — in bytes
  ImageCodecInfo* pArray = (ImageCodecInfo*)(malloc(size));
  if(Encoders)
    GetImageEncoders(num, size, pArray);
  else
    GetImageDecoders(num, size, pArray);

  // Filling map
  CodecsList codecs;
  for(UINT j=0; j < num; ++j)
    codecs[pArray[j].FormatID]=pArray[j].Clsid;

  free(pArray);
  return codecs;
}
```

In this case, a conversion from PNG to JPEG will look something like this:

```
Bitmap bm(L"test.png");
CodecsList codecsList = ReadCodecsList(TRUE);
GUID JpegId = codecsList[ImageFormatJPEG];
...  // Working with the bitmap image
bm.Save(L"test2.jpg", JpegId); // See the warning that follows
```

.NET programmers can relax here: this functionality has already been implemented for them. All the dirty work of creating `FormatID` and `CLSID` will be done in the innards of the .NET library (in the `FindEncoder` method). All that needs to be passed to the `Save` method is the named property of

Chapter 5: Operations with Bitmaps and Graphics Formats in GDI+ 121

the `System.Drawing.Imaging.ImageFormat` class containing the `FormatID` value of the corresponding codec, as follows:

```
Bitmap bm = new Bitmap("test.png");
... // Working with the bitmap image
bm.Save("test2.jpg", ImageFormat.Jpeg);
```

IMPORTANT

The `Save()` method will not work if the name of a file already opened using GDI+ is passed to it. This happens because the file remains in use until the `Bitmap` destructor is executed.

Another problem arises if the file is available for writing but its length exceeds the resulting image size. `Save()` will not truncate it, and there will be garbage left at the end of the file.

Microsoft is aware of these problems. The second one has already been entered into the Knowledge Base—*"PRB: Save Method of Bitmap Class Does Not Truncate File Size"* (Q312119).

A Practical Example: Saving Screen Contents to a Graphics File

To test the GDI+ magic, we've written a C++ program (Listing 5.6) that saves the visible screen contents in the BMP and PNG formats (the latter compresses graphics files efficiently without quality loss). To have effective access to the screen pixels, we resorted to GDI. To avoid the bother of initializing GDI+, we used the `InitGdiPlus` class described in *Chapter 1*. To compile the example, in addition to the source file, supply the initgdiplus.cpp name to the compiler.

Listing 5.6. Saving screen contents in BMP and PNG formats [C++]

```
// Compilation:
// cl grab.cpp initgdiplus.cpp user32.lib kernel32.lib gdi32.lib
// VC7 users: Add the "/link /delayload:gdiplus.dll" key

#define STRICT
#include <windows.h>
#include <gdiplus.h>
#include "initgdiplus.h"

// Warning: In future GDI+ versions, codec GUIDs may change.
```

```cpp
static const GUID guidPng = 
{ 0x557cf406, 0x1a04, 0x11d3, { 0x9a, 0x73, 0x00, 0x00, 0xf8, 0x1e, 0xf3,
  0x2e } };

static const GUID guidBmp = 
{ 0x557cf400, 0x1a04, 0x11d3, { 0x9a, 0x73, 0x00, 0x00, 0xf8, 0x1e, 0xf3,
  0x2e } };

int CALLBACK WinMain(HINSTANCE hInstance, HINSTANCE hPrevInstance,
                    LPSTR lpCmdLine, int nShowCmd )
{
  HDC hdc = ::GetDC(NULL);
  RECT rc = {0, 0, GetSystemMetrics(SM_CXFULLSCREEN),
    GetSystemMetrics(SM_CYFULLSCREEN)};
  HDC hdcMem = CreateCompatibleDC(hdc);

  HBITMAP hBitmap = CreateCompatibleBitmap(hdc, (int)rc.right,
    (int)rc.bottom);
  HBITMAP hOldBmp = (HBITMAP)SelectObject(hdcMem, hBitmap);
  BitBlt(hdcMem, 0, 0, (int)rc.right, (int)rc.bottom, hdc,
    0, 0, SRCCOPY);
  hBitmap = (HBITMAP) SelectObject(hdcMem, hOldBmp);
  DeleteDC(hdcMem);
  RSDN::InitGdiPlus init;
  if(init.Good())
  {
    Gdiplus::Bitmap bitmap(hBitmap, NULL);
    bitmap.Save(L"c:\\screen.png", &guidPng);
    bitmap.Save(L"c:\\screen.bmp", &guidBmp);
  }
  else
    MessageBox(0, " GDI+ initialization error", 0, MB_OK|MB_ICONHAND);
  DeleteObject(hBitmap);
  return 0;
}
```

As you can see, file saving takes only one line of code. We did not use the clever ways to look up codecs in the table described previously. Instead, we simply hardwired into the code the values taken from the window of the Codecs program.

The resulting utility has a practical use: it allows us to take shots of the monitor screen and can be used, for example, when writing computer books. Hopefully, you will also find it useful.

Of interest are the comparative sizes of the resulting files. At the 1024 × 768 screen resolution and the True Color screen mode, the BMP file turned out to be 3 MB. A compressed PNG of the same resolution was only 68 KB, or 45 times smaller! Of course, the more complex the image being output to the screen, the lower the compression ratio will be.

5.4. Specific Capabilities of File Formats

In this section, the additional capabilities made available by various GDI+ file codecs and ways to avoid some problems will be considered.

5.4.1. Saving a GIF with Transparency

This is the most popular discussion subject in the newsgroups associated with GDI+ graphics formats. Indeed, the use of GIF files with transparent areas has become widespread in the Web. Loading a transparent GIF file presents no difficulties: the codec correctly recognizes the transparent areas and sets their alpha channel values to zero.

But this causes problems when saving the image. Conversion of GIF files into the 32-bit format when loading is the problem, because saving GIF files requires a palette. The codec can save this type of bitmap image only in the halftone palette—a standard table of 216 common colors. The necessary colors here are obtained by pixel dithering. The image starts looking rather ugly, and any semblance of transparency becomes out of the question.

If you need to save transparent bitmap images without encountering unnecessary difficulties, make use of the 32-bit format (PNG or TIFF with alpha channel).[i]

Nevertheless, it is possible to create a transparent GIF using GDI+. This will require direct work with the image bits, because the image must have no more than 256 colors and must remain in the index format. Only then will the codec recognize as transparent the first item in the color table, with 0 in the alpha field, and save the

---

[i] Keep in mind that many browsers incorrectly display the PNG format; in particular, Internet Explorer does not understand PNG with alpha channel.

file correctly. The following Knowledge Base articles give a complete description of this process' technology:

"INFO: GDI+ GIF Files Are Saved Using the 8-Bpp Format" (Q318343)
"HOW TO: Save a .gif File with a New Color Table By Using GDI+" (Q315780)
"HOW TO: Save a .gif File with a New Color Table By Using Visual C# .NET" (Q319061)

5.4.2. Loading and Saving Multiframe Files

Some graphics formats allow you to save more than one image in one file. For example, TIFF files can hold several images of the same page scanned at different resolutions.

Another reason for the multiframe formats' existence is animation. Those moving images flashing on millions of Web pages most often are animated GIF images.

It used to be difficult to load such a file from disk without low-level disassembling of its format. For example, the `OleLoadPicture` API function could not load animated GIF files on its own. Now, all work is done by a GDI+ codec, and loading a multiframe image is no different from loading a standard graphics file.

The `Image::GetFrameCount` function can be used as follows to find the number of frames in the loaded bitmap image:

```
UINT GetFrameCount(
  const GUID* dimensionID
);
```

For the parameters, it takes a pointer to the GUID constant defining the type of the stored files. The available values of `dimension ID` are described in the GDI+ header files. For GIF files, the `FrameDimensionTime` constant needs to be passed. The `FrameDimensionPage` constant for TIFF files is as follows:

```
frameCount = bitmap.GetFrameCount(&FrameDimensionTime);
```

Before drawing a frame, it must be made active with the help of the `Image::SelectActiveFrame` function. The details of how to do this can be found in the documentation and the source code of the demonstration applications.

Saving files is more difficult. In GDI+ 1.0, multiframe saving is implemented only for TIFF files. Unfortunately, animated GIF files cannot be saved this way.

So, consider the step-by-step procedure for creating a multiframe TIFF file:

1. Create an `Image` object, which will manage the saving process. It must contain the first frame of the multiframe image.

Chapter 5: Operations with Bitmaps and Graphics Formats in GDI+ 125

2. Using the `Image::Save` method, save the first frame. This step is no different from the previously-described version for a single frame.
3. To save the subsequent frames into the same file, call the `SaveAdd` method from the main `Image` object, passing it the necessary frame.

NOTE

Some variations are possible here. If all the necessary frames are in the source `Image` object, they simply need to be made current in succession (using the `SelectActiveFrame` method). Then, the version of the `SaveAdd` method that takes only a pointer to the `EncoderParameters` structure is called.

Frames of other bitmap images can be added to the file being saved by calling the `SaveAdd` method version that, with the parameters, takes a pointer to an `Image` class object.

4. To finish the process, call the version of the `SaveAdd` method that takes the special `EncoderValueFlush` saving parameter (Listing 5.7).

Listing 5.7. Finishing saving a multiframe file [C++]

```
ULONG value;
EncoderParameters params = {1}; // One parameter
params.Parameter[0].NumberOfValues = 1;
params.Parameter[0].Guid   = EncoderSaveFlag;
params.Parameter[0].Type   = EncoderParameterValueTypeLong;
params.Parameter[0].Value  = &value;
... // Saving frames
value = EncoderValueFlush; // Finishing the sequence

myImage.SaveAdd(&encoderParameters);
```

5.4.3. Thumbnail Images

GDI+ provides a convenient mechanism for creating thumbnail images. Because such images are small and display rapidly, they are used for previewing full-size images on Web pages, in image-viewing applications (e.g., ACDSee), etc.

You already have everything you need to create thumbnail images. All you would need to do is create a `Bitmap` of the necessary size, initialize the device (`Graphics`) for output into this bitmap, and output the image in some acceptable way (e.g., by setting the `InterpolationModeHighQualityBicubic` output mode, which will be described later). The library creators deemed this not good enough, and they added the `GetThumbnailImage` method to the `Image` class, which does all this work:

```
Image* GetThumbnailImage(
  UINT thumbWidth,
  UINT thumbHeight,
  GetThumbnailImageAbort callback,
  VOID* callbackData
);
```

The `thumbWidth` and `thumbHeight` parameters pass the needed thumbnail size to this function. The `callback` and `callbackData` parameters are used when there needs to be a capability to interrupt the thumbnail creation process. By default, they are set to `NULL` and this capability is ignored.

What are the advantages of this technique? At first glance, only its simplicity (and, accordingly, its limited capabilities). But in reality the `GetThumbnailImage()` method is the most rapid way to create thumbnails. Most graphics formats allow a thumbnail of the image to be embedded in the same file with the full-size image. If 0 is passed in the `thumbWidth` and `thumbHeight` parameters, the format codec will try to extract exactly this thumbnail (of course, when using an unsuitable GDI+ format, you will have to create a thumbnail on your own). Moreover, when creating a miniature image from the start, this method may provide other optimizations that the `DrawImage` method does not.

The .NET Framework `System.Drawing.Image` class has an analogous method. The only difference is that instead of a pointer to the `GetThumbnailImageAbort` function, the `Image.GetThumbnailImageAbort` delegate must be passed in .NET:

```
public Image GetThumbnailImage(
    int thumbWidth,
    int thumbHeight,
    Image.GetThumbnailImageAbort callback,
    IntPtr callbackData
);
```

Because the C# example of using this function is compact, the complete source code of a thumbnail-creating application is given in Listing 5.8.

Listing 5.8. Creating thumbnails [C#]

```csharp
using System;
using System.Drawing;
using System.Drawing.Drawing2D;
using System.Drawing.Imaging;

class ThumbnailExtractor
{
  public static void Main(string[] args)
  {
    foreach(string arg in args) // Searching the array elements
      SaveThumbnail(arg);
  }

  static void SaveThumbnail(string name)
  {
    try
    {
      Bitmap bm = new Bitmap(name);
      Image thumb = bm.GetThumbnailImage(0, 0, null, IntPtr.Zero);
      thumb.Save(name + "_tn.jpg", ImageFormat.Jpeg);
    }
    // Has a problem arisen?
    catch(Exception e)
    {
      Console.WriteLine(e); // An implicit call to e.ToString()

    }
  }
};
```

This program creates (or extracts) thumbnails of all files specified in the command line and saves them in the JPEG format in the same folder, adding the *_tn.jpg* suffix to the file name.

NOTE

The MSDN states that an instance of the Image.GetThumbnailImageAbort delegate must be created even if you do not want to use it (pointing to a dummy function). However, the code in Listing 5.8 works perfectly, passing a null instead of the delegate.

5.4.4. Working with Image Metadata

Along with the image itself, many applications store supplementary information in graphics files. It is common practice to call this collection of nonessential fields *metadata* (indeed, they are in some respects similar to the metadata stored in .NET assemblies). These can be the date the picture was taken, copyright to the image, resolution parameters, etc. Practically all graphics formats provide for storage of such information.

GDI+ simplifies work with metadata, abstracting the details of various formats and making available a sufficiently flexible and convenient access mechanism. It is done with the help of the `PropertyItem` class, which is a wrapper for any type of data stored in a file:

```
class PropertyItem
{
public:
    PROPID  id;      // A unique number
    ULONG   length;  // Field length in bytes
    WORD    type;    // Value type (one of the
                     // PropertyTagTypeXXXX types)
    VOID*   value;   // Pointer to the data

};
```

The value of the `id` field defines the type of the stored information. Each graphics format has a corresponding set of available identifiers defined in the gdiplusimaging.h header file.

Listing 5.9 shows the source code for a small example program to demonstrate working with metadata written in C# and outputting a list of the information fields for the specified graphics file.

Listing 5.9. Enumerating image metadata [C#]

```
using System;
using System.Drawing;
using System.Drawing.Drawing2D;
using System.Drawing.Imaging;
```

Chapter 5: Operations with Bitmaps and Graphics Formats in GDI+

```
class ImageProperties
{
  public static void Main(string[] args)
  {
    foreach(string arg in args)
    {
      Bitmap bm = new Bitmap(arg);
      foreach(PropertyItem i in bm.PropertyItems)
        Console.WriteLine("Property #{0}: type = {1}, len = {2}",
          i.Id, i.Type, i.Len);
    }
  }
};
```

5.5. Using Bitmaps When Working with Graphics Objects

The current library implementation operates with 32-bit color for any color calculations. Bitmaps, in which colors are represented differently, are converted to the 32-bit format before they are processed. Consequently, a good way to save processor resources and system memory is to work with 32-bit bitmaps from the start (the default offering). For example, when creating a `Graphics` instance from a GDI device context (`HDC`), a 32-bit intermediate buffer is created, into which the bitmap is output; only then this buffer is copied into the context. If the device context has a different color depth, additional conversions will have to be performed, which will lower the level of performance. Moreover, this organization of operations with graphics contexts dictates its own limitations on referencing the context using GDI: it cannot be done during the `Graphics` lifetime.

5.5.1. Image Output and Geometric Transformations

We described transforming coordinates in GDI+ in *Chapter 3*. This library also provides special tools for geometric image transformations during image output. These tools will be considered in this section.

The `DrawImage` method of a `Graphics` object is responsible for outputting bitmaps. Hold it: We wrote "the method." It would be more correct to use the plural form here: there are 18 of these methods! Based on the purpose, these overloaded functions are divided into two main groups:

- Methods to output an image or a part of an image into a rectangular area with a two-axis scaling capability. By their actions, these methods are similar to the GDI StretchBlt function but have additional capabilities: for example, interpolating the resulting image. As parameters, these methods are passed different type coordinates of the rectangular source and destination areas:

```
void PaintFlower(Graphics& g, Rect& rc)
{
    ...
    g.DrawImage(flowerImage, flowerPos.X, flowerPos.Y,
        flowerImage->GetWidth(), flowerImage->GetHeight());
}
```

Specifying the initial bitmap pixel size explicitly tells GDI+ that no scaling needs to be performed, and the output will go faster.

- Methods to output an image or part of an image into a parallelogram with the corresponding transformation of the coordinates of all points of the original bitmap. GDI lacks similar functionality (in the NT family, a somewhat similar operation is performed by the PlgBlt function.) These methods require for their work an array of any three vertex points of the parallelogram (the fourth vertex is calculated from them).

Note that with the latter technique, rotation is a special case of transformation: it is enough to specify three coordinates of the parallelogram rotated to any angle. The order of the points in the array must correspond to the order of the *A1*, *B1*, and *C1* points, as shown in the diagram in Fig. 5.3.

But in most cases, it will be easier to use the already considered GDI+ coordinate transformations to rotate the bitmap being output.

Moreover, images can be rotated to a multiple of a 90-degree angle or flipped relative to their symmetry axes by the Status RotateFlip(RotateFlipType rotateFlipType); method, taking an element of the RotateFlipType enumeration as the parameter. All possible GDI+ enumeration versions are stored in the gdiplusenums.h file.

Chapter 5: Operations with Bitmaps and Graphics Formats in GDI+ 131

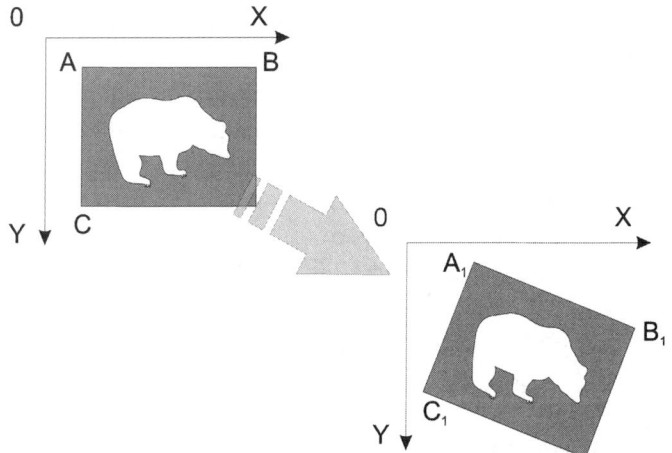

Fig. 5.3. Diagram for outputting bitmaps with affine transformations

The versions of the `DrawImage` method that take a pointer to an `ImageAttributes` class object provide more flexible control over the image output. Most parameters specified in the `ImageAttributes` object deal with color correction, which is described later. At present, of interest may be the `Status SetWrapMode( WrapMode wrap, const Color& color, BOOL clamp );` method of this class that affects the geometry of the images being output.

It allows you to specify how the output area outside of the bounds of the output image is to be filled. The type of filling is defined by the `wrap` parameter from the `WrapMode` enumeration. In particular, specifying `WrapModeTile` produces tiled output. Setting the `WrapModeClamp` mode fills the outside area with the color specified in the `color` parameter. The `clamp` parameter in the current implementation is ignored.

This is true not only for bitmaps but also for outputting `Metafile` objects, which also are descendants of the `Image` class.

Having mentioned the `SetWrapMode` method of the `ImageAttributes` class, the same name methods of the `LinearGradientBrush`, `PathGradientBrush`, and `TextureBrush` classes cannot be left unmentioned. They perform analogous functions when specifying area-fill parameters.

5.5.2. Image Quality

Magnifying, stretching, and distorting the original image may produce some ugly results: jagged image edges, staircase lines, etc. The reason for this lies in the nature of the raster graphics: the information that the image contains is limited to the selected resolution.

Nevertheless, there are various interpolation algorithms that allow you to significantly improve the quality of the resulting image, or rather its quality as perceived by a human. Some of these were built into the GDI+ library from the beginning.

The `Graphics::SetInterpolationMode` allows you to specify the interpolation mode (or algorithm) used when outputting an image with a new pixel size. The constants of the available modes are described in the `InterpolationMode` enumeration.

The corresponding tool in the .NET version of a `Graphics` object is the `InterpolationMode` property.

The quality gain in the given case leads to a speed loss; consequently, when the mode is used with the highest quality, `InterpolationModeHighQualityBicubic`, slow computers may take several seconds to output a large image.[i] But only this method can adequately reproduce an image reduced to 25% (and less) of the original. This mode can be useful for various automatic ASP.NET thumbnail generators.

The quality (and speed) of bitmap output is affected by some other settings of `Graphics` objects settings. Brief descriptions of these are given in Table 5.1.

Table 5.1. GDI+ Quality Mode Control Methods

Method	Function
`SetSmoothingMode`	Sets the antialiasing method when outputting primitives: lines and geometric shapes.
`SetCompositingMode`	Determines whether transparency is accounted for when overlaying raster images.
`SetCompositingQuality`	Controls the quality of color component calculations when overlaying raster images.
`SetPixelOffsetMode`	Sets the method of calculating the pixel offset during interpolation. Roughly speaking, this determines whether the coordinates of pixels (or of pixel centers) are handled as integers during the calculations.
`SetRenderingOrigin`	Sets the position of the origin point in color dithering in 8- and 16-bit modes.

---

[i] This pertains to screen output, that is, moderately large images. Bicubic interpolation of graphic art resolution images can take minutes for even the most modern computers to perform.

Chapter 5: Operations with Bitmaps and Graphics Formats in GDI+   133

Analogous methods prefixed by Get are employed to obtain values of the corresponding settings. In the .NET Framework environment, the Graphics class has analogous properties without prefixes (e.g., SmoothingMode and PixelOffsetMode).

5.5.3. Flicker Removal

A common problem when creating rapidly changing dynamic graphics (and in particular animation) is *flicker*. It has been fought traditionally using double buffering, a capability also available in GDI+. A Graphics object can be created with an existing Bitmap instance as a back buffer (Image, actually, but we are interested in bitmaps at the moment):

```
Graphics( Image* image );
static Graphics* FromImage( Image* image );
```

All output operations, which involve such an object, will reflect on the contents of the Bitmap instance used as the back buffer. This presents a simple capability of double-buffered output: the image is prepared "behind the scenes" and almost instantaneously placed on the screen, eliminating the annoying flicker when images are prepared directly on the physical screen (Listing 5.10).

Listing 5.10. Double-buffered output in GDI+ [C++]

```
void OnPaint(HDC hdc, RECT& rc)
{
  Graphics g(hdc);
  Rect paintRect(0, 0, rc.right, rc.bottom);
  // Creating a temporary buffer
  Bitmap backBuffer(rc.right, rc.bottom, &g);
  Graphics temp(&backBuffer);
  // Drawing an image in the buffer
  PaintBackground(temp, paintRect);
  PaintFlower(temp, paintRect);
  PaintButterfly(temp, paintRect);
  // Moving the image to the screen
  g.DrawImage(&backBuffer, 0, 0, 0, 0,
    rc.right, rc.bottom, UnitPixel);
}
```

Not every raster image is suitable for creating a `Graphics` object with a back buffer. In particular, this is impossible for the index and `Grayscale` raster images. This has to do with the limitations of the GDI+ core.

IMPORTANT

Even using double buffering may not eliminate flicker. When a window is refreshed, it is first sent the `WM_ERASEBKGND` message. The default handler of this message fills the area that needs refreshing with the `hbrBackground` brush, specified in the properties of the window's class. This type of flicker is eliminated by first suppressing the area filling by the default message handler. This is done by blocking `WM_ERASEBKGND` or specifying zero `hbrBackground` brush when registering the window's class. Then, when drawing the image, the entire window is filled through your means.

WinForms already provides a double buffering mode. To enable it, the `UserPaint`, `AllPaintingInWmPaint`, and `DoubleBuffer` flags of the `System.Windows.Forms.ControlStyles` enumeration must be set in the window, in which the drawing is done (e.g., a control element or a form), as shown in Listing 5.11.

Listing 5.11. Setting styles for WinForms double buffering [C#]

```
protected override void OnLoad(EventArgs e)
{
  SetStyle(ControlStyles.UserPaint, TRUE);
  SetStyle(ControlStyles.AllPaintingInWmPaint, TRUE);
  SetStyle(ControlStyles.DoubleBuffer, TRUE);
  ... // Another initialization
  base.OnLoad(e);
}
```

By the way, in WinForms double buffering, the output noticeably speeds up (despite the additional transfer to the screen): the demonstration application started to produce 75 to 80 frames per second instead of the previous 70.

5.5.4. Efficiency

At present, efficiency is the Achilles' heel of the library. GDI+ was designed with a goal of hardware acceleration, but in version 1.0 it has not been implemented.

Chapter 5: Operations with Bitmaps and Graphics Formats in GDI+

We can only hope that this shortcoming will be eliminated soon, because pixel-by-pixel calculations of semitransparency and antialiasing are not the fastest operations.

Because we started talking about speed, it would be appropriate to mention that GDI+ outputs bitmaps most rapidly when optimized for the particular device format represented by the CachedBitmap class. When such bitmaps are created, the original bitmap and the device onto which the resulting image is to be output need to be specified:

```
CachedBitmap(Bitmap* bitmap, Graphics* graphics);
```

Certain limitations are placed on this constructor. In particular, the Graphics output device must not be linked to the HDC of a printer or a metafile. Furthermore, when the output device characteristics are changed (e.g., when the resolution or the color depth is adjusted), CachedBitmap must be created anew to work with the new device; otherwise, the output will not occur.

To output optimized bitmaps to the screen, the Graphics::DrawCachedBitmap is used:

```
Status DrawCachedBitmap( CachedBitmap* cb, INT x, INT y);
```

This method speeds up output not only to the screen but also to memory because it dispenses with many intermediate calculations.

Good news: DrawCachedBitmap supports transparency and alpha channel (we have verified this).

Bad news: The application of coordinate transformation to an output device is not supported (except for coordinate translation). In particular, optimized bitmaps unfortunately cannot be rotated during output. If the image must be rotated, use an intermediate output with rotation to memory and only then cache the obtained Bitmap. This trick will not work if the rotation angle changes dynamically (in this case, it would be better to dispense with caching to avoid wasting time creating the intermediate image every time).

IMPORTANT

So how do you cache animated (multiframe) images? It is easy: you will need exactly as many CachedBitmap objects as there are frames in the animation. To cache the next frame, make that frame active (as before, it is output to the screen) with the help of the Image::SelectActiveFrame method. The source code given in Listing 5.12 demonstrates this technique.

Listing 5.12. Caching a multiframe GIF image [C++]

```cpp
// Required variables
Bitmap *butterflyImage;         // Animated butterfly image
CachedBitmap **cachedFrames;
// Cached frames will be placed here.
int frameCount;
int activeFrame;
...
// Initialization
frameCount = butterflyImage->GetFrameCount(&FrameDimensionTime);
cachedFrames = new CachedBitmap*[frameCount];
// Creating a Graphics object based on the Desktop
// window and assuming that the current video mode
// will not change
Graphics g(GetWindowDC(0));

// Caching proper
for(int i=0; i<frameCount; i++)
{
  butterflyImage->SelectActiveFrame(&FrameDimensionTime, i);
  cachedFrames[i] = new CachedBitmap(butterflyImage, &g);
}
activeFrame = 0;
butterflyImage->SelectActiveFrame(&FrameDimensionTime, 0);
```

Before using `CachedBitmap`, think about potential inconveniences: you will have to keep track of the moment the video mode changes and correspondingly reset all optimized bitmaps. Moreover, the efficiency gain of frames output per second is not that great: in our tests, it did not exceed 9% (even after many other performance-impeding operations were removed). Taking the operation of creating the `Graphics` intermediate context out of the `OnPaint` function and moving it into the initialization code turned out to be far more profitable although not a cure-all: this buffer needs to be created anew when the window size changes.

Finally, we did not found anything resembling the `DrawCachedBitmap` technique in the .NET environment. But .NET programmers should not despair: the timing results of `CachedBitmap` output suspiciously match the timing results of raster image output in the `ImageFormat.Format32bppPArgb` format (the champion of processing efficiency for GDI+ raster images). Most likely, the `CachedBitmap` class owes the lion's share of its speed gain to the preliminary multiplication of the raster image color component by the alpha channel value; this format is also available in .NET.

5.5.5. Demonstration Applications

To conclude this section on using bitmaps when working with graphics objects, consider two small demonstration applications, whose source code can be found on the accompanying CD-ROM.

The first application was written using the C++ version of the library. It illustrates the application of many described techniques: delayed loading of gdiplus.dll, loading GIF bitmaps from program resources, and using double buffering to eliminate flicker. Moreover, the source code contains an example (albeit a simplified one) of working with an animated GIF image.

You can also use this application as proving grounds for testing GDI+ capabilities on your own. The `InvalidateRect` function is called at once in the handler of the main window `WM_PAINT` message, guaranteeing the arrival of the next `WM_PAINT` message, and the number of frames output per second is calculated.

The other application is written in C# and is an example of outputting animated GIF files in a window of a WinForms program. It also implements an efficiency tracker (using the `System.Timers.Timer`) and double buffering.

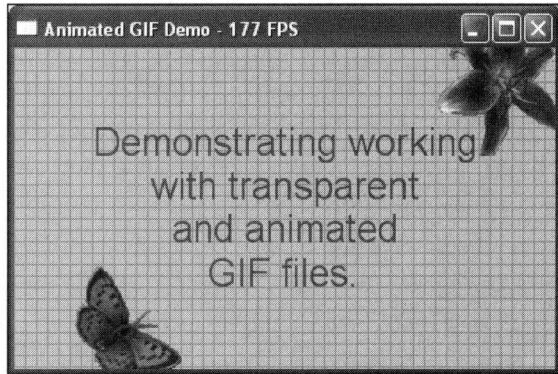

Fig. 5.4. C++ demonstration program

Fig. 5.5. C# demonstration program

In both applications, animation is intentionally output with the maximum possible speed to clearly demonstrate efficiency. To output animation with the needed speed in a real application, though, you will have to obtain the frame delay parameters from the graphics file (by calling the `Image::GetPropertyItem` function with the `PropertyTagFrameDelay` parameter). Moreover, .NET has a special auxiliary class, `System.Drawing.ImageAnimator`, that makes the animation task easier.

5.6. Direct Work with Raster Data

Unfortunately, the GDI+ library has limitations. Some of them are caused by bugs in the current implementation and probably will disappear soon. Others stem directly from the library's new architecture, in which an attempt was made to get rid of the accursed legacy of some GDI anachronisms. Regardless, direct access is often needed to the bitmap data inside of these pretty wrappers that are the GDI+ classes for the GDI+ flat API. In this section, you will learn the capabilities for doing this offered by GDI+.

5.6.1. The Color Class

In the 32-bit color model, a use for the fourth byte has finally been found: it is no longer used as simple alignment padding (e.g., as in the `RGBQUAD` structure) but stores the alpha value—technically speaking, the pixel transparency value. This was

Chapter 5: Operations with Bitmaps and Graphics Formats in GDI+   139

taken into account when designing the `Color` class, which acquired a corresponding constructor:

```
Color(
   BYTE a, // Alpha
   BYTE r, // Red
   BYTE g, // Green
   BYTE b // Blue
);
```

If the more traditional three-component `Color` constructor form is used, the alpha value is set to 255 (complete transparency). Moreover, a large selection of named color constants is defined in the `Color` class (e.g., `Color::AliceBlue`); their alpha value also equals 255.

In the .NET environment, a somewhat different approach is taken: for initialization, the `Color` structure has many static color value properties (e.g., `DeepSkyBlue`) and methods (e.g., the `FromArgb` method family). When the `FromArgb` method is used, the value of each of the four-color constituents cannot be larger than 8 bits:

```
public static Color FromArgb(int, int, int, int);
```

The .NET color structure also has the useful possibility of converting colors into the hue, saturation, and brightness model:

```
public float GetBrightness();
public float GetHue();
public float GetSaturation();
```

It also implements the standard `ToString` method, making it possible to obtain a string with the color's name or with the enumeration of its ARGB components:

```
public override string ToString();
```

5.6.2. Direct Pixel Access

To obtain and set the color of a bitmap pixel, the `Bitmap` class has the `GetPixel` and `SetPixel` methods available, respectively:

```
Status GetPixel(INT x, INT y, Color* color);
Status SetPixel(INT x, INT y, const Color& color);
```

What can be said about them? Use them only when necessary: their performance is terrible (as, by the way, is the performance of the analogous GDI functions). If you are overcome by a desire to draw an image in this way, it is better to draw it once in a `Bitmap` object and then output to the screen a cached image of the obtained bitmap.

By the way, a `Graphics` object has no means for changing the color of a specific pixel as can be done in GDI through the `SetPixel/GetPixel` functions working with the HDC. What could be the reason for this? Mainly, this was an attempt to achieve graphics independence of the output device (see the *"INFO: Resolution-Independence in GDI+"* (Q311460) MSDN article for details).

A faster way of changing the color of a specific pixel is to access some rectangular area of the bitmap by using the `Bitmap::LockBits` method:

```
Status LockBits(
   IN const Rect* rect,                 // Bitmap area to be accessed
   IN UINT flags,                       // Access parameters (read, write)
   IN PixelFormat format,               // PixelFormat enumeration constant
   OUT BitmapData* lockedBitmapData     // Output data area
);
```

The `flags` parameter is formed from the constants of the `ImageLockMode` enumeration. In addition to the type of access to the bitmap, it may hold the `ImageLockModeUserInputBuf` flag indicating that the `lockedBitmapData->Scan0` field already contains a pointer to a sufficient buffer allocated by the user. A detailed description of this function as well as examples of its use can be found in the platform SDK documentation.

NOTE

Calling `LockBits` causes the specified area to be copied into a temporary buffer. Modifying the bitmap data in this buffer will reflect on the `Bitmap` contents only after a back call of `UnlockBits` with the same `lockedBitmapData` pointer as the parameter.

When doing this, if the specified format of the temporary buffer (`PixelFormat`) is different from the format of the original raster, the `LockBits/UnlockBits` calls will need additional conversions.

To access the bitmap of the original image, the following (undocumented) feature can be taken advantage of. In GDI+ 1.0, the `Bitmap::GetHBitmap` method always returns a device-independent bitmap (DIB) section. It is sufficient to call `GetObject()` for this `HBITMAP` to receive bitmap data and the necessary `BITMAPINFO` structures (see article Q186221, *"SAMPLE: DibSectn.exe Uses DIB Sections in Win32,"* for an example of working with DIB sections). However, this behavior cannot be relied on in the future versions of the library.

5.6.3. Transparency Support

If there is a need to set a certain color of a bitmap to transparent, this can be done in several ways. The first way is to apply direct color replacement with the help of the `GetPixel` and `SetPixel` functions. With this method, all image pixels will have to be visited and the pixels of the selected color must be replaced with transparent pixels. As already mentioned, this is not the fastest way of doing this. The second way is to resort to direct memory access by calling `LockBits`.

In .NET, it is not necessary to replace colors and raw bitmaps returned by `LockBits` calls. The `System.Drawing.Bitmap` class implements the `MakeTransparent` method that makes all bitmap pixels of the selected color transparent.

```
Bitmap bm = new Bitmap("test.bmp");
// Assuming the color of the bitmap's first pixel is transparent
Color backColor = bm.GetPixel(0, 0);
bm.MakeTransparent(backColor);
```

But what if the original image cannot be modified? You can take advantage of the `Bitmap::Clone` method by cloning the bitmap or part of it and replacing the pixels in the clone. However, GDI+ has a simpler way of supporting transparency only when outputting images. For this, an instance of the `ImageAttributes` class (which you already encountered with the `Graphics::DrawImage` methods) needs to be created. This class can be used to correct many color parameters of the output image. In particular, the `SetColorKey` method can be used to specify that a certain color spectrum (or rather all pixels whose color components lie in this range) will become transparent during the output. Look, for example, at what happens to the butterfly from the demonstration project if a fragment of the `PaintButterfly` method is modified this way:

```
ImageAttributes attr;
// All colors in the (0, 0, 0, 0)-(100, 100, 100, 100) range will
// become transparent.
attr.SetColorKey(Color(0, 0, 0, 0), Color(100, 100, 100, 100));
Rect destRect(butterflyPos, Size(butterflyImage->GetWidth(),
   butterflyImage->GetHeight()));
g.DrawImage(butterflyImage, destRect, 0, 0,
   butterflyImage->GetWidth(),
   butterflyImage->GetHeight(),UnitPixel, &attr);
```

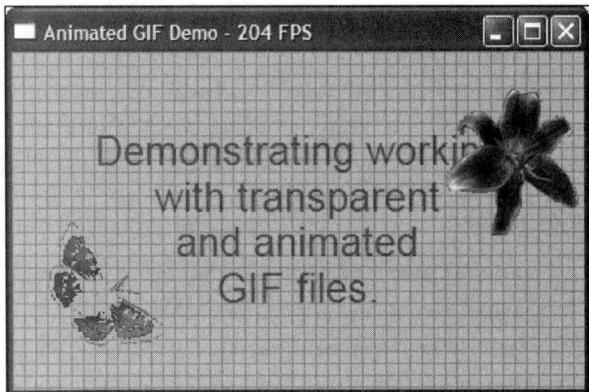

Fig. 5.6. Assigning a color key to a bitmap color range

NOTE If you insert this piece of code into the demonstration program, you will discover an annoying bug in the current GDI+ version. If a nonzero pointer to the `ImageAttributes` class is passed to the `Graphics::DrawImage` method, the animation output starts only from the first frame even though any other frame may be active.

In addition to direct color replacement, the `ImageAttributes` class supports recoloring: employing matrix algebra to perform calculations on each color component of the pixels. Because the alpha component plays a key role in the color calculations, recoloring can be used, for example, to increase the transparency level of the entire image twofold. The appropriate matrix is as follows:

$$\begin{bmatrix} 1 & 0 & 0 & 0 & 0 \\ 0 & 1 & 0 & 0 & 0 \\ 0 & 0 & 1 & 0 & 0 \\ 0 & 0 & 0 & 0.5 & 0 \\ 0 & 0 & 0 & 0 & 1 \end{bmatrix}$$

Each element of this matrix is a coefficient in the [0,1] range. The 0.5 number on the main diagonal in the fourth row means that multiplying a five-element vector (four color elements and one dummy element necessary for the calculations) by this matrix will make the fourth element of the product vector equal to the original value of the fourth element multiplied by 0.5. That is the alpha component. The following code prepares this conversion:

```
ColorMatrix colorMatrix =
{
```

```
    1.0f, 0.0f, 0.0f, 0.0f, 0.0f,
    0.0f, 1.0f, 0.0f, 0.0f, 0.0f,
    0.0f, 0.0f, 1.0f, 0.0f, 0.0f,
    0.0f, 0.0f, 0.0f, 0.5f, 0.0f,
    0.0f, 0.0f, 0.0f, 0.0f, 1.0f
};
attr.SetColorMatrix(&colorMatrix,
    ColorMatrixFlagsDefault,
    ColorAdjustTypeBitmap);
```

Fig. 5.7 shows the results of its use in the demonstration project.

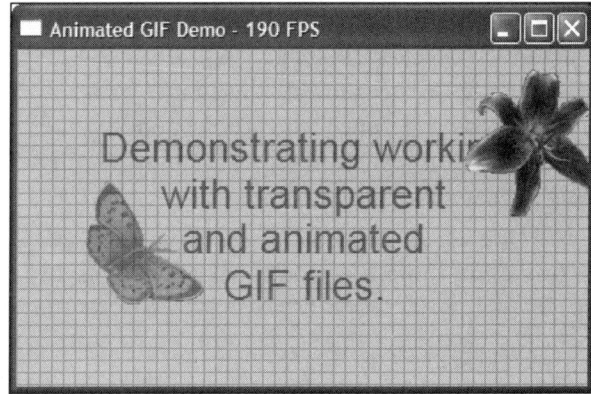

Fig. 5.7. Output of a bitmap with additional alpha overlay

5.6.4. Raster Operations

A common question in forums and Usenet newsgroups is as follows: How can GDI+ be made to use raster operations defined in GDI? For example, to select a collection of objects on the screen, it would be nice to invert them (or to color them with a reversible rectangle). In computer-aided design systems, an inverse shape or an outline of the future object may need to be drawn. Moreover, the R2_XOR mode makes it possible to restore images under objects by redrawing the object in the same place.

Microsoft specialists usually reply to this: "You do not really need this capability. The XOR graphics is simply ugly. Modern 32-bit graphics video modes allow images to be selected and overlaid using the alpha channel. Using various ROP [raster operation] codes to obtain transparency is also outdated: transparency is implemented in GDI+ ab initio." Indeed, GDI+ does not support raster operations. If the device context is force-set (e.g., the R2_XOR mode), it will be ignored during the output.

C++ programmers still have good old GDI; they only must not forget the already mentioned interoperability problems described in the MSDN article *"INFO: Interoperability Between GDI and GDI+"* (Q311221). But what are .NET developers to do? It turns out that the System.Windows.Forms.ControlPaint class is not part of the GDI+ hierarchy. For drawing reversible lines and rectangles, it makes the DrawReversibleLine, DrawReversibleFrame, and FillReversibleRectangle methods available.

However, a popular utility named *Anakrino* has been available for downloading from the Internet for a long time. It disassembles .NET assemblies into the source code of the initial high-level languages: C# and C++. Applied to the helpless FillReversibleRectangle method, all the magic of ControlPaint is unveiled in no time. Its methods reference the corresponding low-level gdi32.dll tools (SafeNativeMethods is simply the internal namespace, in which these GDI functions are defined):

Listing 5.13. Unveiling the ControlPaint class secrets [C#, pseudocode]

```
public static void FillReversibleRectangle(
  Rectangle rectangle, Color backColor)
{
  int local0;
  int local1;
  IntPtr local2;
  IntPtr local3;
  int local4;
  IntPtr local5;

  local0 = ControlPaint.GetColorRop(backColor, 10813541, 5898313);
  local1 = ControlPaint.GetColorRop(backColor, 6, 6);
  local2 = UnsafeNativeMethods.GetDCEx(
    UnsafeNativeMethods.GetDesktopWindow(), IntPtr.Zero, 1027);
  local3 = SafeNativeMethods.CreateSolidBrush(
    ColorTranslator.ToWin32(backColor));
  local4 = SafeNativeMethods.SetROP2(local2, local1);
```

Chapter 5: Operations with Bitmaps and Graphics Formats in GDI+

```
    local5 = SafeNativeMethods.SelectObject(local2, local3);
    SafeNativeMethods.PatBlt(local2, rectangle.X, rectangle.Y,
       rectangle.Width, rectangle.Height, local0);
    SafeNativeMethods.SetROP2(local2, local4);
    SafeNativeMethods.SelectObject(local2, local5);
    SafeNativeMethods.DeleteObject(local3);
    UnsafeNativeMethods.ReleaseDC(IntPtr.Zero, local2);
}
```

As can be seen, the "forbidden" `SetROP2` method is used to achieve the necessary effect.

How can you use these methods? Instructions and corresponding examples can be found in the following MSDN Knowledge Base articles:

"HOW TO: Draw a Rubber Band Rectangle or Focus Rectangle in Visual C#" (Q314945)

"HOW TO: Draw a Rubber Band or Focus Rectangle in Visual Basic .NET" (Q317479)

Fig. 5.8 is our C# example that allows part of an image to be inverted. Try to launch the example; click the left mouse button in the free area of the form and drag the cursor. The selected area is inverted even outside of the form limits: a clear demonstration of the interoperability between the high-level GDI+ and the low-level GDI.

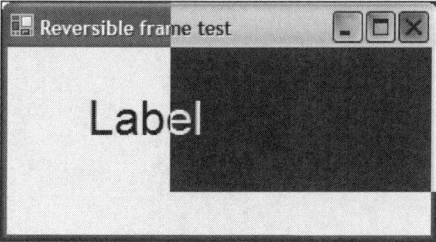

Fig. 5.8. Outputting inverse graphics using .NET

The source code and the compiled application of this demonstration example are available on the accompanying CD-ROM.

As you can see, the GDI+ library makes most powerful tools for raster work available to programmers. In *Chapter 6*, we will consider creating graphics filters for processing bitmap images.

Chapter 6: Viewing and Editing Bitmap Images

In this chapter, the following subjects are considered:

- ❐ Creating a multidocument application
- ❐ Executing a multithread program
- ❐ Using GDI+ tools to load images from different format files
- ❐ Outputting bitmap images to the screen
- ❐ Image scaling modes
- ❐ Using an image histogram
- ❐ Editing images using point and spatial filters
- ❐ Implementing transformations using software (the *BMViewer* program)

All the source codes within this chapter are written in C++.

6.1. Creating an Application

Your brief action plan is as follows:

1. Create a program framework to experiment with.
2. Give the program image-loading and image-saving capabilities.
3. Add image-editing filters.

Before creating the application, a brief familiarization with its architecture is in order.

6.1.1. The Document/View Architecture

The *Document/View* architecture is the main architecture used for building Visual C++ projects. The main idea of this type of program structure is to separate data from their representation on the screen. The Document/View architecture is implemented by creating two classes in addition to the main window class and the application class: a *document* class and a *view* class. The document and view classes are derived from the MFC library classes. The base class for the document class is the CDocument class; for the view class, the base class is the CView class. A document is any data aggregate: text, audio, video, etc. There are two types of applications built using the Document/View architecture: *Single Document Interface* (SDI) and *Multiple Document Interface* (MDI). The SDI applications allow only one document at a time to be edited. The standard Windows programs Notepad and Paint are examples of single-document applications. MDI applications, as their classification name suggests, allow several documents at a time to be edited. Adobe Photoshop is an example of an MDI application. Moreover, the documents supported by MDI applications can be of different types. For example, the Microsoft Visual C++ environment allows several documents of different types to be edited at the same time: program source code, resources (such as menus, dialog windows, icons, and bitmap images), etc.

The advantage of the Document/View architecture lies in that it allows data to be separated from their visual representation. In applications of this type, the same data stored in a document object can be simultaneously represented in different ways with the help of different view objects. For example, a certain graph (the same collection of data) can be presented as a table of values in one window, as a curve in another window, and as a diagram in yet another window.

The pivotal objects in this architecture are one or several document objects. Each document is accompanied by at least one view object (there can be more than one view object of the same document, as explained in the previous example). A view is an object whose function is to display the document data on the screen and to provide interaction with the user. The user observes and edits the data visualized by the view object. The view object accepts the user's control actions, communicates with the document object, and changes the data in it using document methods.

6.1.2. Creating a Multidocument Application

Delve deeper into the process of creating an MDI application. You will not have to make a great effort to do this because most of the work will be done by the *AppWizard*.

The framework application for viewing and editing images is created as follows:

1. Navigating down the **File New Projects MFC AppWizard (exe)** menu sequence, start creating the application. Give the project a name—*BMViewer*, for example.
2. In the first step of the AppWizard, select the **Multiple documents** type of application.
3. In the second through the fifth steps, accept all default settings.
4. In the sixth step of the AppWizard, change the base class of the view from the default `CView` to `CScrollView`. This substitution will give the application the capability of scrolling oversized images in the view window. In the same step, you can change the names of the files, in which the application classes will be stored. For example, the default *mbviewerview.h* can be changed to the more succinct *mbview.h*.

That's it; the framework application is ready. All that remains to be done is to flesh it out with some functional properties.

6.2. The Bitmap Class

Because the program will work with bitmap images, you will need a mechanism for loading, storing, and accessing bitmap data.

Fortunately, the GDI+ library has a class for working with bitmap images that has a complete set of the functions needed. This is the `Bitmap` class, described in *Chapter 5*.

Thus, data for the program will be objects of the `Bitmap` class. Next, look into the changes to the application framework necessary for it to be able to work with these objects. In brief, the following tasks need to be done:

1. In the `CBMApp` class, which creates the application, attach the GDI+ library, provide for its initialization when launched and cleanup when finished, and get the description of the codecs (because images will be loaded and stored).
2. In the `CBMDoc` document class, define `Bitmap` objects for storing bitmap data and implement methods for creating, editing, and removing these data.
3. In the `CBMView` view class, implement methods for visualizing images.

6.3. Attaching GDI+ and Modifying the Application Class

To attach the GDI+ library, you will use the mechanism described in *Section 1.3.3* and add the *initgdiplus.h* and *initgdiplus.cpp* files to the project. In the interface of the CBMApp class, which creates the application, define the m_GdiPlusInit object of the InitGdiPlus class. Thus, the GDI+ library has been attached. To make sure that the library initializes successfully, add a couple of code lines to the CBMApp::InitInstance() method, which is called when the application is started:

```
BOOL CBMApp::InitInstance()
{
   if(!m_GdiPlusInit.Good())
   {
      AfxMessageBox("GDI+ Initialization error ");
      return FALSE;
   }
...
```

When the application terminates, the m_GDIPlusInit object will be destroyed and the GDI+ library will be cleaned up and closed in the destructor of this object.

You have created a multidocument application, that is, an application that can work with several images at the same time. Every time a new image is opened, a new document object will be created that will load and control bitmap data. To know what file formats the Bitmap class can load, you have to obtain a description of the image codecs installed on the machine. It is advisable to perform this operation only once; therefore, implement it in the application class and execute it when the program is launched. It must be noted that the list of *image decoders* (modules that load images) can differ from the list of *image encoders* (modules that save images). To keep matters simple, limit the program to obtaining only the list of the encoders because these modules also load images. How to work with the codecs is examined in detail in *Section 5.3.1*.

Thus, to store the description of the image codes, add to the CBMApp class a pointer to the ImageCodecInfo and a variable to store the number of codecs:

```
ImageCodecInfo* m_pCodecInfoArray;
UINT m_nCodecNum;
```

Moreover, you will need a method to populate the list; call it ReadCodecsInfo() (see Listings 6.1 and 6.2).

When the program is launched, the framework application automatically creates a new blank document. However, you want to load and edit only existing images. To prevent the creation of a new document, use **ClassWizard** to define in the CBMApp class a method to handle messages of the ID_FILE_NEW command; leave the body of this method blank. If you want your program to have the function to create new documents, this command will have to be handled in some other way.

You will also have to define a method to process the **File Open** menu command (the ID_FILE_OPEN identifier). This method will be used to organize a list of the supported file format extensions and to display the open file name selection dialog. Then the OpenDocumentFile() method of the CWinApp base class is called, which creates a new document and calls for it the OnOpenDocument() method with the specified file name as the parameter. Finally, the OnOpenDocument() class is redefined for the document class and loads the image.

Take a look at the listings. The modified interface of the CBMApp class is shown in Listing 6.1, and its implementation is shown in Listing 6.2. (Only the source code of the modified methods is shown; the complete source code is available on the accompanying CD-ROM.)

Listing 6.1. The CBMapp class interface [BMViewer.h]

```
class CBMApp : public CWinApp
{
   RSDN::InitGdiPlus m_GdiPlusInit;

   // Defining the image load and save codecs
   ImageCodecInfo* m_pCodecInfoArray;
   UINT m_nCodecNum;
protected:
   // Obtaining the image load and save codecs
   void ReadCodecsInfo();

public:
   CBMApp();
   ~CBMApp();

   // Provides a pointer to the codecs definition array
   UINT GetCodecsArrayPtr(ImageCodecInfo ** pCodecs)
   {*pCodecs = m_pCodecInfoArray; return m_nCodecNum;};
```

Part II: Bitmap Graphics

```
    // Overrides
        // ClassWizard generated virtual function overrides.
        //{{AFX_VIRTUAL(CBMApp)
        public:
        virtual BOOL InitInstance();
        //}}AFX_VIRTUAL

    // Implementation
        //{{AFX_MSG(CBMApp)
        afx_msg void OnAppAbout();
        afx_msg void OnFileNew();
        afx_msg void OnFileOpen();
        //}}AFX_MSG
        DECLARE_MESSAGE_MAP()
};
```

Listing 6.2. Implementing the CBMApp class [BMViewer.cpp]

```
#include "stdafx.h"
#include "bmviewer.h"

#include "mainfrm.h"
#include "childfrm.h"
#include "bmdoc.h"
#include "bmview.h"
#include <atlbase.h>

#ifdef _DEBUG
#define new DEBUG_NEW
#undef THIS_FILE
static char THIS_FILE[] = __FILE__;
#endif

/////////////////////////////////////////////////////////////////////
// CBMApp

BEGIN_MESSAGE_MAP(CBMApp, CWinApp)
    //{{AFX_MSG_MAP(CBMApp)
    ON_COMMAND(ID_APP_ABOUT, OnAppAbout)
```

```
   ON_COMMAND(ID_FILE_NEW, OnFileNew)
   ON_COMMAND(ID_FILE_OPEN, OnFileOpen)
   //}}AFX_MSG_MAP
   // Standard file-based document commands
   ON_COMMAND(ID_FILE_NEW, CWinApp::OnFileNew)
   ON_COMMAND(ID_FILE_OPEN, CWinApp::OnFileOpen)
   // Standard print setup command
   ON_COMMAND(ID_FILE_PRINT_SETUP, CWinApp::OnFilePrintSetup)
END_MESSAGE_MAP()

/////////////////////////////////////////////////////////////////////////
// CBMApp construction

CBMApp::CBMApp()
{
   // TODO: Add construction code here, and
   // place all significant initialization in InitInstance.
}

CBMApp::~CBMApp()
{
   // TODO: Add construction code here, and
   // place all significant initialization in InitInstance,
   // releasing memory.
   if(m_pCodecInfoArray != NULL)
      free(m_pCodecInfoArray);

}

/////////////////////////////////////////////////////////////////////////
// The one and only CBMApp object

CBMApp theApp;

/////////////////////////////////////////////////////////////////////////
// CBMApp initialization

BOOL CBMApp::InitInstance()
{
   if(!m_GdiPlusInit.Good())
```

```
        {
            AfxMessageBox("GDI+ initialization error");
            return FALSE;
        }
        // Get the codecs list.
        ReadCodecsInfo();
...
// (The unmodified source code generated by
// the AppWizard for the rest of the program.)
...

}
void CBMApp::ReadCodecsInfo()
{

    UINT size;
    // Finding the number of codecs installed in the system
    GetImageEncodersSize(&m_nCodecNum, &size);

    // Allocating memory for definition
    m_pCodecInfoArray = (ImageCodecInfo*)(malloc(size));

    // Getting the codecs description
    GetImageEncoders(m_nCodecNum, size, m_pCodecInfoArray);
}

/////////////////////////////////////////////////////////////////////
// CBMApp message handlers

void CBMApp::OnFileNew()
{

}

void CBMApp::OnFileOpen()
{
    // Creating a list of the supported file formats
    CString Descr, Filter;
    USES_CONVERSION;
    for(UINT j=0; j < m_nCodecNum; ++j)
```

```
{
    Descr.Format("%s (%s)|%s|",
                OLE2T(m_pCodecInfoArray[j].FormatDescription),
                OLE2T(m_pCodecInfoArray[j].FilenameExtension),
                OLE2T(m_pCodecInfoArray[j].FilenameExtension));
    Filter += Descr;
}
Filter += "All Files (*.*)|*.*||";
CFileDialog OpenFDlg(TRUE, NULL, NULL,
            OFN_HIDEREADONLY|OFN_FILEMUSTEXIST,
            Filter.GetBuffer(Filter.GetLength()), AfxGetMainWnd());
Filter.ReleaseBuffer();

// Calling the dialog
if(OpenFDlg.DoModal() != IDOK)
    return;

// Getting the file name
CString FilePath = OpenFDlg.GetPathName();

// Calling the CWinApp class method
// A document object will be created
// and the CBMDoc::OnOpenDocument() method will be called.
OpenDocumentFile(FilePath);
}
```

6.4. Modifying the Document Class to Work with Images

To only display an image on the screen, it is enough to define one `Bitmap` class object in the document class, load images into it, and then display them. However, for a program to have some image-editing capabilities, at lease two objects are needed: one to store the original image and one, in which to place the modified image.

The procedure for working with two `Bitmap` objects is as follows:

1. The image is loaded into the first `Bitmap` object and is displayed until it is modified by the user issuing some image-editing instruction.

2. The modified image is placed into the second `Bitmap` object, and this image object is displayed.
3. The user may not like the changes made to the image and may want to have an **Undo Changes** function available. This is easily done: the objects are simply switched. If the user wants to undo more than one change, several image object copies reflecting all changes to be undone must be created. The image object copies storing the changes can be stored in a last-in-first-out stack, with the last change stored at the top.

The complete application source code is given on the CD-ROM included with the book; only the key parts necessary for understanding the main ideas are considered in the book.

Returning to the program, create in the `CBMDoc` document class two pointers to the `Bitmap` objects that will store the original and the modified images:

```
Bitmap *m_pBM[2];    // Two image buffers
Bitmap *m_pCurBM;    // Pointer to the current buffer
```

The `m_pCurBM` pointer will store the address of the current image, the one that you will display.

To load an image, redefine the `OnOpenDocument()` method of the `CBMDoc` class (Listing 6.3). This can be done using ClassWizard. We assume that you have already learned how to use the class generator, and we will not explain it here.

Listing 6.3. The `OnOpenDocument()` method of the `CBMDoc` class [BMDoc.cpp]

```
BOOL CBMDoc::OnOpenDocument(LPCTSTR lpszPathName)
{
   if (!CDocument::OnOpenDocument(lpszPathName))
      return FALSE;

   CComBSTR fname;
   fname.Append(lpszPathName);

   // Loading the image into the first buffer
   m_pBM[0] = Bitmap::FromFile(fname);
   m_pCurBM = m_pBM[0];

   // GDI+ always creates an object;
   // therefore, check whether an image is present.
   return (m_pCurBM != NULL && m_pCurBM->GetWidth());
}
```

As can be seen in Listing 6.3, the image is loaded into the first `Bitmap` object. This object becomes the current one, and its address is stored in the `m_pCurBM` variable. Next, check whether the created image has dimensions.

6.5. Using a Virtual Screen

The *virtual screen* concept is extensively used in programming screen output. Before the image is displayed on the physical monitor, it is prepared on this virtual screen. The preparation may take a long time and may include several operations that the user has no need to be aware of. The image from the virtual screen is copied to the physical one in one operation, which takes much less time than building the image.

In this case, the image can be drawn using the `DrawImage()` method of the `Graphics` class (see *Section 1.2.5*), which performs output to the device context. However, before the image is output to the screen, the latter must be cleared of the old contents. If these operations are carried out sequentially in the current display context, the screen will flicker unpleasantly. To avoid this effect, a virtual screen is created in the program and the image is first output to it. The image will have to be redrawn most often in the view object—for example, when processing scrolling messages, redrawing the window after it is overlapped by other windows, or changing the window size. In this case, the image is simply copied from the virtual screen to the display device context using the fast `CDC::BitBlt` method.

There are different ways to implement the virtual screen. In the subsequent presentation, consider an implementation, in which the screen size is the same as the size of the image being scaled. The advantage of this approach is that the entire ready-for-output image can be placed on the virtual screen. If the entire image does not fit into the output window, all that needs to be done is the starting point must be offset by the scroll value and the right part of the image must be displayed in the window.

The disadvantage of this method is that a large amount of memory is needed to reflect the virtual screen bitmap. Assume that you have a 100 × 100-pixel image. At 32-bit color depth, the virtual screen bitmap for this image will require 40 KB, whereas the virtual screen bitmap for the image scaled up tenfold will require 4 MB. Consequently, problems may arise with outputting large images.

You can manage without a large virtual screen. A screen the size of the maximum possible output window is sufficient. In this case, only the needed part of the image will have to be displayed on this virtual screen.

The advantage of this approach is that you save memory and can scale images up without worrying about running out of memory for the virtual screen.

Its drawback is that additional processing of the image scrolling or the window-size change messages will have to be performed and that the needed part of the image must be output to the virtual screen every time such a message arrives. This may slow down image scrolling.

Because the CBMView view class is responsible for displaying images in the program, the task of servicing the virtual screen will be laid on it. The changes that need to be done for this are considered in the next section.

6.6. Modifying the View Class

To implement a virtual window, declare two variables in the view object:

```
CBitmap    m_VirtScreenBitmap;
CDC        m_VirtScreenDC;
```

The m_VirtScreenBitmap object will be used to store the virtual screen bitmap, and the m_VirtScreenDC object will serve as the virtual screen context.

The virtual screen context must be compatible with the context of the image output window. Add the WM_CREATE message handler to the CBMView class and create the compatible context in it (see Listing 6.4).

Listing 6.4. Creating a virtual window context [BMView.cpp]

```
int CBMView::OnCreate(LPCREATESTRUCT lpCreateStruct)
{
   if (CScrollView::OnCreate(lpCreateStruct) == -1)
      return -1;

   // TODO: Add your specialized creation code here.

   // Create compatible context for the virtual screen.
   CPaintDC dc(this);
   m_VirtScreenDC.CreateCompatibleDC(&dc);

   return 0;
}
```

Chapter 6: Viewing and Editing Bitmap Images 159

The only thing left is to output the image to the virtual screen. To solve this problem, you will have to do the following:

1. Add a method that will output the image in the document object to the virtual screen. Name it, for example, `UpdateVirtualScreen()`. The same method will create the virtual screen bitmap large enough to output the entire image.
2. To the `CBMView::OnDraw()` method, add code for copying the virtual screen to the client portion of the output window. Copying will take the position of the scroll box into account.
3. Using ClassWizard, redefine the `OnUpdate()` virtual method so that it sets the size of the scroll area corresponding to the image size, accounting for the scaling coefficient. This needs to be done so that the user could observe any part of the image by scrolling it in the window. The `OnInitialUpdate()` method added to the class by AppWizard when creating the framework application can be deleted, or just the code to set the scroll area size can be commented out in it. In the former case, do not forget to delete the declaration of this method in the class interface. The method is no longer needed because the implementation of the `OnInitialUpdate()` in the base class calls the `OnUpdate()` method that has already been properly modified.
4. Using ClassWizard, define the `WM_ERASEBKGND` message-handling method to control redrawing (clearing) of the background of the view window. This will get rid of flicker when you redraw the view window.

The source code of these methods is shown in Listing 6.5.

Listing 6.5. Modified view methods [BMView.cpp]

```
// Background fill color
#define GRAY RGB(127, 127, 127)
BOOL CBMView::UpdateVirtualScreen()
{
   CBMDoc* pDoc = GetDocument();
   ASSERT_VALID(pDoc);

   // Pointer to the current image has been obtained.
   Bitmap* pCurBM = pDoc->GetCurrentBMPtr();
   if(pCurBM == NULL) return FALSE;

   // Calculate the image size, accounting for the scale.
```

Part II: Bitmap Graphics

```cpp
    LONG imgw = static_cast<LONG>(pCurBM->GetWidth()*m_dScale);
    LONG imgh = static_cast<LONG>(pCurBM->GetHeight()*m_dScale);

    // If the bitmap exists, get its size.
    BITMAP BMStruct; BMStruct.bmWidth = BMStruct.bmHeight = 0;
    if(m_VirtScreenBitmap.GetSafeHandle( ))
        m_VirtScreenBitmap.GetBitmap(&BMStruct);

    // If the dimensions of the virtual screen are
    // smaller than the image, make the screen larger.
    if(BMStruct.bmWidth < imgw || BMStruct.bmHeight < imgh)
    {
        CPaintDC dc(this);
        // Display dimensions in pixels.
        int scrw = dc.GetDeviceCaps(HORZRES);
        int scrh = dc.GetDeviceCaps(VERTRES);

        // Select a temporary bitmap in the context,
        // which will release the m_VirtScreenBitmap
        // (if it was selected in the context)
        // and will allow its deletion.
        CBitmap TempBM; TempBM.CreateCompatibleBitmap(&dc, 1, 1);
        m_VirtScreenDC.SelectObject(&TempBM);

        // Destroy the old bitmap.
        m_VirtScreenBitmap.DeleteObject();
        // In its place, build a new one
        // no smaller than the display dimensions.
        if(!m_VirtScreenBitmap.CreateCompatibleBitmap(&dc,
                    (imgw < scrw?scrw:imgw), (imgh < scrh?scrh:imgh)))
            return FALSE;
        // The new bitmap is selected in the virtual screen context.
        m_VirtScreenDC.SelectObject(&m_VirtScreenBitmap);
    }

    // Clear the virtual screen.
    CBrush FonBrush(GRAY); // Background fill brush
    m_VirtScreenBitmap.GetBitmap(&BMStruct);  // Determine the screen dimensions.
```

Chapter 6: Viewing and Editing Bitmap Images

```cpp
        m_VirtScreenDC.FillRect(&CRect(0,0, BMStruct.bmWidth,
                            BMStruct.bmHeight), &FonBrush);
    // Create a Graphics object for the virtual screen.
    Graphics g(m_VirtScreenDC.m_hDC);
    // Set the scaling mode.
    g.SetInterpolationMode(m_nStretchMode);
    // Image output
    g.DrawImage(pCurBM, Rect(0, 0, imgw, imgh), 0, 0, pCurBM->GetWidth(),
            pCurBM->GetHeight(), UnitPixel);
    // Refresh the image on the screen.
    Invalidate();
    return TRUE;
};

void CBMView::OnDraw(CDC* pDC)
{
    // TODO: Add your specialized code here, call the base class, or both.
    CBMDoc* pDoc = GetDocument();
    ASSERT_VALID(pDoc);

    // Get the dimensions of the client part of the window.
    CRect ClientRect;
    GetClientRect(&ClientRect);

    // Copy the contents of virtual screen,
    // taking the position of the scroll box into account.
    CPoint ScrollPos = GetScrollPosition();
    pDC->BitBlt(ScrollPos.x, ScrollPos.y,
            ClientRect.Width(), ClientRect.Height(),
            &m_VirtScreenDC, ScrollPos.x, ScrollPos.y, SRCCOPY);
}

void CBMView::OnInitialUpdate()
{
   CScrollView::OnInitialUpdate();
//   CSize sizeTotal;
//   TODO: Calculate the total size of this view.
//   sizeTotal.cx = sizeTotal.cy = 100;
//   SetScrollSizes(MM_TEXT, sizeTotal);
```

```
}

void CBMView::OnUpdate(CView* pSender, LPARAM lHint, CObject* pHint)
{
    CBMDoc* pDoc = GetDocument();
    ASSERT_VALID(pDoc);

    // Refresh the image on the virtual screen.
    if(UpdateVirtualScreen())
    {
       // Scroll area size
       CSize ScrollSize;

       // Scroll area is the entire image size, accounting for scaling.
       ScrollSize = pDoc->GetCurrentBMSize();
       ScrollSize.cx = static_cast<LONG>(ScrollSize.cx*m_dScale);
       ScrollSize.cy = static_cast<LONG>(ScrollSize.cy*m_dScale);
       SetScrollSizes(MM_TEXT, ScrollSize);
    }
    else
       AfxMessageBox("Error outputting to the virtual screen");

    // Call the base class method.
    CScrollView::OnUpdate(pSender, lHint, pHint);
}
```

Now, examine how this code works. When TRUE is returned by the OnOpenDocument() method of the document object, the framework application creates a view object and sends to it a message to display the document contents. In this case, the message is processed by the CBMView::OnUpdate() method, which in turn calls the CMBView::UpdataVirtualScreen(). The UpdateVirtualScreen() method creates a properly-sized bitmap, attaches it to the virtual screen descriptor, requests the current image from the document object, and outputs the image to the virtual screen. The image is output using the m_dScale and m_nStretchMode variables that specify the scale and the interpolation mode. Add these variables to the CBMView class to do some scaling experiments. The variables are defined in the class interface as follows:

```
double             m_dScale;
InterpolationMode  m_nStretchMode;
```

Chapter 6: Viewing and Editing Bitmap Images 163

NOTE

The `m_nStretchMode` variable is of the `InterpolationMode` enumeration type and sets the interpolation mode when outputting the bitmap image to the screen. See *Section 5.5.2* for details.

In the constructor, these variables are initialized with the starting values:

```
CBMView::CBMView()
{
   m_dScale = 1.0;
   m_nStretchMode = InterpolationModeHighQualityBicubic;
}
```

After the image has been output to the virtual screen, the `Invalidate()` method is called, which tells the view to refresh the image on the physical screen. Having received this message, the view calls its `OnDraw()` message, which copies the image from the virtual screen to the physical screen.

That's it. Now the images can be loaded and viewed. Fig. 6.1 shows the program with four images loaded (this is a multidocument application).

Fig. 6.1. Viewing images in the **BMViewer** program

Moreover, in MDI programs, a document can have more than one view object, as is shown in Fig. 6.2. A new document view can be created with the **Window New Window** menu command sequence. Changing data of the document object will be reflected in all windows (by all view objects). This property can be used, for example, to show the same image scaled at different ratios in different windows; you will see later on how this is done. We recommend a book by Herbert Shildt [9] for further study of the SDI and MDI application features.

Fig. 6.2. One of the pictures is shown in two windows

To change the scale of the output image, add the **Zoom In** and **Zoom Out** commands to the **View** menu; to set the scaling interpolation mode, the **Stretch BICUBIC** and **Stretch NEIGHBOR** instructions are used (Fig. 6.3).

Several modes are defined in the InterpolationMode enumeration. To demonstrate clear differences between two modes, we will use only two of them, called InterpolationModeHighQualityBicubic and InterpolationModeNearestNeighbor.

Chapter 6: Viewing and Editing Bitmap Images 165

Command handlers are added to the view class using ClassWizard (Listing 6.6). These functions change the state of the m_dScale and m_nStretchMode variables. These commands can also be assigned hotkeys (or shortcuts).

The OnUpdateViewStretchBicubic() and OnUpdateViewStretchNeighbor() methods are added to process the UPDATE_COMMAND_UI message from the scaling mode commands. These functions can be used to control the state of the corresponding commands in the program interface (e.g., depending on the program status, the commands can be disabled). In this case, we simply mark the corresponding scaling mode.

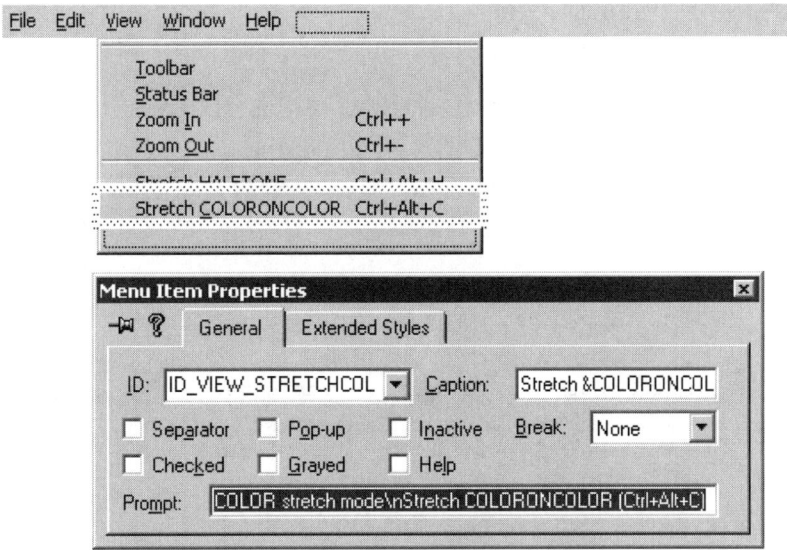

Fig. 6.3. Adding scaling commands to the program menu

Listing 6.6. Processing scaling commands [BMView.cpp]

```
void CBMView::OnViewZoomin()
{
    // TODO: Add your command handler code here.
    m_dScale *= 2;
    OnUpdate(NULL, 0, NULL);
}

void CBMView::OnViewZoomout()
```

```
{
    // TODO: Add your command handler code here.
    m_dScale /= 2;
    OnUpdate(NULL, 0, NULL);
}

void CBMView::OnViewStretchBicubic()
{
    // TODO: Add your command handler code here.
    m_nStretchMode = InterpolationModeHighQualityBicubic;
    OnUpdate(NULL, 0, NULL);
}

void CBMView::OnUpdateViewStretchBicubic(CCmdUI* pCmdUI)
{
    // TODO: Add your command update unique identifier (UI) handler code here
    pCmdUI->SetCheck(m_nStretchMode == InterpolationModeHighQualityBicubic);
}

void CBMView::OnViewStretchNeighbor()
{
    // TODO: Add your command handler code here.
    m_nStretchMode = InterpolationModeNearestNeighbor;
    OnUpdate(NULL, 0, NULL);
}

void CBMView::OnUpdateViewStretchNeighbor(CCmdUI* pCmdUI)
{
    // TODO: Add your command update UI handler code here.
    pCmdUI->SetCheck(m_nStretchMode == InterpolationModeNearestNeighbor);
}
```

The split-window mechanism can be used in MDI applications. This mechanism allows several views to be shown in one window frame. For this, you only need to teach the frame of the child window of the application to work with several views. This is easily done. When creating a framework application, in AppWizard step 4, open the **Advanced Options** dialog window by pressing the **Advance** button, open the **Window Styles** tab, and check the **Use split window** checkbox. If you did not do this during the framework application creation process, it is no big problem: open the `CChildFrame` class interface and manually add an object variable of the `CSplitterWnd` class:

```
// Attributes
protected:
    CSplitterWnd m_wndSplitter;
```

Then, use ClassWizard to redefine the `OnCreateClient` virtual method in the `CChildFrame` class and touch up its code as shown in Listing 6.7.

Listing 6.7. The corrected `CChildFrame::OnCreateClient` method [ChildFrm.cpp]

```
BOOL CChildFrame::OnCreateClient(LPCREATESTRUCT lpcs, CCreateContext* pContext)
{
    // TODO: Add your specialized code here, call the base class, or both.

// return CMDIChildWnd::OnCreateClient(lpcs, pContext);
    return m_wndSplitter.Create( this,
        2, 2,                   // Maximum number of rows and columns
        CSize( 10, 10 ),        // Minimum window size
        pContext );
}
```

Voilà! In one window frame you can see four window views of the image at different scale ratios and in different interpolation modes (Fig. 6.4). To obtain this effect, grab the slider in the left part of the horizontal scroll bar with the mouse and drag it to where you want it to be. The vertical scroll bar slider serves the same purpose but only in the vertical dimension.

Although the `CSplitterWnd::Create()` method has parameters for setting the maximum number of rows and columns in the split window, according to the official documentation, each must not be greater than two. However, increasing these values at your own risk, the split window can be broken into nine views.

The last view clicked with the mouse is considered the active one and is the one acted on by the scaling commands. The upper row of Fig. 6.4 shows enlarged parts of the image. The left one is in the `InterpolationModeHighQualityBicubic` mode, and the right one is in the `InterpolationModeNearestNeighbor` mode. It can be seen that the `InterpolationModeNearestNeighbor` mode is not trying to fight the staircase effect.

Fig. 6.4. Four views of one document object are displayed in one window frame

6.7. Editing Images

Finally, you have reached the most interesting part. The transformation magic is the big joy made available by digital image processing. Using the image-editing features of such programs as Adobe Photoshop or Ulead Photoimpact, even a person without great artistic skills can transform a most ordinary photograph into something more intriguing. Although their powerful features are easy to use, the extensive image-processing features of the programs are the results of a programmer's laborious work based on sound mathematical principles. Continue your study by examining the following two types of transformations:

❑ *Point transformations*—The new value of an image element (pixel) is calculated based only on its old value.

❑ *Spatial (matrix) transformations*—Taken into account when calculating its new value is not only the old value of a pixel but also the values of the pixels within a certain area around it.

To perform point transformations, lookup tables come in handy; these are considered in *Section 6.7.3*.

Spatial transformations usually involve calculating the convolution of the values of a group of pixels. The convolution is calculated by multiplying the pixel values within the transformation area by their weight coefficients and then summing the products. The values of the weight coefficients are supplied by the elements of the transformation matrix. The values of the matrix elements determine the transformation type. The dimensions of the transformation matrix correspond to the area occupied by the pixels that will be involved in the transformation. The central element of the matrix is the weight coefficient of the pixel being transformed. Therefore, transformation matrices usually have odd dimensions (e.g., 3 × 3 or 5 × 5 elements). Convolutions often have deep and sophisticated mathematical meanings, which fortunately can be given a simple and understandable practical interpretation. For example, consider a convolution using the following *M* matrix:

$$M = \begin{bmatrix} 1 & 1 & 1 \\ 1 & 1 & 1 \\ 1 & 1 & 1 \end{bmatrix}$$

The new value of the *P(x, y)* pixel can be calculated using the following pseudocode:

```
MX = 3; // X-dimension of the transformation matrix
MY = 3; // Y-dimension of the transformation matrix
CountCoeffSumm = 0; // Transformation matrix coefficient sum counter
NewP = 0; // The new pixel value
for(j = -MY/2; j <= MY/2; j++)
   for(i = -MX/2; i <= MX/2; i++)
       {
           NewP = NewP + P(x+i, y+j)*M(i, j);
           CountCoeffSumm = CountCoeffSumm + M(i, j);
       }
P(x, y) = NewP/CountCoeffSumm;
```

Integer division is assumed here—that is, MX/2 produces 1.

During the transformation process, the transformation matrix coefficients are added; after the new value of the pixel has been calculated, it is divided by this sum. This is necessary to bring the result within the value range of the summed pixels.

The just-described convolution using an identity matrix corresponds to the blurring transformation (sharpness reduction) of an image. This effect is obtained by averaging the values of the group of pixels encompassed by the transformation matrix. If the value of the (x, y) pixel is below the average, it will decrease; if it is above the average, it will increase. However, this does not mean that the entire image will become flat, because as the transformation matrix moves along the image following the (x, y) coordinates, the average changes. In the following material, use of various transformation matrices will be considered.

Into separate transformation categories are placed frame-by-frame and geometric processes. Frame-by-frame transformations involve two or more images. An example of a frame-by-frame transformation is subtraction to find the difference between two images. Subtraction can be used to determine similarities (find differences) between images. Frame-by-frame transformations are widely used in processing and compressing video data streams.

The very name of the process—*geometric*—says that the essence of the transformation is in changing its location or other geometric characteristics. Examples of geometric transformations are image rotation, shift, interpolation, and scaling.

All transformation types are examined in a book by Craig Lindley [3]. The detailed examination of the classical bitmap-image transformations, including the underlying theory, and of their software implementations are the strong points of this book. Basic image-processing theory and more information about the internal workings and practical application of digital filters can be found in books by David Rogers [7, 8].

The following material will consider the essence of some bitmap-image transformation procedures that have become classical. For this, endow the BMViewer program with image-editing capabilities. The program will implement several transformations, but it is no less important that you will try to structure it to be able to easily add to it implementations of any new transformations.

6.7.1. Image Brightness Histogram

A histogram is a bar graph. An *image brightness histogram* is a graph that shows the relative frequency of various brightness pixels in an image. Say you have a 16-pixel image. Let 8 pixels have a brightness of one, 2 pixels have a brightness of four, and the remaining 6 pixels have a brightness of seven. On a one-to-ten brightness scale, a histogram of this image may look like what is shown in Fig. 6.5.

Real images usually comprise a lot more pixels, and their brightness is measured on a 0-to-255 scale.

The brightness of an RGB pixel is calculated using the following formula:

Brightness = $0.3 \times Red + 0.59 \times Green + 0.11 \times Blue$

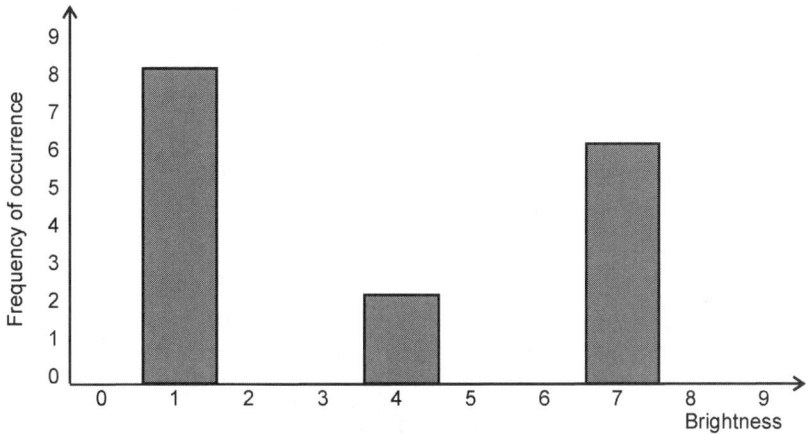

Fig. 6.5. Brightness histogram of the imaginary 16-pixel image

As you can see, in this formula, different colors have different weight coefficients. This is because human eye perceives different color components with different degrees of sensitivity.

The brightness histogram is widely used for analyzing and editing images.

To build the histogram, add the `GetHistogram` method to the `CBMDoc` class. The `GetHistogram()` method receives two parameters (see Listing 6.10):

❑ `DWORD *pHist`—A pointer to the array, in which the histogram values will be stored

❑ `int Range`—The array size, also functioning as the brightness range

The subscript of a value in the `pHist` array corresponds to the brightness, and the element's value corresponds to the frequency, with which this brightness occurs in the image. A histogram is easily calculated by processing all image pixels in a loop. In the loop body, first the brightness of the next image pixel is calculated and then the value of the corresponding element in the `pHist` array is incremented by one.

After calculating the histogram, all that is left is to display in on the screen. The first step is to add a special dialog window to the program (Fig. 6.6). If you have forgotten how to do this, remember that a new dialog-window template is added using the **Insert Resource Dialog New** command sequence. Assign the `IDD_HIST` identifier to the template and add a frame to it (a *picture* element of the *frame* type). You will need this element to draw the histogram; therefore, give it the `IDC_HIST_VIEW` identifier. Two sliders (*slider* element) are also added to the template, as well as two *static* elements, in which the histogram values will be displayed as text.

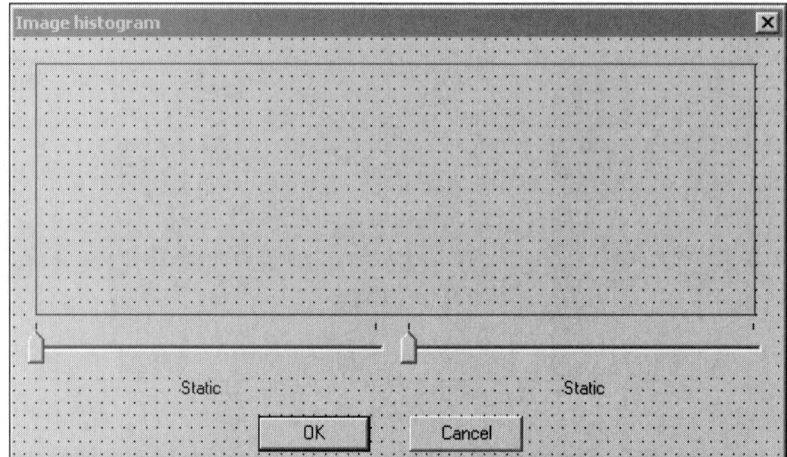

Fig. 6.6. Template of the image histogram dialog window

In principle, the histogram image can be drawn right over the dialog window by defining in the dialog class the message handler WM_PAINT and doing the corresponding plotting in it. However, a greater degree of flexibility can be obtained by creating a specialized class to output the histogram into a specified Windows window. This class is created using the same ClassWizard.

In the MFC ClassWizard window, press the **AddClass New** buttons. In the **New Class** window that appears, give the new class a name—for example, CHistView (Fig. 6.7). Specify the CStatic class as its base class. This MFC library class provides the functionality of the Windows static control elements, such as frame, bitmap, and icon. You will redefine the WM_PAINT message handler in the CHistView class and teach it to draw histograms. Then you will be able to associate an object inherited from the CHistView class with the IDC_HIST_VIEW control element. These actions will allow you to place the histogram image in the right part of the dialog window without specifying corresponding coordinates in the program code. In the same window, several histogram elements can be displayed (e.g., for different color channels) without modifying the program to display the histogram.

The sliders added to the dialog will be needed later to edit the histogram. These two elements are described here so that we can avoid describing this dialog twice. Using ClassWizard, create a CHistDlg class to service the dialog (just press the <Ctrl> + <W> key combination while in the dialog-window template editor). Associate the created control elements with the objects in the dialog class (Fig. 6.8); the object of the created CHistView class should be associated with the IDC_HIST_VIEW element.

Chapter 6: Viewing and Editing Bitmap Images

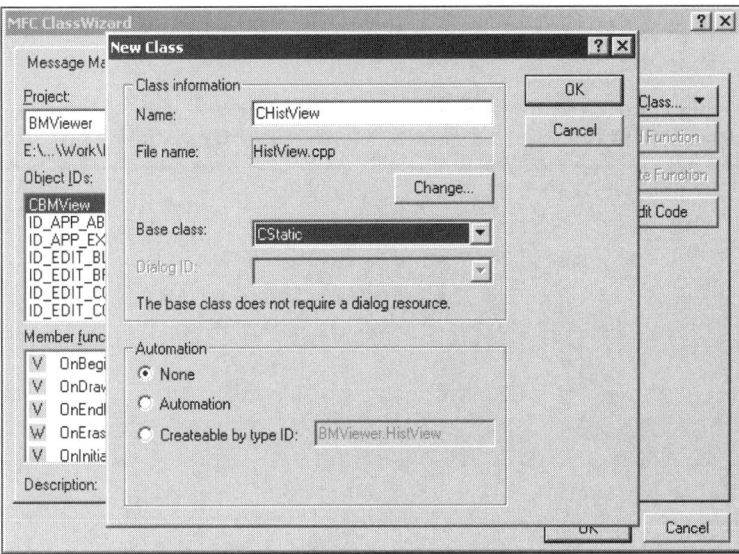

Fig. 6.7. Creating the `CHistView` class

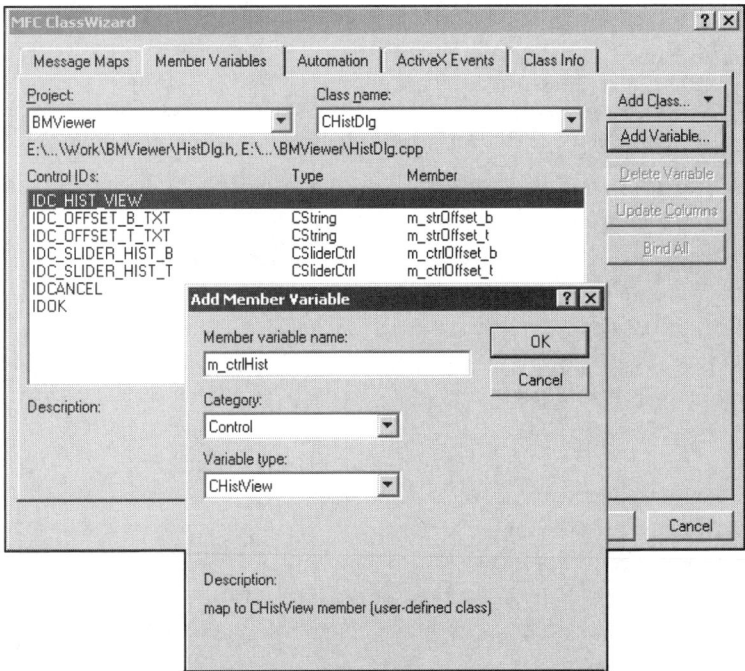

Fig. 6.8. Variables of the `CHistDlg` class

To draw the histogram, using ClassWizard again, add a message handler `WM_PAINT` to the `CHistClass` (Listing 6.8).

Listing 6.8. The `CHistView::OnPaint()` method [HistView.cpp]

```
void CHistView::OnPaint()
{
    CPaintDC dc(this); // Device context for painting

    // TODO: Add your message handler code here.

    if(m_pHist == NULL || m_iRange == 0 ) return;

    // Find the average.
    DWORD MaxBright = 0, SumBright = 0;
    for(int i=0; i < m_iRange; i++)
        SumBright += m_pHist[i];

    // Let the maximum (shown in the drawing) value
    // be three times greater than the average.
    MaxBright = 3*SumBright/m_iRange;
    if(MaxBright == 0) return;

    // Pen to draw the histogram
    CPen HistPen(PS_SOLID, 2, m_Color);
    CPen *pOldPen = dc.SelectObject(&HistPen);
    CGdiObject *pOldBrush = dc.SelectStockObject(NULL_BRUSH);

    // Find the output window coordinates.
    CRect FrameRect;
    GetWindowRect(&FrameRect);
    ScreenToClient(&FrameRect);

...// Draw the histogram in the window.
    dc.Rectangle(&FrameRect);
    FrameRect.bottom -= 1;
    double kx = ((double)FrameRect.Width())/m_iRange;
    double ky = ((double)FrameRect.Height())/MaxBright;

    int x=0, y=0;
```

```
        for(i=0; i < m_iRange; i++)
    {
        x = FrameRect.left+(kx*i);
        y = FrameRect.bottom;
        dc.MoveTo(x, y);
        y = FrameRect.bottom -(ky*m_pHist[i]);
        if(y < FrameRect.top) y = FrameRect.top;
        dc.LineTo(x, y);
    }
    if(pOldPen)
        dc.SelectObject(pOldPen);
    if(pOldBrush)
        dc.SelectObject(pOldBrush);

    // Do not call CStatic::OnPaint() to paint messages.
}
```

Every time the window (in this case, the window is the control element associated with the `CHistView` class object) is to be shown on the screen, Windows sends to it the `WM_PAINT` message. The program processes this message and draws the histogram.

As you have undoubtedly noticed, the values for drawing the histogram are stored in the array pointed to by the `m_pHist` variable, with the `m_iRange` variable setting the array's dimension. These variables are added to the interface of the `CHistView` class (Listing 6.9) with the `SetData()` method to set them.

Listing 6.9. Interface of the `CHistView` class [HistView.h]

```
class CHistView : public CStatic
{
// Construction
public:
    CHistView();

// Attributes
public:
    int         m_iRange;    // Dimension of the histogram array
    const DWORD *m_pHist;    // Pointer to the histogram data
    COLORREF    m_Color;     // Color for drawing the histogram

// Operations
```

```
public:
   // Sets data to be displayed
   void SetData(const DWORD *pHist,  int Range)
            {m_pHist = pHist; m_iRange = Range;};
   // Sets the color for drawing the histogram
   void SetColor(const COLORREF &c) {m_Color = c;};

// Overrides
   // ClassWizard generated virtual function overrides.
   // {{AFX_VIRTUAL(CHistView)
   // }}AFX_VIRTUAL

// Implementation
public:
   virtual ~CHistView();

   // Generated message map functions
protected:
   // {{AFX_MSG(CHistView)
   afx_msg void OnPaint();
   // }}AFX_MSG

   DECLARE_MESSAGE_MAP()
};
```

For the dialog to work, it must be called somewhere in the program. For this purpose, add a **Histogram** command to the program menu item **Edit** and a method to handle this command to the document class (Listing 6.10).

Listing 6.10. Methods of the CBMDoc class to work with the histogram [BMDoc.cpp]

```
BOOL CBMDoc::GetHistogram(DWORD *pHist, int Range)
{
   // Bitmap data
   BitmapData Data;

   // Obtaining access to the data
   if(!m_pCurBM || m_pCurBM->LockBits(&Rect(0, 0, m_pCurBM->GetWidth(),
        m_pCurBM->GetHeight()), ImageLockModeRead, PixelFormat32bppRGB,
        &Data) != Ok)
```

Chapter 6: Viewing and Editing Bitmap Images 177

```
      return FALSE;

   // Zeroing out the table
   for(int i=0; i < Range; i++)
      pHist[i] = 0;

   for(UINT y=0, x=0; y < Data.Height; y++)
      for(x=0; x < Data.Width; x++)
   {
      // Pixel address        BYTE*
pPix = ((BYTE*)Data.Scan0) + Data.Stride*y + x*4;

      BYTE Brightness = Y(pPix)*Range/256;
      pHist[Brightness] += 1;
   }

   if(m_pCurBM->UnlockBits(&Data) != Ok )
      return FALSE;

   return TRUE;
};

void CBMDoc::OnEditHistogram()
{
   const int Range = 256;
   DWORD Hist[Range]; // Histogram from the Range brightness gradations
   // Requesting the histogram from the current image
   if(!GetHistogram(Hist, Range))
      return;
   // Creating the dialog object
   CHistDlg HDlg;
   // Passing the histogram to the dialog
   HDlg.SetData(Hist, Range);
   // Displaying the histogram
   if(HDlg.DoModal() == IDCANCEL) return;
   // Contrast needs to be corrected.
 if(HDlg.m_iOffset_b != 0 || HDlg.m_iOffset_t != 0)
   {
      // Adjusting the histogram filter
      m_HistogramFilter.Init(HDlg.m_iOffset_b, HDlg.m_iOffset_t);
      // Activating the histogram filter
```

```
        m_pCurFilter = &m_HistogramFilter;
        // Doing the transformation
        Transform();
    }
}
```

In Listing 6.10, everything up to the `// Contrast needs to be corrected.` line ought to be clear. What this contrast correction is will be explained later.

Another moment that needs to be explained is how the histogram data are passed into the dialog object. This is done using the `SetData(Hist, Range)` method, and the dialog object passes the data directly to the element that displays the histogram. This method is added to the interface of the `CHistDlg` class and looks as follows:

```
void SetData(const DWORD *pHist, int Range)
         {m_ctrlHist.SetData(pHist, Range);};
```

Here, `m_ctrlHist` is an object inherited from the `CHistView` class. The complete source code of the class interface is given on the accompanying CD-ROM.

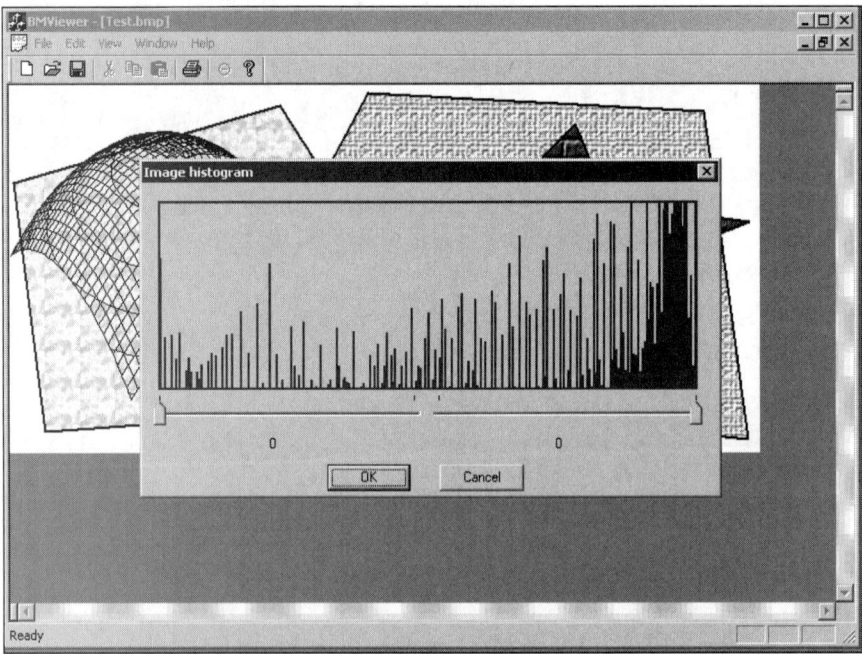

Fig. 6.9. Histogram of the test image created in Painter 4.2

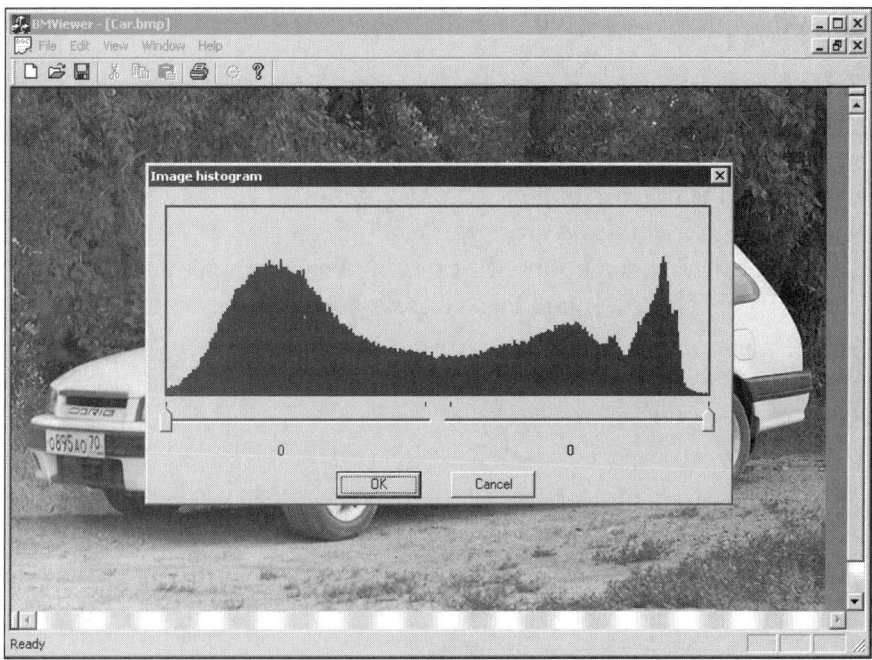

Fig. 6.10. Brightness histogram of a photograph

Now, take a look at the brightness histograms of the images. One example (Fig. 6.9) is the histogram of the test image that you created in the Painter 4.2 program in *Chapter 4*.

The histogram in Fig. 6.9 shows that the brightness in this image is distributed unevenly (shifted toward the light hues) and that many brightness values are missing. This is understood because the image is artificial and far from all colors and hues were used to create it. Photographic images have smoother histograms over a wide brightness range, like the one shown in Fig. 6.10.

Examining the histogram in Fig. 6.10, you can see that although the brightness range is broad, it does not cover the entire range. Consequently, you can try to improve the way this photograph looks. We will look into how histograms can be used to increase image contrast, but first we have to describe the internals of the software implementing transformations.

6.7.2. Software Procedure for Implementing Transformations and Graphics Filters

Because you are going to implement a series of image-transformation procedures, you have to think hard about how they are going to interact with each other and with the rest of the program modules. Judging by the interface of many graphics editors and the organization of video data processing software, the *filter* concept is widely used in multimedia programming. What is a filter? A filter is a program that transforms data in some way while passing them through itself. In this case, data are the color values of image pixels. This approach appears to work well because it makes it possible to design precisely constructed program modules. Assume that you have a set of filters passing bitmap data through which various effects can be achieved (Fig. 6.11).

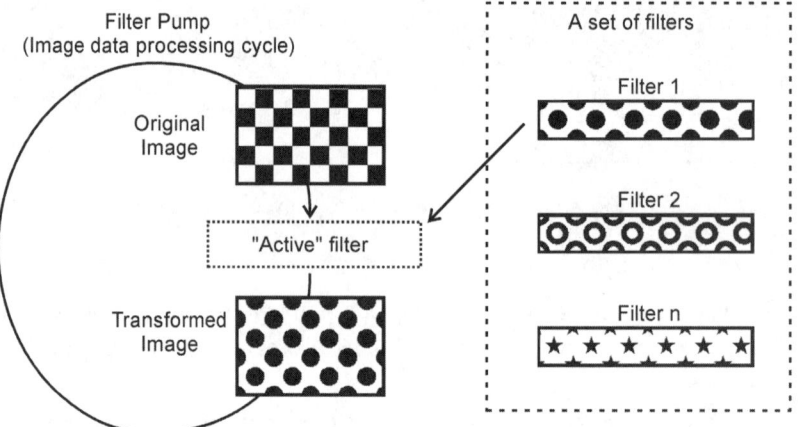

Fig. 6.11. Diagram of how to use filters to transform images

To obtain a desired effect, the program only needs to be informed, which filter to consider current. Somewhere in the program there must be a *filter pump:* a procedure that will pump data through filters.

Filters can be implemented as classes derived from a base class. A set of methods shared by all filters is defined in the base class. In the program, define a variable to serve as the pointer to the current filter. The filter pump will use this pointer to reference the necessary filter.

The image filtration can be implemented in various ways. For example, the entire initial image can be passed to the filter for processing and outputting a transformed image. Another method is to pass the initial image through the filter one pixel at a time. In the latter case, the cycle for processing the entire image does not have to be duplicated in each filter and the filter calling procedure completely controls the image area to be transformed.

Of these two ways of organizing the filter pump, implement the second one. In doing this, you will remove the image-transformation process into a separate program execution thread (we will call it the *work thread*). Doing this will give you, the user, the capability to control not only the filter application area but also the duration of the filtering operation. For example, if you become impatient waiting until the transformation is completed, you can stop the process.

The general transformation method in this case looks as follows:

1. When a transformation command arrives, a work thread is created.
2. The view objects are informed of the start of the transformation. The view starts the timer; from time to time, it checks how much of the work has been done and informs the user of the progress.
3. The transformation is performed in the work thread with the completion percentage increasing.
4. When the transformation has been completed (or interrupted by the user), messages are sent to the view objects to announce that the work has been completed; subsequently, the transformed image is displayed.

Because the CBVDoc class controls data in the BMViewer program, the filter pump will be placed into it. To create the work thread, the following methods have to be added to the CBMDoc class:

- `Transform()`—Creates the work thread
- `ThreadProc()`—The thread function; launches the filter pump for a specific document object
- `TransformLoop()`—The filter pump
- `CreateCompatibleBuffer()`—Creates a buffer for the transformed image
- `InformAllViews()`—Sends messages to all document views

The source code for all of these methods is given on the accompanying CD-ROM; here, briefly examine only the `TransformLoop()` and `CreateCompatibleBuffer()` methods (Listing 6.11).

Listing 6.11. The `CBMDoc::TransformLoop()` method [BMDoc.cpp]

```cpp
void CBMDoc::TransformLoop()
{
   if(m_pCurFilter == NULL) return;
   if(!CreateCompatibleBuffer()) return;

   m_EventDoTransform.SetEvent();
   m_bEditable = FALSE;
   InformAllViews(UM_STARTTRANSFORM);

   Bitmap   *pSBM = GetCurrentBMPtr(),         // Source
            *pDBM = GetBufferBMPtr();          // Destination
   // The filter is informed of the transformation's source and
   // destination
   if(!m_pCurFilter->SetBuffers(pSBM, pDBM))
   {
      m_EventDoTransform.ResetEvent();
      m_bEditable = TRUE;

      AfxMessageBox("Data cannot be accessed");
      return;
   };

   UINT width = pSBM->GetWidth();
   UINT height = pSBM->GetHeight();

   for(UINT y=0; y < height; y++)
   {
      // Completion percentage
      InterlockedExchange(&m_lExecutedPercent, 100*y/height);
      // Check whether the user wishes to interrupt transformation.
      if(!m_EventDoTransform.Lock(0))
        {
            m_pCurFilter->ReleaseBuffers();
            InformAllViews(UM_ENDOFTRANSFORM, FALSE, 0);
            m_bEditable = TRUE;
            return;
        }

      // Transform using the current filter.
```

Chapter 6: Viewing and Editing Bitmap Images 183

```cpp
        for(UINT x=0; x < width; x++)
        {
            // If the "process half of the string" flag is set, then
            // simply copy the first part of the string.
            if(m_bEditHalf && x == 0)
            {
               m_pCurFilter->CopyPix(x, width/2, y);
               x = width/2-1;
            }
            else
                m_pCurFilter->TransformPix(x, y);
        }
    }

    m_EventDoTransform.ResetEvent();
    m_bEditable = TRUE;

    if(!m_pCurFilter->ReleaseBuffers())
    {
       AfxMessageBox("Buffers cannot be released");
       return;
    };

    SwapBM();          // Make the buffer the current image.
    SetModifiedFlag();  // "Data have been changed" flag

    InformAllViews(UM_ENDOFTRANSFORM, TRUE, 0);
    return;
};

BOOL CBMDoc::CreateCompatibleBuffer(UINT width/*=0*/, UINT height/*=0*/)
{
    if(!m_pCurBM) return FALSE;

    Bitmap *pBuff=GetBufferBMPtr();

    // Delete the incompatible buffer.
    if( pBuff && width && height && (width != pBuff->GetWidth() ||
        height != pBuff->GetHeight()))
    {
```

```
        delete pBuff;
        pBuff = NULL;
    }

    // There is no buffer, so create one.
    if(!pBuff)
    {
        PixelFormat format = m_pCurBM->GetPixelFormat();
        pBuff = new Bitmap( m_pCurBM->GetWidth(),
                            m_pCurBM->GetHeight(), format);
    }

    SetBufferBMPtr(pBuff);
    return pBuff != NULL;
};
```

The `TransformLoop()` method first uses the `CreateCompatibleBuffer()` method to obtain a buffer to receive the transformed image. The `CreateCompatibleBuffer()` method checks that the buffer is available; if it is not, then the method creates it. The buffer is created using the `new` operator. Recall the specificity of using this operator to create GDI+ objects in MFC applications, described in *Section 1.3.2*. To avoid problems when compiling a debug version of the program, the following line was commented out in the bmdoc.cpp file: `//#define new DEBUG_NEW`

Next, the executing transformation event (`m_EventDoTransform` object derived from the `CEvent` class) is set. After this, the current filter is informed, which image is to be the source and which the destination (addresses of the `Bitmap` objects). Then the loop is started, in which image pixels are pumped through the filter. The current filter is pointed to by the `m_pCurFilter` variable declared in the `CBMDoc` class for this purpose. This variable is a pointer to the object of `CFilter` class. The actual data transformation is done by the `CFilter::TransformPix()` method. The `CFilter` class is the base class for all filters. It is described in *Section 6.7.4*.

During the transformation process, before the next pixel line is processed, the completion percentage is calculated as a percentage of the already processed image pixel lines. Using the API `InterlockedExchange()` function, the calculated value is stored in the `m_lExecutedPercent` variable. This function allows the variable to be referenced simultaneously from different threads. Then, a check for the `m_EventDoTransform` event being set is carried out. Only after this line are pixels processed. At this stage in the program, for demonstration purposes, the user observes the transformation effect on only half of the image. If the `m_bEditHalf` flag is set, the first half of the line is copied without modification.

After all image pixels have been processed, the `m_EventDoTransform` flag is cleared and the filter is informed that the transformation has been completed. The image in the buffer becomes the current image, and the `UM_ENDOFTRANSFORM` message with the `TRUE` parameter is sent to all views. The `TRUE` parameter means that the transformation has been completed and the images in the views' windows must be refreshed.

The messages sent to the views informing them of the beginning and the end of the transformation are defined in the bmdoc.h file as follows:

```
#define UM_STARTTRANSFORM    WM_USER+ 0x8000
#define UM_ENDOFTRANSFORM    UM_STARTTRANSFORM+1
```

`WM_USER` is a special constant, from which (to the 0xBFFFh value) the programmer can define messages to be used in the application without worrying that they will conflict with Windows messages. However, the MSDN library says that some of the redefined Windows classes can use the values in the range up to 0x7FFFh for their own purposes. Apparently, this is why some sources suggest that user values should be defined as `WM_USER+7` and higher, which basically works. But the reason why +7 was chosen is unknown to us. Therefore, we can take this a step further for caution and define messages in the range starting from 0x8000h.

To process the messages in the view class, the following needs to be done:

1. To the interface of the `CBMView` class (the bmview.h file), the following methods must be added:

   ```
   afx_msg LONG OnStartTransform(UINT wParam, LONG lParam);
   afx_msg LONG OnEndTransform(UINT wParam, LONG lParam);
   ```

2. To the message map of the `CBMView` class (the bmview.cpp file), the following macrocommands are added:

   ```
   ON_MESSAGE(UM_STARTTRANSFORM, OnStartTransform)
   ON_MESSAGE(UM_ENDOFTRANSFORM, OnEndTransform)
   ```

3. To the `CBMView` class (the bmview.h file), implementation of the following methods are added:

   ```
   LONG CBMView::OnStartTransform(UINT wParam, LONG lParam)
   {
       OnStartTimer();
       return 0;
   ```

```
   }

   LONG CBMView::OnEndTransform(UINT wParam, LONG lParam)
   {
      OnStopTimer();
      if(wParam)
         // Refresh the image on the virtual screen.
         UpdateVirtualScreen();
      return 0;
   }
```

As can be seen from the source code of the methods, upon receiving UM_STARTTRANSFORM, the OnStartTimer() method is called in the view object. This method creates a timer. To process the WM_TIMER messages sent by the timer, using ClassWizard, the OnTimer() method is added to the CBMView class. This method requests the operation completion percentage and refreshes this information. The operation completion percentage will be shown in the view window header. A progress bar could be placed into the status line; however, as you will see later, the program will allow you to transform several images simultaneously; in this case, it is unclear how a single progress indicator can be shared.

Arrival of the UM_ENDOFTRANSFORM message is processed by the OnEndTransform() method, which, depending on whether the value of the wParam argument is TRUE or FALSE, does one of the following:

❒ TRUE (transformation successfully completed)—The screen is refreshed.
❒ FALSE (user interrupted the operation)—The screen is not refreshed.

Then it calls the OnStopTimer() function, which destroys the timer.

The complete source code of these methods is given on the accompanying CD-ROM.

The flowchart of object and stream interaction is shown in Fig. 6.12.

Removing "long play" data-processing operations into a separate execution thread allows the user to retain control over the program execution—that is, the program will not hang on this type of task. In this application, having launched filtration of one of the open images, the user can switch to viewing and editing another image. If necessary, the user can stop the transformation process. To allow this, provide a command in the program that will clear the m_EventDoTransform flag. When this flag is cleared, the CBMDoc::TransformLoop() execution loop is interrupted, the thread function terminates, and the work thread ceases to exist.

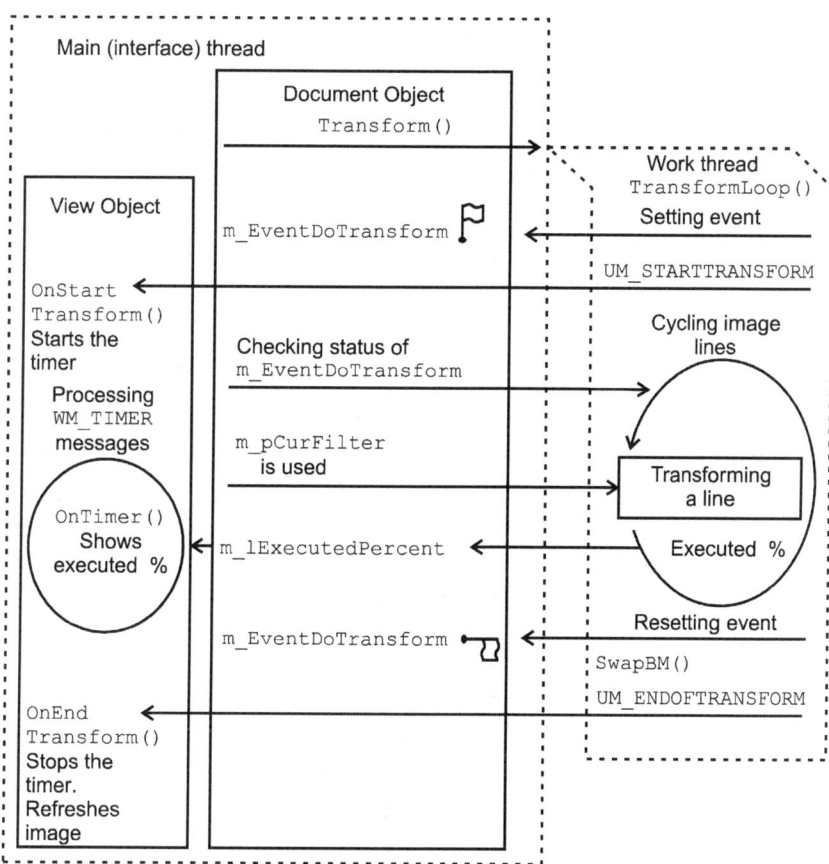

Fig. 6.12. Flowchart of the program image transformation operation

6.7.3. Lookup Tables

A *lookup table* is simply an array filled with values. The array dimensions equal the maximum value that a quantity to be transformed can take on. Such a table is a convenient and speedy means to substitute one value with another. Lookup tables are suitable for situations, in which the new value is produced from a single old value, that is, in *point* transformations.

Suppose that you need to transform a pixel's brightness. In this case, the old brightness value plays the role of the element index in the table and the value of this element is the new brightness value. A transformation formula may look like the following:

```
V = TransformTable[V];
```

Here, V is the brightness value and `TransformTable` is the lookup table. Of course, the lookup table must be filled with values before it is used.

Consider, for example, how the image's colors can be inverted.

Each 8-bit color component can take on values in a 0-to-255 range.

Create a 256-element lookup table and fill it with values from 255 to 0 (Fig. 6.13).

Index	0	1	2	3	4		253	254	255
Value	255	254	253	252	251		2	1	0

Fig. 6.13. Inversion-type lookup table

Having performed transformation by the previously-described formula using the table (see Fig. 6.13), the 255 brightness will be changed to 0, 254 to 1, etc. For such a simple transformation as color inversion, using a lookup table may not necessarily produce speed gains worth talking about; however, if the new pixel values must be computed by a more complex formula (i.e., other than $V = 255 - V$), the speed gains will be noticeable. Moreover, employing lookup tables makes it possible to use a uniform approach to performing various transformations.

6.7.4. The Filter Class

The structure shown in Fig. 6.11 presupposes the existence of a filter object in the program. Filters perform various transformations, but the filter pump views them all as the same and, accordingly, treats them in the same way. Therefore, you need to define a `CFilter` base class for a filter with a minimal but fundamental set of methods that will be used for communications with the other program components. The interface of such a class is shown in Listing 6.12.

Listing 6.12. The `CFilter` base class for filters [Filter.h]

```
#define SOURCE 0
#define DEST 1

// Virtual base class
class CFilter
{
protected:
    // Pointers to the source and destination images
    Bitmap *m_pBM[2];
    // Bitmap data
```

```
        BitmapData m_Buffer[2];

protected:
    BYTE* GetPixelPointer(UINT x, UINT y, BOOL t = SOURCE)
    {
        if(!m_Buffer[t].Scan0 || x >= m_Buffer[t].Width ||
            y >= m_Buffer[t].Height) return NULL;
        // Calculating the number of bytes per pixel
        BYTE bpp = (BYTE)(m_Buffer[t].PixelFormat>>8)/8;
        // Determining the address
        return ((BYTE*)m_Buffer[t].Scan0) + m_Buffer[t].Stride*y + x*bpp;
};


public:
    CFilter()
    {
        m_pBM[SOURCE] = m_pBM[DEST] = NULL;
    }

    // Setting the source and destination images
    // Obtaining access to the data
    BOOL SetBuffers( Bitmap *pSource, Bitmap *pDest);
    // Releasing buffers
    BOOL ReleaseBuffers();

    virtual BOOL CopyPix(UINT x1, UINT x2, UINT y);
    // The virtual pixel transformation method
    // will be redefined in the derived classes.
    virtual BOOL TransformPix(UINT x, UINT y) = 0;
};
```

The class has the following data:

- m_pBM[SOURCE]—The address of the source image object supplying data for transformation
- m_pBM[DEST]—The address of the destination image object receiving the transformed data
- m_Buffer[2]—Two structures defining bitmap data of the Bitmap objects

The class' methods are as follows:

- `SetBuffers()`—Conveys the addresses of the source and destination images to the filter. This method provides direct access to the bitmap data of the images by using the `Bitmap::LockBits()` method (see *Section 5.6.2*). It is convenient to perform transformations on the RGB values of pixels; therefore, a `PixelFormat24bppRGB` buffer is requested:

```
BOOL CFilter::SetBuffers( Bitmap *pSource, Bitmap *pDest)
{
   m_pBM[SOURCE] = pSource;
   m_pBM[DEST] = pDest;
   // Verification
   if(!m_pBM[SOURCE] || !m_pBM[DEST])
      return FALSE;
   // Obtaining direct access to the data
   if(// The source data are read only,
      m_pBM[SOURCE]->LockBits(&Rect(0, 0, m_pBM[SOURCE]->GetWidth(),
      m_pBM[SOURCE]->GetHeight()), ImageLockModeRead,
       PixelFormat24bppRGB, &m_Buffer[SOURCE]) != Ok ||
      // the destination is write only.
      m_pBM[DEST]->LockBits(&Rect(0, 0, m_pBM[DEST]->GetWidth(),
      m_pBM[DEST]->GetHeight()),
      ImageLockModeWrite, PixelFormat24bppRGB, &m_Buffer[DEST]) != Ok)
      return FALSE;
      return TRUE;
}
```

- `ReleaseBuffers()`—Tells the filter to release the image buffers:

```
BOOL CFilter::ReleaseBuffers()
{
   // Checking    if(!m_pBM[SOURCE] || !m_pBM[DEST])
      return FALSE;
   // Releasing buffers

  if(m_pBM[SOURCE]->UnlockBits(&m_Buffer[SOURCE]) != Ok ||
     m_pBM[DEST]->UnlockBits(&m_Buffer[DEST])    != Ok )
     return FALSE;
   return TRUE;
}
```

- `TransformPix()`—Transforms data of one pixel with *(x, y)* coordinates. Must be redefined in the derived classes.

The `m_pCurFilter` variable pointer to the `CFilter` class object is defined in the `CBMDoc` class. This variable is assigned the address of the current filter. Methods to filter were defined in the `CFilter` class; the same methods are used in the `CBMDoc::TransformLoop()` method (see Listing 6.11). Because the `CFilter::TransformPix()` method was defined as virtual, in the `TransformLoop()` method, the real method for transforming the current filter will be called.

To implement point transformation methods, create a `CDotFilter` class as shown in Listing 6.13.

Listing 6.13. The `CDotFilter` base class for point filters [Filter.h]

```
// Base class for point filters
class CDotFilter: public CFilter
{
protected:
   // Color components lookup tables    BYTE BGRTransTable[3][256];
public:
   // Pixel transformation method    BOOL TransformPix(LONG x, LONG y);
};
```

Data for this class are three RGB component lookup tables. In principle, defining one table would be sufficient for the transformation methods considered; nevertheless, a more common approach is defining three tables. This is because transformations of the image color spectrum (its hues) may have to be performed. That is where three tables will come in handy.

The `TransformPix()` method is redefined for the point filter. This method will be shared by most of the point filters considered. The method's source code is shown in Listing 6.14.

Listing 6.14. The `CDotFilter::TransformPix()` method [Filter.cpp]

```
BOOL CDotFilter::TransformPix(UINT x, UINT y)
{
   // Source
   BYTE *pSPix = GetPixelPointer(x, y, SOURCE);
   // Destination
   BYTE *pDPix = GetPixelPointer(x, y, DEST);
```

```
    if(!pSPix || !pDPix)
       return FALSE;

    // Transforming the pixel and placing it in the destination image
    pDPix[0] = BGRTransTable[0][pSPix[0]];
    pDPix[1] = BGRTransTable[1][pSPix[1]];
    pDPix[2] = BGRTransTable[2][pSPix[2]];

    return TRUE;
};
```

Although the 24-bit color mode is called RGB, color components are stored in the buffer in reverse order. This is not especially important, but you must be aware of this and take it into account; this is done when the new value of a pixel's color is produced.

All that remains to be done in the classes derived from the `CDotFilter` class that define various effects is to devise a way to initialize the tables.

To implement spatial (matrix) transformation methods, create a `CMatrixFilter` class. The interface of this class is shown in Listing 6.15.

Listing 6.15. Interface of the `CMatrixFilter` base class for matrix filters [Filter.h]

```
// Spatial (matrix) filters
// Base class
class CMatrixFilter: public CFilter
{
protected:
    int m_rangX; // X- and Y-dimensions of the matrix
    int m_rangY;
    const int *m_pMatrix; // Pointer to the matrix
public:
    // Pixel transformation method
    BOOL TransformPix(LONG x, LONG y);
};
```

Data for the class are the transformation matrix dimensions and the pointer to the matrix. As a rule, square transformation matrices are used. However, you never know whether a nonsquare matrix may be useful; therefore, horizontal and vertical matrix dimensions are specified. Matrix dimensions determine the area of pixels surrounding an *(x, y)* pixel that will be involved in the calculation of the new value of this pixel. The `m_pMatrix` pointer to the transformation matrix will be assigned the address of the matrix that will be used in the transformation.

The implementation of the `CMatrixFilter::TransformPix()` method is shown in Listing 6.16.

Listing 6.16. The `CMatrixFilter::TransformPix()` method [Filter.cpp]

```
// Spatial filters
BOOL CMatrixFilter::TransformPix(UINT x, UINT y)
{
   // Determining the overlapping area of the image and
   // the transformation matrix; this is needed for
   // processing pixels located at image edges
   int x_start = 0;
   int dx = m_rangX/2, dy = m_rangY/2;

   if(x-dx < 0) x_start = dx-x;

   int y_start = 0;
   if(y-dy < 0) y_start = dy-y;

   int x_finish = m_rangX;
   if(x+dx > m_Buffer[SOURCE].Width)
      x_finish -= (x+dx-m_Buffer[SOURCE].Width);

   int y_finish = m_rangY;
   if(y+dy > m_Buffer[SOURCE].Height)
      y_finish -= (y+dy-m_Buffer[SOURCE].Height);

   // Calculating new pixel color value,
   // taking into account adjacent pixels
   // falling into the transformation matrix coverage area
   int NewBGR[3];
   int count = 0;
   for(int c=0, mx=0, my=0; c<3; c++)
   {
      NewBGR[c] = 0; count = 0;
      for(my = y_start; my < y_finish; my++)
         for(mx = x_start; mx < x_finish; mx++)
```

```cpp
        {
            // Source
            BYTE *pSPix = NULL;
            if((pSPix = GetPixelPointer(x+(mx-dx), y+(my-dy),
                SOURCE))!= NULL)
            {
                NewBGR[c] += (m_pMatrix[my*m_rangX+mx] * pSPix[c]);
                count += m_pMatrix[my*m_rangX+mx];
            }
        }
    }
    // Pixel address in the destination image
    BYTE *pDPix = GetPixelPointer(x, y, DEST);

    // Bringing the value within the allowed range and
    // placing it into the destination
    if(pDPix)
    for(c=0; c<3; c++)
    {
        if(count != 0)
        NewBGR[c] = NewBGR[c]/count;
        if(NewBGR[c] < 0)
            NewBGR[c] = 0;
        else if(NewBGR[c] > 255)
            NewBGR[c] = 255;

        pDPix[c] = NewBGR[c];
    }

    return TRUE;
};
```

In the `CMatrixFilter::TransformPix()` method, first the area, in which the image and the transformation matrix overlap, is determined. This step is needed because pixels located at image edges may have no neighboring pixels on one or two sides. Fig. 6.14 shows some situations, in which not all matrix coefficients are involved in the transformation. Matrix index 5 corresponds to the pixel being transformed.

The new pixel value is produced taking into account the values of all pixels and transformation matrix coefficients falling into the image–matrix overlapping area.

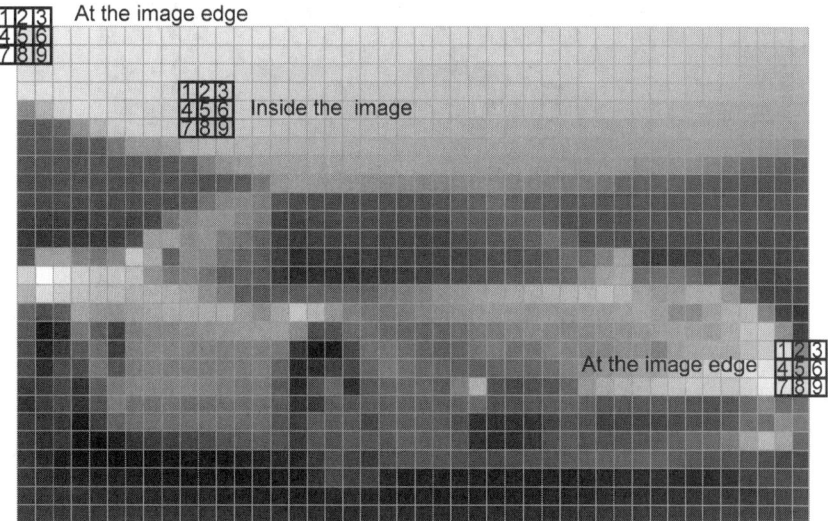

Fig. 6.14. Image–matrix overlap

6.7.5. Using a Brightness Histogram and the Histogram Filter

A histogram shows to what extent the brightness range is used in the image. Histograms of low-contrast images have their values concentrated within a small range. Histograms of such images may be shifted to the dark or light area but may also lie in the center of the brightness range (Fig. 6.15).

Histograms of normal-contrast images, as a rule, lie over the entire brightness range (Fig. 6.16). Such images are usually perceived as being better quality.

Histograms of high-contrast images also cover the entire brightness range. They can, however, have peaks because of large dark and light pixel areas.

Consider how the brightness distribution information can be used to correct image contrast. For example, the photograph in Fig. 6.10 has practically no black or near-white pixels.

You can try to correct the situation by stretching the brightness of the image pixels over the 0-to-255 range. This process will cause the dark pixels to become darker (up to black), and the light pixels will become lighter (up to white).

The template of the **Histogram** window (IDD_HIST) has two slider controls. Use them to define the lower and the upper limits of the brightness value range.

Fig. 6.15. Low-contrast image

Fig. 6.16. Normal-contrast image

Fig. 6.17. High-contrast image

First, using ClassWizard, add a message handler of the `WM_INITDIALOG` message to the `CHistDlg` class. The `WM_INITDIALOG` message is sent to a dialog window immediately before the latter is displayed on the screen. In the message handler of this message, set the initial slider control parameters and the sliders' positions (Listing 6.17).

Listing 6.17. Processing the `WM_INITDIALOG` message in the `CHistDlg` class [HistDlg.cpp]

```
BOOL CHistDlg::OnInitDialog()
{
   CDialog::OnInitDialog();
   // Lower limit slider control
   m_ctrlOffset_b.SetRange(0, 127);
   // Slider in the extreme left position
   m_ctrlOffset_b.SetPos(0);
   // Upper limit range
   m_ctrlOffset_t.SetRange(128, 255);
   // Slider in the extreme right position
   m_ctrlOffset_t.SetPos(255);
   // Text
   m_strOffset_b = "0";
   m_strOffset_t = "0";
   UpdateData(FALSE);
   return TRUE;
}
```

You should recall that `m_ctrlOffset_b` and `m_ctrlOffset_t` are objects derived from the `CSliderCtrl` class and are associated with the slider controls; `m_strOffset_b` and `m_strOffset_t` are objects derived from the `CString` class and are associated with the static elements in the dialog window (see Figs. 6.6 and 6.8).

Next, add to the `CHistDlg` class message handlers for two more messages. The `WM_HSCROLL` message is sent to the window when a slider is moved (Listing 6.18). The other message is sent when the user presses the **OK** button in the dialog window (Listing 6.19). When the `WM_HSCROLL` message is processed, the positions of the sliders will be displayed in the dialog window. When the "OK button pressed" message is processed, the positions of the sliders are stored in the `m_iOffset_b` and `m_iOffset_t` variables. These integer variables were added to the `CHistDlg` class for the purpose of extracting from it the information about the sliders' position after the window closed.

Listing 6.18. Processing the WM_HSCROLL message in the CHistDlg class [HistDlg.cpp]

```
void CHistDlg::OnHScroll(UINT nSBCode, UINT nPos, CScrollBar* pScrollBar)
{
   m_strOffset_b.Format("%d", m_ctrlOffset_b.GetPos());
   m_strOffset_t.Format("%d", 255-m_ctrlOffset_t.GetPos());
   UpdateData(FALSE);
   CDialog::OnHScroll(nSBCode, nPos, pScrollBar);
}
```

Listing 6.19. Processing the "OK button pressed" message in the CHistDlg class [HistDlg.cpp]

```
void CHistDlg::OnOK()
{
   m_iOffset_b = m_ctrlOffset_b.GetPos();
   m_iOffset_t = 255-m_ctrlOffset_t.GetPos();
   CDialog::OnOK();
}
```

Now that all preparations are done, you know what brightness value range needs to be stretched. All that remains is to create the right filter and pass it the information about this range.

Brightness correction is a point-wise process. Consequently, derive a CHistogram histogram filter class from the CDotFilter class (Listing 6.20).

Listing 6.20. Interface of the CHistogram class [Filter.h]

```
// The histogram
class CHistogram: public  CDotFilter
{
public:
   BOOL Init(int offset_b, int offset_t);
};
```

Only one new method, Init(), is declared in this class. The offsets from the lower and upper brightness range limits are passed to this method (Listing 6.21).

The `Init()` method fills the lookup tables with the new values. In the process, the full brightness range from 0 to 255 is distributed evenly over the range specified in the Histogram dialog window.

Listing 6.21. The `CHistogram::Init()` method [Filter.cpp]

```cpp
BOOL CHistogram::Init(int offset_b, int offset_t)
{
   int range = 0;
   // Set to 0 all table elements with indices
   // ranging from 0 to the lower limit.
   for(int i=0, t=0; t<3; t++)
      for(i=0; i < offset_b; i++)
      {
         BGRTransTable[t][i] = 0;
      }
   // Set to 255 all table elements with indices
   // ranging from 255 to the upper limit.

   for(t=0; t<3; t++)
      for(i=255; i >= 256-offset_t; i--)
      {
         BGRTransTable[t][i] = 255;
      }
   // All table elements with indices ranging from
   // the lower to the upper limits are evenly
   // distributed over the 0-to-255 range.
   double step = 256./(256 - (offset_b + offset_t));
   for(t=0; t<3; t++)
   {
      double value = 0.;
      for(i = offset_b; i < 256-offset_t; i++)
      {
         BGRTransTable[t][i] = (int)((value)+0.5);
         value += step;
      }
   }
   return TRUE;
};
```

Go back to Listing 6.10 and examine what happens after the `// Contrast needs to be corrected` line.

After the user presses the **OK** button in the Histogram dialog window, a check is made for whether the sliders have been moved. If this event has taken place, the `m_HistogramFilter` object (declared in the interface of the `CBMDoc` class) is initialized and made current. Then the `CMBDoc::Transform()` method is called and in turn launches the work thread that performs the transformation (see Listing 6.11).

Take a look at the effect produced by the brightness corrections. By setting the sliders as shown in Fig. 6.18, the brightness range to be stretched is specified.

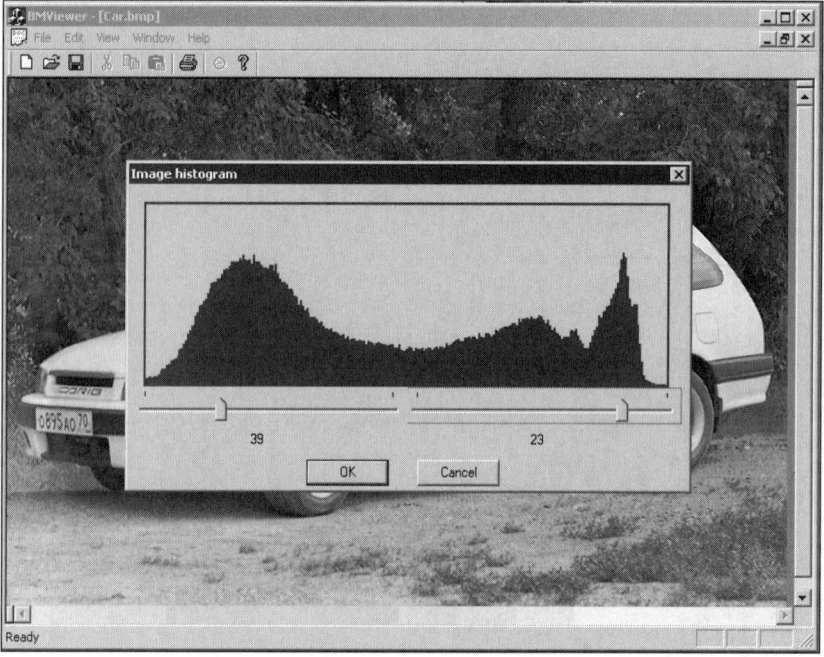

Fig. 6.18. Brightness correction

The result of the brightness correction operation is shown in Fig. 6.19, and the histogram of the corrected image is shown in Fig. 6.20. To make the transformation effect more visible, only half of the image was transformed (Fig. 6.19). The `CBMDoc::Transform()` method has such a capability (Listing 6.11). The histogram in Fig. 6.20 is for a fully corrected image.

Fig. 6.19. Results of the brightness correction operation

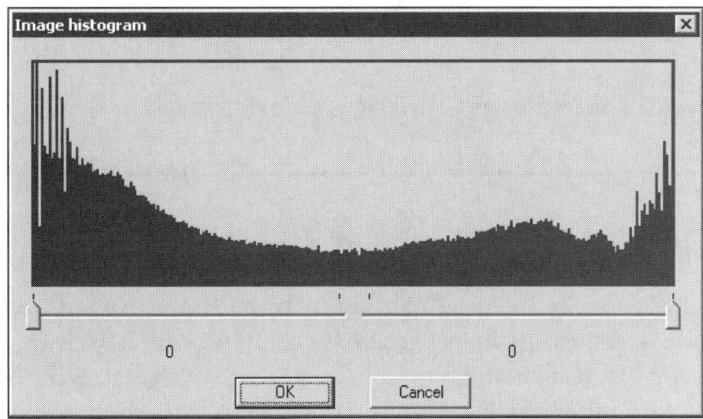

Fig. 6.20. Brightness histogram after the correction

The brightness correction process just considered is a manual one. But the same operation can be done automatically. In the automatic brightness correction, the algorithm must determine the borders of the range to be corrected. For this, first some threshold brightness value must be specified (e.g., defined relative to the average brightness). Next, the correction range is determined by scanning the image histogram and finding indices of those histogram elements whose values lie at the specified threshold. Then, the correction is done exactly like in the manual version of the process.

6.7.6. The Brightness/Contrast Filter

Many graphics editors have capabilities for changing image brightness and contrast. Brightness is changed by simply increasing or decreasing the brightness of all pixels by a specified value (a constant). The change is expressed by the brightness diagram shift to the left or right of the brightness scale. The same as the image brightness, its contrast can be increased or decreased.

This type of transformation is of the point type. To implement it, add a `CBrightCont` class (derived from the `CDotFilter` class) to the program to serve as the **Brightness/Contrast** filter. The interface of this class is shown in Listing 6.22.

Listing 6.22. Interface of the `CBrightCont` class [Filter.h]

```
// Brightness/contrast
class CBrightCont: public    CDotFilter
{
public:
    BOOL Init(int b_offset, int c_offset);
};
```

The interface of the `CBrightCont` class is the same as that of the `CHistogram` class (Listing 6.20). However, the values of the `b_offset` and `c_offset` parameters of the `CBrightCont::Init()` method can be both positive and negative, reflecting increasing or decreasing image brightness/contrast, respectively.

The implementation of the `CBrightCont::Init()` method is shown in Listing 6.23. This method initializes the lookup tables. First, the brightness is shifted by the specified value, and then the brightness range is either compressed or stretched. Brightness values do not change uniformly during compression and stretching; instead, they change proportionally to their distance from the gray median specified by the `CONTRAST_MEDIAN` constant.

The value of `CONTRAST_MEDIAN` equal to 159 specifies a lighter shade of gray (than, for example, the brightness range arithmetic mean of 127) and produces good results for many images. You can experiment using different values of this constant and observe the results. A more correct approach, however, is not to specify the brightness range median by a constant but to define it based on the histogram of the source image.

A brightness range is stretched as described in the previous section except that the top and bottom offsets of brightness scale are equal and specified by the `c_offset` parameter. Another difference is that, after completing the brightness correction operation, the contrast correction operation is performed using the values of the lookup table that are assumed to be indices of the table obtained after performing the brightness correction.

A third difference is that the coefficient tables are first transformed to correct brightness and then changed to take into account the contrast correction.

Listing 6.23. The `CBright::Init()` method [Filter.cpp]

```cpp
// The gray median
#define CONTRAST_MEDIAN 159
BOOL CBrightCont::Init(int b_offset, int c_offset)
{
   int i=0,   // Color index in the lookup table
       t=0,   // Table index
       // Index of the color corresponding to the
       // lower brightness limit
       t_index = 0,
       // Index of the color corresponding to the
       // upper brightness limit
       b_index = 0,
       value_offset; // Color value offset
   double value = 0.; // New color value
   // Changing brightness
   for(i, t=0; t<3; t++)
      for(i=0; i<256; i++)
      {
         if( i+b_offset > 255) BGRTransTable[t][i] = 255;
         else if( i+b_offset < 0) BGRTransTable[t][i] = 0;
         else BGRTransTable[t][i] = i + b_offset;
      }
  // Changing contrast
  if(c_offset < 0)// Reducing contrast
  {
```

```
      for(i=0, t=0; t<3; t++)
      for(i=0; i<256; i++)
      if(BGRTransTable[t][i] < CONTRAST_MEDIAN)
      {
         // Calculating the offset based on the
         // color distance from the gray median
         value_offset = (CONTRAST_MEDIAN-BGRTransTable[t][i])*c_offset/128;
         if(BGRTransTable[t][i] - value_offset > CONTRAST_MEDIAN)
            BGRTransTable[t][i] = CONTRAST_MEDIAN;
         else BGRTransTable[t][i] -= value_offset;
      }
      else
      {
         // Calculating the offset based on the
         // color distance from the gray median
         value_offset = (BGRTransTable[t][i]-CONTRAST_MEDIAN)*c_offset/128;
         if(BGRTransTable[t][i] + value_offset<CONTRAST_MEDIAN)
            BGRTransTable[t][i] = CONTRAST_MEDIAN;
         else BGRTransTable[t][i] += value_offset;
      }
}
else   if(c_offset > 0)
// Increasing contrast
{
   // Calculating the lower color limit
   int offset_b = c_offset*CONTRAST_MEDIAN/128;
   // All table values below the lower limit
   // will be assigned values of 0.
   for(t=0; t<3; t++)
   for(b_index = 0; b_index < 256; b_index ++)
   {
      if(BGRTransTable[t][b_index] < offset_b)
         BGRTransTable[t][b_index] = 0;
      else break;
   }
  // Calculating the upper color limit
   int offset_t = c_offset*128/CONTRAST_MEDIAN;
   // All table values above the upper limit
   // will be assigned values of 255.
   for(t=0; t<3; t++)
```

```
            for(t_index = 255; t_index >= 0; t_index --)
            {
                if(BGRTransTable[t][t_index] + offset_t>255)
                    BGRTransTable[t][t_index] = 255;
                else break;
            }
            // Calculating the step of the brightness intensity change
            double step = 256./(256 - (offset_b + offset_t));
            // Stretching the intensity of the colors
            // between the lower and the upper limits to make
            // them occupy the entire 0-to-255 range
            for(t=0; t<3; t++)
            {
                value = 0.;
                for(i = b_index; i <= t_index; i++)
                {
                    if(BGRTransTable[t][i] >= offset_b ||
                       BGRTransTable[t][i] < 256-offset_t)
                    {
                        value = (int)((BGRTransTable[t][i] - offset_b)*step + 0.5);
                        if(value > 255) value = 255;
                        BGRTransTable[t][i] = (int)(value);
                    }
                }
            }
        }
        return TRUE;
};
```

To provide the user with a capability to specify brightness and contrast correction values, add the Brightness/Contrast dialog to the program (Fig. 6.21). The way this dialog window is created is not much different from creating the Histogram dialog window.

Assign the dialog the IDD_BRIGHT_CONT identifier and create the CbrightContDlg class; assign variables to the control elements (Fig. 6.22).

To call the dialog, add the **Edit Brightness and Contrast** command to the menu and a handler for this command to the CBMDoc class (Listing 6.24). This method first creates the dialog; if the user presses the **OK** button, the **Brightness/Contrast** filter is initialized (the m_BrightContFilter object of the CBrightCont class is defined in the interface of the CBMDoc class). Then, the filter is made current and the filter pump (implemented by the CBMDoc::Transform() method) is called.

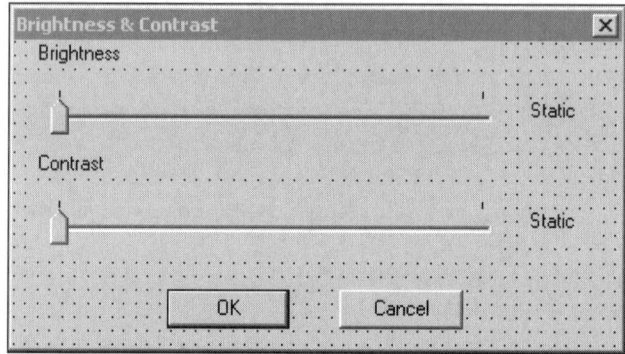

Fig. 6.21. Brightness & Contrast correction dialog window template

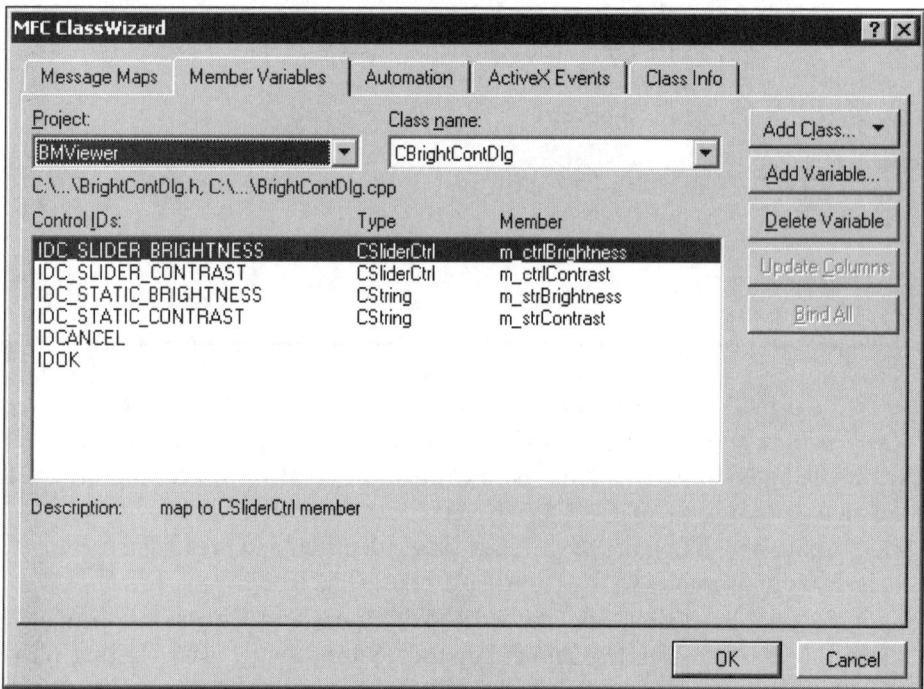

Fig. 6.22. Variables of the CBrightCont class

Listing 6.24. Method to handle the Edit→Brightness and Contrast command [BMDoc.cpp]

```
void CBMDoc::OnEditBrightnessandcontrast()
{
    CBrightContDlg BCDlg;
    if(BCDlg.DoModal() == IDCANCEL) return;

    if(BCDlg.m_iBrightnessOffset != 0 || BCDlg.m_iContrastOffset != 0)
    {
        m_BrightContFilter.Init(BCDlg.m_iBrightnessOffset,
                       BCDlg.m_iContrastOffset);
        m_pCurFilter = &m_BrightContFilter;
        Transform();
    }
}
```

Fig. 6.23. Photograph after brightness correction

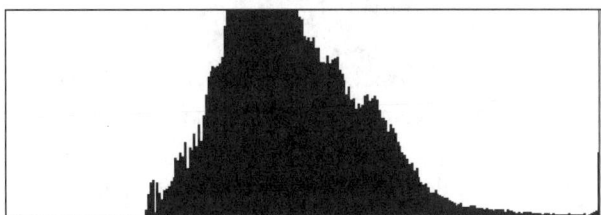

Fig. 6.24. Brightness histogram after brightness correction

Take a look at the effects produced by the Brightness/Contrast filter. First, try to increase slightly the brightness of the photograph shown in Fig. 6.15. Fig. 6.23 shows the same photograph, but the brightness of half of it is increased by 30 correction units.[i]

A histogram of the image (reflecting correction to its entire area) is shown in Fig. 6.24. From this figure, notice that compared with the histogram in Fig. 6.15, it has shifted into the lighter area.

Continue editing the photograph and try to change its contrast. The tools provided by the Histogram contrast correction dialog can be used for this; instead, battle test the new ones. Increase the contrast by 20 correction units. The results are shown in Fig. 6.25.

Fig. 6.25. Photograph after brightness and contrast correction

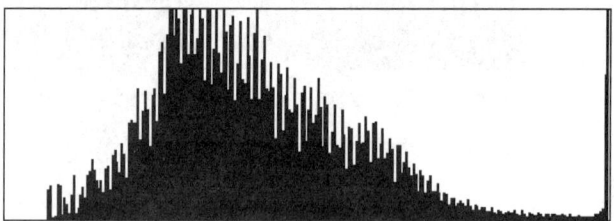

Fig. 6.26. Brightness histogram after brightness and contrast correction

---

[i] The correction range is assumed to be half of the brightness range (255/2=127), but on the slider control it is represented by the MAX_CORRECTION_OFFSET value. Therefore, one correction unit equals 127/MAX_CORRECTION_OFFSET. This is simply a peculiarity of the program implementation.

The brightness histogram after contrast correction of the entire image is shown in Fig. 6.26. The image has greater contrast, and the histogram covers a wider range of values.

The brightness and contrast can also be reduced. Do some experiments with this.

6.7.7. The Color Inversion Filter

Now, consider a simple filter that we described in *Section 6.7.3* when we covered lookup tables. This filter is implemented by the `CInvertColors` class (Listing 6.25).

Listing 6.25. Interface of the `CInvertColors` class [Filter.h]

```
// Color inversion
class CInvertColors: public  CDotFilter
{
public:
   CInvertColors();
};
```

The color inversion operation does not require any setup variables; therefore, lookup tables are initialized in the class constructor (Listing 6.26).

Listing 6.26. The `CInvertColors` class constructor [Filter.cpp]

```
CInvertColors::CInvertColors()
{
   for(int i=0, t=0; t<3; t++)
      for(i=0; i < 256; i++)
      {
         BGRTransTable[t][i] = 255-i;
      }
};
```

What a filter! It is so easy to implement, but what an effect it produces (Fig. 6.27).

Of course, as with the other filters, a `CInvertColors` class object was added in the CBMDoc class, a corresponding command was added to the menu, and a handler method was added to the CBMDoc class. In short, what the rest of the gang has, this filter has.

Fig. 6.27. The half of the image processed by the **Inversion** filter

6.7.8. The Emboss Filter

Next, consider another point filter, which can also be classified as a spatial type (and upon closer scrutiny, features of both frame-accurate and geometric processes can be noticed in it). This filter can be implemented by either with or without matrices. Consider the "without" version. After being processed by the filter, the image will look as if it had stone embossing. The **Emboss** filter is a regular tool in many graphics editors.

The embossing effect is obtained by subtracting the pixel brightness from the brightness of a pixel located a few pixels from the pixel being transformed—for example, offset sideways or upward. The obtained difference is then shifted into the gray tones area.

The Emboss filter is implemented by the CEmboss class (Listing 6.27).

Listing 6.27. Interface of the CEmboss class [Filter.h]

```
// Emboss
class CEmboss: public  CDotFilter
{
public:
    BOOL TransformPix(LONG x, LONG y);
};
```

Because the transformation performed by the `CEmboss` filter is different from the point-type transformation, the `CDotFilter::TransformPix()` method had to be redefined. Here is where the advantages of object-oriented programming become evident: The rest of the filter operation procedure remains unchanged.

The source code of the `TransformPix()` method is shown in Listing 6.28. The `STONE_OFFSET_X` and `STONE_OFFSET_Y` constants specify the distance and direction, with which the subtrahend pixel (the pixel being subtracted) is offset in relation to the minuend pixel (the pixel being subtracted from) and the influence the obtained effect. It is possible to create a dialog providing means to modify these parameters at will. In the presented implementation of the `CEmboss::TransformPix()` function, all color components are assigned the same intensity. This does not have to be this way; the result can be painted any shade, as it is done, for example, in the Ulead Photoimpact graphics editor.

Listing 6.28. The `CEmboss::TransformPix()` method [Filter.cpp]

```
// Direction and distance of pixel offset
#define STONE_OFFSET_X 3
#define STONE_OFFSET_Y -3
BOOL CEmboss::TransformPix(UINT x, UINT y)
{
   // Source
   BYTE *pSPix = GetPixelPointer(x, y, SOURCE);
   // Destination
   BYTE *pDPix = GetPixelPointer(x, y, DEST);
   if(!pSPix || !pDPix)          return FALSE;

   int x2 = x + STONE_OFFSET_X; if(x2 < 0) x2 = 0;
   int y2 = y + STONE_OFFSET_Y; if(y2 < 0) y2 = 0;

   // The offset pixel
   BYTE *pSPix2 = NULL;
   if( (pSPix2 = GetPixelPointer(x2, y2, SOURCE)) == NULL)
      pSPix2 = pSPix;

   // Brightness calculation
   BYTE Y1, Y2;
   Y1 = Y(pSPix);
   Y2 = Y(pSPix2);
```

```
    // Finding the difference and shifting it into the gray area
    BYTE d = (Y1-Y2+255)/2;

    // The pixel is assigned new values.
    pDPix[0] = d;
    pDPix[1] = d;
    pDPix[2] = d;

    return TRUE;
};
```

The result of applying the filter is shown in Fig. 6.28.

Fig. 6.28. Half of the image processed by the **Emboss** filter

6.7.9. The Blur Filter

The **Blur** filter performs spatial transformations. The essence of the transformation was considered in *Section 6.7*, and all difficulties ended in the CMatrixFilter::TransformPix() method (see Listing 6.16); therefore, there ought to be no problems implementing this filter. Applying this filter blurs image details. You might ask, why take a perfectly good image and mess it up? Well, some people like this sort of effect; moreover, sometimes the blur effect can be useful, as you shall see later.

The filter is implemented by the `CBlur` class (Listing 6.29).

Listing 6.29. Interface of the `CBlur` class [Filter.h]

```
class CBlur: public CMatrixFilter
{
public:
   CBlur();
};
```

All particular features of this filter reside in its constructor (Listing 6.30).

Listing 6.30. The `CBlur::CBlur method` [Filter.cpp]

```
const int BlurMatrix[25]=
    {   1,   1,   1,   1,   1,
        1,   1,   1,   1,   1,
        1,   1,   1,   1,   1,
        1,   1,   1,   1,   1,
        1,   1,   1,   1,   1
    };

CBlur::CBlur()
{
   m_pMatrix = BlurMatrix;
   m_rangX = 5;
   m_rangY = 5;
};
```

The `BlurMatrix` matrix specifies the blur transformation; the `CBlur()` constructor simply stores its address and dimensions.

The effect of applying the **Blur** filter is shown in Fig. 6.29.

To make the effect noticeable in the picture, the filter had to be applied several times.

Fig. 6.29. Half of the image processed by the **Blur** filter

6.7.10. The Contour Filter

The **Contour** filter is used for making high-frequency image elements stand out. It is extensively used in image-recognition and machine-vision problems. A high-frequency image element is, for example, a light pixel on the dark background or vice versa. The theoretical information on this subject can be found in the previously-mentioned literature. In practice, everything is simple. The transformation matrix (Listing 6.31) defines the weight coefficients of the pixels in the addition operation (Listing 6.16).

Listing 6.31. The contour transformation matrix

```
// The border sharpness coefficient
// can be easily specified in a dialog.
#define CONTOUR_COEFF 3
const int ContourMatrix[9] =
    {   -1*CONTOUR_CEFF,   -1*CONTOUR_COEFF,   -1*CONTOUR_COEFF,
        -1*CONTOUR_COEFF,   8*CONTOUR_COEFF,   -1*CONTOUR_COEFF,
        -1*CONTOUR_COEFF,  -1*CONTOUR_COEFF,   -1*CONTOUR_COEFF
    };
```

Assume that the brightness of the pixels falling within the matrix coverage area is about the same. This means that the addition result will be close to zero. But if the brightness of the pixel being transformed (its corresponding matrix element is the central one) is higher than the brightness of the surrounding pixels, the addition result will be greater than zero. Note that the sum of the matrix elements equals zero. Therefore, the image will transform into black with white contours (outlines). But giving the central matrix element the value, for example, of 9 will leave the image colors basically unchanged, making only the borders stand out.

The filter is implemented by the CContour class (Listing 6.32).

Listing 6.32. Interface of the CContour class [Filter.h]

```
class CContour: public CMatrixFilter
{
public:
    CContour();
};
```

Fig. 6.30. Half of the image processed by the **Contour** filter

The constructor of this class stores the necessary matrix and its dimensions (Listing 6.33). Actually, filters such as **Blur** and **Contour** can be implemented by one class by simply initializing them with different matrices.

Listing 6.33. The `CBlur::CBlur()` method [Filter.cpp]

```
CContour::CContour()
{
   m_pMatrix = ContourMatrix;
   m_rangX = 3;
   m_rangY = 3;
}
```

The result of applying the Contour filter is shown in Fig. 6.30.

6.7.11. The Sharpen Filter

The **Sharpen** filter is an illustration of opposites' coexistent unity and struggle: For increasing image sharpness, the filter makes use of the Blur matrix. The task of increasing image sharpness consists of making high-frequency image details stand out by making the light parts lighter and the dark parts darker. To accomplish this, the image is first blurred; then, the difference between the original and the blurred image is determined and the brightness of the original image is changed by the amount of this difference. Thus the homogeneous areas of the image will not change, whereas the areas containing high-frequency details will become more contrast.

The filter is implemented by the `CSharp` class (Listing 6.34).

Listing 6.34. Interface of the `CSharp` class [Filter.h]

```
class CSharp: public CMatrixFilter
{
public:
   CSharp();
   BOOL TransformPix(LONG x, LONG y);
};
```

The `TransformPix` method is redefined in the `CSharp` class; its implementation is shown in Listing 6.35.

Listing 6.35. Methods of the `CSharp` class [Filter.cpp]

```cpp
CSharp::CSharp()
{
   m_pMatrix = BlurMatrix;
   m_rangX = 5;
   m_rangY = 5;
};
// The coefficient increasing sharpness
// can be easily specified in a dialog.
#define SHARP_COEFF 3
BOOL CSharp::TransformPix(LONG x, LONG y)
{
   // Blurring a pixel
   if(!CMatrixFilter::TransformPix(x, y))
      return FALSE;
   BYTE *pDPix = NULL, *pSPix = NULL;

   pSPix = m_pSourceBM->GetPixPtr(x,y);
   pDPix = m_pDestBM->GetPixPtr(x, y);
   int d = 0;
   for(int c=0; c<3; c++)
   {
      // Finding the difference
      d = *(pSPix+c) - *(pDPix+c);
      // Amplifying the difference
      d *= SHARP_COEFF;
      // Assigning the pixel a new value
      if(*(pDPix + c) + d < 0)
         *(pDPix + c) = 0;
      else
         if(*(pDPix + c) + d > 255)
            *(pDPix + c) = 255;
      else
         *(pDPix + c) += d;
   }
   return TRUE;
}
```

The result of applying the filter is shown in Fig. 6.31.

Fig. 6.31. Half of the image processed by the **Sharpen** filter

6.7.12. The Denoise Filter

Graphics editors often use filters intended for removing all types of noise from images. The function of these filters is to restore the original state. The operation methods used by this type of filters can vary significantly, but all of them have two stages. First, the noise pixel is identified (as a rule, identifying the noise is the most difficult part). Then, the value of the noise pixel is substituted with a new one (as a rule, it is calculated based on the surrounding pixels). The simplest example of such a filter is the **Blur** filter. The noise-determination criteria used in it is extremely explicit: All pixels are considered noise. The substitution method is not intricate: The arithmetic mean is used. In several cases, however, applying this filter produces a positive effect.

Consider how a more complex filter (we will call it the **Entropy** filter) is implemented. The idea of this filter consists in the following: a group of pixels, for example, 5 × 5 elements, is involved; the central pixel of the matrix is tested. During the test, the deviation of the pixel brightness from the average brightness value is calculated and the influence of this deviation on the entropy of the examined image area is evaluated. If the filter decides that there should not be such a pixel, its noise value is substituted with a new one, calculated based on the surrounding pixels.

The noise definition criterion of this method is as follows:

1. A number of pixels, n pixels, falling within the examined area are tested. The deviation of each pixel's brightness from the average brightness is determined, then all deviations are summed.

$$S = \sum_{i=0}^{n-1} \Delta_i \qquad 6.1$$

Here, $\Delta_i = |\bar{b} - b_i|$, b_i is the value of the ith pixel, and $\bar{b} = \sum_{i=0}^{n-1} b_i / n$ is the pixel's average brightness.

2. The relative contribution of the deviation Δ_k of the tested pixel to the S value is determined:

$$p_k = \frac{\Delta_k}{S} \qquad 6.2$$

Here, k is the number of the pixel being tested.

3. It is obvious that $\sum_{i=0}^{n-1} p_i = 1$. If the pixel brightness in the examined image fragment is distributed more or less evenly, then the p_i values will not differ significantly from $1/n$. A noise pixel, as a rule, stands out because its brightness differs significantly from the brightness of the surrounding it pixels. The Δ_k value of this pixel is larger than that of the rest of the pixels, meaning that the pixel's contribution to the value calculated by the 6.1 formula will be greater and, as a result, that the p_k value will be greater than $1/n$. This is then the criterion of a noise pixel:

$$\text{If } p_k > \frac{1}{n}, \text{ then pixel } k \text{ is a noise.} \qquad 6.3$$

A more scientific definition of this criterion can also be offered. The properties of the p_i values and the way they are calculated impel us to call this quantity a *probability*. In the information theory, to evaluate the information quantity, the entropy measure is used that is a probability function and that assumes its maximum value in uniform distribution—in this case, when $p_i = \frac{1}{n}$, $i = 0, ..., n - 1$. But if one of the p_k values exceeds $1/n$, the entropy decreases. Consequently, this pixel can be considered noise interrupting the fluent information flow presented by the image to the observer.

The practice of using this criterion shows that it is advisable to modify the 6.3 condition as follows:

$$p_k > c \frac{1}{n} \qquad 6.4$$

Here, *c* is the coefficient (we will call it the *threshold* coefficient) affecting the criterion sensitivity.

When *c = 1*, the 6.4 condition transforms into the 6.3 condition. Practice shows that the best results are obtained at *c* values of 1.5 to 2.0. But you can experiment with the values of this coefficient yourself.

After the offending pixel has been identified, the decision needs to be made about what to do with it. There are several courses of action:

- Substitute the noise pixel value with the average value $\bar{b}$.
- Substitute the noise pixel with the average value calculated based on the values of all pixels with the exception of the offending pixel.
- Substitute the noise pixel with the average value calculated based on the values of all pixels that do not meet the noise-definition criterion. In this case, it is assumed that more than one pixel meeting the noise criterion can fall within the examined area and these pixels values are not taken into account when calculating the new value.

Other methods of calculating substitution are probably possible. In the implementation considered in Listing 6.36, the last approach is used.

The filter processes a group of pixels, which is very similar to the matrix transformation; therefore, the class, by which it is implemented, (call it CDenoise) is inherited from the CMatrixFilter class (Listing 6.36).

Listing 6.36. Interface of the CDenoise class [Filter.h]

```
class CDenoise: public CMatrixFilter
{

public:
   double m_dK;
   int m_nWhatToDo;

   CDenoise();
   BOOL TransformPix(LONG x, LONG y);
};
```

Chapter 6: Viewing and Editing Bitmap Images 221

However, the operations performed by the filter differ from the operations implemented in the `CMatrixFilter::TransformPix()` method; therefore, it will have to be redefined (Listing 6.37).

Listing 6.37. Methods of the `CDenoise` class [Filter.cpp]

```
CDenoise::CDenoise()
{
   m_pMatrix = NULL;
   m_rangX = 5;
   m_rangY = 5;

   m_dK = 2.0;
   m_nWhatToDo = 0;
};

BOOL CDenoise::TransformPix(UINT x, UINT y)
{
   // Source
   BYTE *pSPix=GetPixelPointer(x, y, SOURCE);
   // Destination
   BYTE *pDPix = GetPixelPointer(x, y, DEST);

   if(!pSPix || !pDPix)
      return FALSE;
   // Determining the image-transformation matrix overlap area;
   // this is needed for processing pixels located at the
   // image's borders.

   int x_start = 0;
   int dx = m_rangX/2, dy = m_rangY/2;

   if(x-dx < 0) x_start = dx-x;

   int y_start = 0;
   if(y-dy < 0) y_start = dy-y;

   int x_finish = m_rangX;
   if(x+dx > m_Buffer[SOURCE].Width)
      x_finish -= (x + dx - m_Buffer[SOURCE].Width);
```

```
int y_finish = m_rangY;
if(y+dy > m_Buffer[SOURCE].Height )
   y_finish -= (y + dy - m_Buffer[SOURCE].Height);

// Determining the average brightness value
int mx = 0, my = 0;
int avgY = 0, count = 0;

for(my = y_start; my < y_finish; my++)
   for(mx = x_start; mx < x_finish; mx++)
   {
      if((pSPix = GetPixelPointer(x+(mx-dx), y+(my-dy), SOURCE))!= NULL)
      {
         avgY += Y(pSPix);
         count++;
      }
   }

// Determining the sum of abmodalities
int sumVar = 0;
for(my = y_start; my < y_finish; my++)
   for(mx = x_start; mx < x_finish; mx++)
   {
      if((pSPix = GetPixelPointer(x+(mx-dx), y+(my-dy), SOURCE))!= NULL)
      {
         sumVar += abs(avgY - count*Y(pSPix));
      }
   }

// Pixel address in the source image
pSPix = GetPixelPointer(x, y, SOURCE);
double Pi = sumVar>0?fabs(avgY - count*Y(pSPix))/sumVar:0;

// Pixel address in the destination image
pDPix = GetPixelPointer(x, y, DEST);

BYTE NewValue = 255;

int NewBGR[3], count2 = 0;
```

```
switch(m_nWhatToDo)
{
   case 0: // Removing noise
      if(Pi > m_dK/count) // Noise
      {
         NewBGR[0] = NewBGR[1] = NewBGR[2] = 0;
         count2 = 0;

         // Finding the sum value of all nonnoise pixels
         for(my = y_start; my < y_finish; my++)
         for(mx = x_start; mx < x_finish; mx++)
         {
            if((pSPix = GetPixelPointer(x+(mx-dx), y+(my-dy),
               SOURCE))!= NULL &&
    ((sumVar > 0 ? fabs(avgY-count*Y(pSPix))/sumVar:0) <= m_dK/count))
            {
               for(int c=0; c<3; c++)   NewBGR[c] += pSPix[c];
               count2++;
            }
         }

         // Substituting the noise with the new value
         pSPix = GetPixelPointer(x, y, SOURCE);
         for(int c=0; c<3; c++)
         if(count2)
            // Average value of non-noise pixels
            pDPix[c] = NewBGR[c]/count2;
         else
            // No non-noise pixels found,
            // taking the source pixel value
            pDPix[c] = pSPix[c];
      }
      else // Not noise
         // Simply copying the pixel value
         for(int c=0; c<3; c++)   pDPix[c] = pSPix[c];
   break;
   case 1:    // Isolating noise
      if(Pi > m_dK*1.0/count) // Noise pixel — select
         NewValue = 128;
      for(int c=0; c<3; c++)   pDPix[c] = NewValue;
```

```
        break;
    }

    return TRUE;
}

// Calculating pixel brightness
BYTE Y(PBYTE pPix)
{
    return( (BYTE)(0.11*(*pPix) + 0.59*(*(pPix+1)) + 0.3*(*(pPix+2))) );
}
```

The way the `CDenoise::TransformPix()` method is implemented allows, depending on the value of the `m_nWhatToDo` variable, the noise pixel to be either substituted or shown in gray on the white background. The latter may be useful when determining the optimal value of the threshold coefficient c in condition 6.4.

The only thing remaining now is to do some noise-removal experiments. For this, an image with noise is needed. No need for a flight of fancy here; simply take the car image shown in Fig. 6.10 and, using the Microsoft Paint program, paint with the **Airbrush** some black and white dots on it (Fig. 6.32). This will insert impulse noise in the image: a sharp brightness-level change in isolated pixels.

Fig. 6.32. Image with inserted noise

Now, try to apply the Blur filter to remove the noise (Fig. 6.33). Well, it looks like this is not a case, in which the Blur filter does a good job of noise removal. The reason, probably, is that the noise pixels contribute to the average value.

Try the **Entropy** filter next. Fig. 6.34 shows the image, half of which was processed by this filter with the *c* value of 2.0.

Fig. 6.33. Results of attempting to remove noise using the **Blur** filter

Fig. 6.34. Effect of the **Entropy** noise-removal filter

As can be seen, the filter has done a good job: the bulk of the noise has been removed. Some criticism as to the resulting image quality may be offered because some high-frequency image elements have also been changed. For example, some breaks have appeared in the thin stripe across the car's hood; the same faults can be seen in the lower front spoiler. This is the method's shortcoming. The side effects can be controlled by changing the value of the threshold coefficient.

Although the presented example is a rather artificial one, using this filter can be useful in some real situations—for example, in removing the noise characteristic of low-resolution digital-camera images.

Similar results of filtering out noise in the given image (Fig. 6.32) can be obtained using a less complex filter, called a *median filter*. This method is popular for the processing of digital images and is used in many programs.

The median filtering method was proposed by J. Tukey in 1971 for economic processes analyses. It is heuristic in nature and is not a mathematical solution of a well-defined problem. However, in many cases this filtration method proves to be effective.

The median filtration method is similar to the **Blur** filter considered previously. Like in the **Blur** filter, a pixel area is examined, the pixels' average value is obtained, and the value of the central pixel is substituted with the obtained average. The difference is how this average value is obtained. In the **Blur** filter, the average is determined as the arithmetic mean of the brightness values of all pixels. In a median filter, the brightness values of all pixels of the examined image are simply loaded into a 1D array or a list, the obtained list is sorted, and the value in the middle of the sorted sequence is taken. The examined pixels area can be of various shapes, for example, square or cross-like. The median image filtration process is shown in Fig. 6.35. The pixel being tested is substituted with the median value (taken from the center) of the ordered sequence; therefore, if it has the peak value, it will be substituted with some value closer to the average. The peak value is not taken into account in these calculations. Fig. 6.36 shows the noisy image from Fig. 6.32, half of which has been processed using the **Median** filter in Adobe Photoshop.

The advantage of this method lies in its simplicity and efficiency in removing impulse noise. A shortcoming is image blurring, which in some cases may be unacceptable. As you have probably noticed, the **Median** filter does not have the noise-element identifying stage; consequently, all pixels are transformed, which produces blurring. The median method can be used with the entropy method to determine noise pixels. The dimension and shape of the pixel coverage area are amenable to user control.

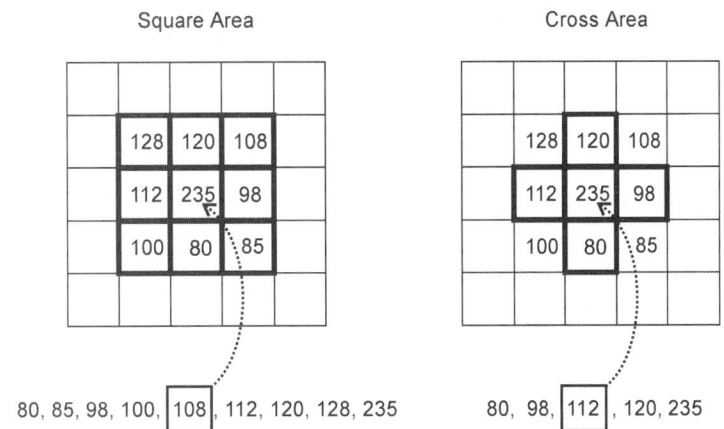

Fig. 6.35. Median filtration process using differently shaped areas

Fig. 6.36. Effect of the **Median** noise-removal filter

The noise-generation problem also is popular in the computer graphics field; an interesting article on this subject can be found at the following Web address: **http://freespace.virgin.net/hugo.elias/models/m_perlin.htm**.

To select the CDenoise filter, a corresponding command was added to the program menu, whose handler—the CBMDoc::OnEditDenoise() method—was placed into the document class (see Listing 6.38). To set up the filter's parameters, the special CDenoiseDlg dialog was added; its template is shown in Fig. 6.37.

228 Part II: Bitmap Graphics

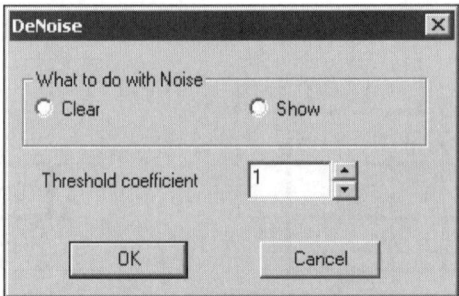

Fig. 6.37. Template of the noise-removal filter dialog

The interface and implementation of the `CDenoiseDlg` dialog are included on the accompanying CD-ROM (the denoisedlg.h and denoisedlg.cpp files).

Listing 6.38. The `CBMDoc::OnEditDenoise()` method. [BMDoc.cpp]

```
void CBMDoc::OnEditDenoise()
{
 static double k = m_DenoiseFilter.m_dK;
 static int what_to_do = 0;
 CDeNoiseDlg DNDlg;
 DNDlg.m_dK = k;
 DNDlg.m_nWhatToDo = what_to_do;

 if(DNDlg.DoModal() != IDOK) return;
 k = m_DenoiseFilter.m_dK = DNDlg.m_dK;
 what_to_do = m_DenoiseFilter.m_nWhatToDo = DNDlg.m_nWhatToDo;

 m_pCurFilter = &m_DenoiseFilter;

 Transform();
}
```

6.7.13. Using Filters

Now that you have learned so much about filters and their internal workings, you can use them with competence. For example, before determining an image's outlines, you can blur the image: This will remove the weak noise that is not noticed during regular viewing but that becomes apparent when outlines are brought out.

The defined outlines can be intensified by the **Sharpen** filter; afterward, the **Inversion** filter used and the final results are obtained as shown in Fig. 6.38.

Fig. 6.38. Half of the image processed by a sequence of several filters

In this way, a remarkable photograph can be made into a unique coal drawing. Of course, the presented example does not limit the application area of the filters considered previously.

6.8. Printing Images

It is likely that the user may desire to immortalize his creation in hard copy—that is, print it out. However, having executed the **File Print Preview** command sequence, the user will discover that the masterpiece he or she created has shrunk to the size of a postage stamp.

But you know the reason for this: You studied this in *Section 4.3.1*. There, the problem was solved by setting another view mode. In the BMViewer program, however, the views operate in the MM_TEXT mode (see Listing 6.5, method CBMView::OnUpdate()). This is satisfactory because one screen pixel corresponds to one image pixel. The problem can be solved by scaling the image size when outputting it to the printer. For this, the virtual CView::OnPrint() method in the CBMView view class is redefined. This can be done using ClassWizard. The new method is shown in Listing 6.39.

Part II: Bitmap Graphics

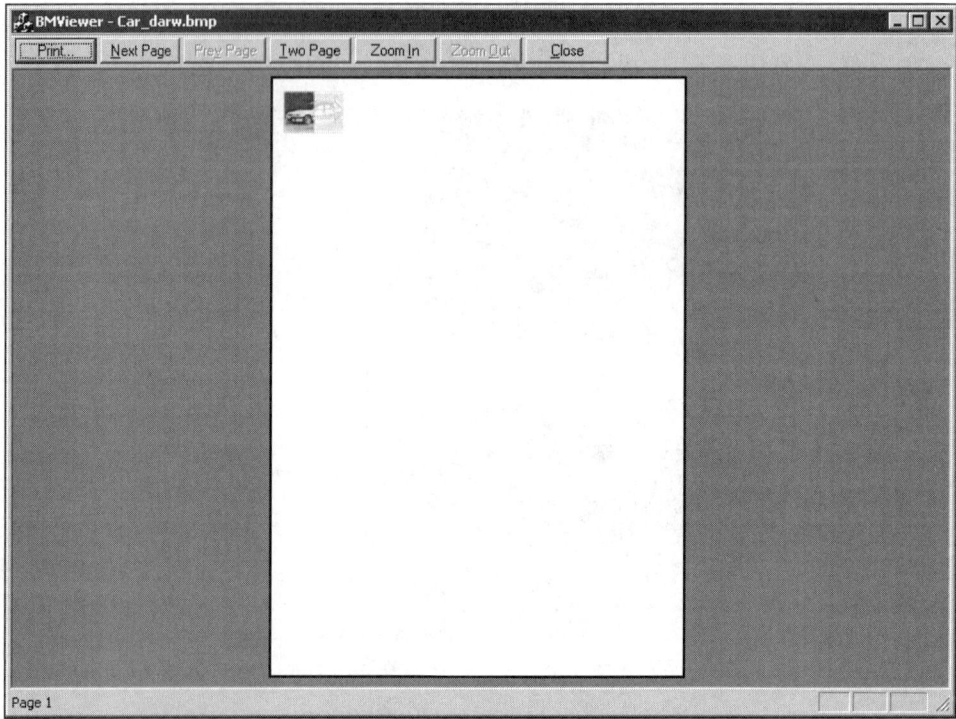

Fig. 6.39. Postage-stamp-sized masterpiece

Listing 6.39. The `CBMView::OnPrint()` method [BMView.cpp]

```
void CBMView::OnPrint(CDC* pDC, CPrintInfo* pInfo)
{
   // Device resolution
   int DXRes = pDC->GetDeviceCaps(LOGPIXELSX);
   int DYRes = pDC->GetDeviceCaps(LOGPIXELSY);

   CBMDoc* pDoc = GetDocument();
   ASSERT_VALID(pDoc);

   Bitmap* pCurBM = pDoc->GetCurrentBMPtr();
   if(pCurBM == NULL) return;

   LONG  height, width;
```

```
    double resx, resy;
// Recalculating the image size to fit the printer resolution
    width = pCurBM->GetWidth();
    height = pCurBM->GetHeight();

    resx = (double)pCurBM->GetHorizontalResolution();
    resy = (double)pCurBM->GetVerticalResolution();
    // Setting reasonable limits
    if(resx <= 0 || resx > 3000) resx = 96;
    if(resy <= 0 || resy > 3000) resy = 96;

    width = (int)(((double)width)*DXRes/resx + 0.5);
    height = (int)(((double)height)*DYRes/resy + 0.5);

    // Creating a Graphics object for the specified context
    Graphics g(pDC->m_hDC);
    // Setting the scaling mode
    g.SetInterpolationMode(m_nStretchMode);
    // Outputting the image
    g.DrawImage(pCurBM, Rect(0, 0, width, height), 0, 0, pCurBM->GetWidth(),
    pCurBM->GetHeight(), UnitPixel);
};
```

In the `OnPrint()` method, using the `CDC::GetDeviceCaps` method, the printer resolution is obtained. This method returns the resolution in dots per inch (dpi). A bitmap image also has the "resolution" parameter, which is recorded in the header of the `BITMAPINFOHEADER` in the `biXPelsPerMeter` and `biYPelsPerMeter` fields. From the names of these fields, you can see that the resolution is recorded in them in dots per meter. This should not scare you; an inch equals 25.4 mm. Therefore, image resolution is later converted to dots per inch. Unfortunately, far from all bitmap programs place values into the `biXPelsPerMeter` and `biYPelsPerMeter` fields. Some programs, for example, Painter 4.2, put 0 in this field (it would be more proper to record the screen resolution in there); other programs leave it uninitialized, containing some random value. This field is checked for the proper contents in the next stage. The image size is then scaled proportionally to the ratio of the image and the printer resolutions. Finally, the remarkable capabilities of the `Bitmap::OnDraw()` method to output images to the device context, scaling them to the specified size, are used.

In principle, a dialog call can be added to the `OnPrint()` method, in which the user could specify the needed printout size.

The results of the program operation using the new `OnPrint()` method are shown in Fig. 6.40. Before printing, the landscape paper orientation is set by the standard dialog called with the **File Print Setup** menu command sequence.

Fig. 6.40. Print preview

6.9. Saving Results

There is no simple way to save edited images into the source file for the reasons explained in *Section 5.3.2*. Therefore, redefine the **File Save As** command sequence in the program to ask the user to supply a new file name. The source code for implementing this method is shown in Listing 6.40. It must be noted that the file format (codec) is chosen by the index of the file type selected in the dialog. No checks that the file extension is correct are made. Subsequently, the image can be saved in the JPEG format even though the file has the BMP extension. When writing commercial software, such mix-ups must be avoided.

Listing 6.40. The `CBMDoc::OnFileSaveAs()` method [BMDoc.cpp]

```
void CBMDoc::OnFileSaveAs()
{
    // TODO: Add your command handler code here.

    if(!m_pCurBM)
        return;

    // Preparing the list of supported file formats
    ImageCodecInfo *pCodecs;
    UINT nCodecNum = ((CBMApp*)AfxGetApp())->GetCodecsArrayPtr(&pCodecs);

    CString Descr, Filter;
    USES_CONVERSION;
    for(UINT j = 0; j < nCodecNum; ++j)
    {
        Descr.Format("%s (%s)|%s|", OLE2T(pCodecs[j].FormatDescription),
                                    OLE2T(pCodecs[j].FilenameExtension),
                                    OLE2T(pCodecs[j].FilenameExtension));
        Filter += Descr;
    }
    Filter += "|";

    // Creating the dialog; by default, the file name
    // coincides with the original file name
    CFileDialog SaveFDlg(FALSE, NULL, GetTitle(), OFN_OVERWRITEPROMPT,
                Filter.GetBuffer(Filter.GetLength()), AfxGetMainWnd());
    Filter.ReleaseBuffer();

    // Setting the original file format and
    // getting the GUID identifying the image format
    GUID FirmatID;
    m_pBM[0]->GetRawFormat(&FirmatID);
    // Find the necessary codec
    for(UINT n=0; n < nCodecNum; n++)
        if(pCodecs[n].FormatID == FirmatID)
```

```
    break;

SaveFDlg.m_ofn.nFilterIndex = n+1;

// Calling the dialog
if(SaveFDlg.DoModal() != IDOK)
    return;

// Getting the file name
CComBSTR fname;
fname.Append(SaveFDlg.GetPathName());

if(m_pCurBM->Save(fname,
        &pCodecs[SaveFDlg.m_ofn.nFilterIndex-1].Clsid) != Ok)
    AfxMessageBox("Image save failure");

return;
}
```

6.10. Conclusion

This chapter was not short, but far from all theoretical and practical riches of digital imagery have been considered in it. This is good: It leaves plenty of room for experiments. We hope that the BMViewer program may serve as a proving ground to test your ideas. The presented implementation of the program can undoubtedly be significantly improved. In the given implementation, the number of filters is limited and they are hard-defined in the CBMDoc class. A method to dynamically attach filters to the program could be devised. In this case, filters can be implemented in DLLs as Jeffrey Richter explains in [5]. This would make it possible to expend the program's capabilities after it was written. This model is used in Adobe Photoshop and many other programs. The dynamic approach requires more serious understanding of the task at hands and planning of the application architecture. Nevertheless, even the method, on which the BMViewer program is based, has implicit possibilities for expanding its functionality. Another program development direction begging to be used is employing the extensive capabilities of the GDI+ library.

We express our thanks to Peter Gubanov for his permission to use in the book pictures from the site **http://www.elecard.com/peter/pictures/**.

PART IV:
USING THE DIRECTX 9 LIBRARY

Chapter 7: Using Direct3D Tools to Work with Graphics 237

Chapter 8: Looking Closer at Direct3D ... 279

Chapter 7: Using Direct3D to Work with Graphics

In this chapter, the following subjects are considered:

- ❐ Components and architecture of the DirectX 9.0 library
- ❐ DirectX 9.0 versions for Windows and the .NET Framework
- ❐ Working with graphics devices
- ❐ Initializing graphical modes
- ❐ Using the Direct3D tools to delete invisible details of images

7.1. Review of the DirectX 9.0 Library

To write complex, high-performance multimedia software, programmers must be able to access the hardware resources. The DirectX library comprises a collection of low-level software interfaces that provide such access for programmers developing applications for the Windows platform. If you are planning to write a captivating network game, a multimedia application, or a 3D graphics screensaver, you ought to start by considering the capabilities provided by DirectX.

The DirectX library has changed greatly over the years. We consider the capabilities of version 9.0 of the DirectX API. In addition to various technological innovations reflecting the new devices, this library introduces the managed interface, the feature that makes DirectX easy to use in the software for the .NET Framework platform.

We begin by familiarizing you with the main library components. They are as follows:

- *DirectX Graphics*—Combines the capabilities of the DirectDraw and Direct3D graphics programming interfaces of the previous versions of DirectX.
- *DirectInput*—Provides the capability to process user input from diverse devices, including the mouse, keyboard, and joystick.
- *DirectPlay*—Contains tools for writing network applications (e.g., multi-user games).
- *DirectSound*, *DirectMusic*, and *DirectX Media Objects*—Combined in version 9.0 under the name *DirectX Audio*, provide tools for audio and MIDI music programming.
- *DirectShow*—Used to capture and reproduce multimedia streams. In version 9.0, *DirectShow Editing Services* were introduced. These are a collection of objects that make it easy to design programs for nonlinear assembly of multimedia streams or audio or video players that use real-time effects and spectacular transitions between clips.
- *DirectX Diagnostics*—A software interface for diagnosing drivers and equipment.
- *DirectSetup*—A software interface enabling users to customize the installation process of DirectX on their systems.

As you can see, DirectX provides facilities for creating diverse graphics and multimedia applications and contains additional software interfaces (unlike its main competitor, the OpenGL library, which is geared exclusively toward graphics).

What programming tools are available to the programmer who decides to use DirectX? This question is answered in the next section.

7.2. The DirectX 9.0 SDK Package

To successfully launch a Star Wars shooter that uses Direct3D capabilities, it is sufficient to install the DirectX Runtime package, which contains a collection of dynamic libraries, device drivers, and configuration files. This entire file collection

Chapter 7: Using Direct3D Tools to Work with Graphics 239

takes about 36 MB of hard disk space and is often included in CDs with drivers for new video cards or with the latest games.

However, for writing your own DirectX 9.0 software, this package falls short. What you need for this task is the DirectX 9.0 SDK package, available for free on the Microsoft site.

This package contains the following:

- A collection of header files and libraries for C++ compilers
- Managed DirectX assemblies for use with .NET compilers
- Lots of reference documentation in the Compiled HTML Help format
- A collection of examples and step-by-step tutorials accessible by categories and languages through the **Sample Browser** application shell (Fig. 7.1)

Fig. 7.1. Application shell to access the DirectX examples and step-by-step tutorials

- AppWizards for creating starter applications in Visual C++, Visual C#, and Visual Basic .NET environments
- Auxiliary utilities for editing DirectX files, viewing system parameters, and monitoring the system
- The execution environment—the Debug and Retail versions of the DirectX Runtime package (the Debug version is slower but has extra checks that catch bugs in the development stage; you can switch easily between these two versions)

You can select specific package components during the installation (Fig. 7.2), but we recommend that you install all of them.

Fig. 7.2. Installing the DirectX 9.0 SDK

We assume that you have successfully installed the package on your system and can move on to the practical part: it's time to learn how to attach the DirectX SDK to your programming projects.

7.3. The First Programs

Start by writing two programs, one for Windows and the other for the .NET environment. Following the step-by-step instructions, you will get full-fledged programs that use DirectX Graphics to create 3D images.

The new technologies used in the example will be explained later. The important thing now is to learn how to properly set up the development environment and to obtain source code for the example programs that can be used as a basis for further studies of the various Direct3D capabilities.

7.3.1. Writing the First Program in C++

Unfortunately, the AppWizards supplied with the DirectX 9.0 SDK package can only be used in the Visual Studio 6.0 and 7.0 environments. Therefore, we will show you how to attach the DirectX SDK to the Microsoft Visual Studio .NET 2003 (7.1) package.

Launch the Visual Studio environment and create a new **Win32 Project** (Fig. 7.3). Name the project (**DX_Sample** in the example), select the **Empty Project** option, and confirm creation of the project by pressing the **Finish** button.

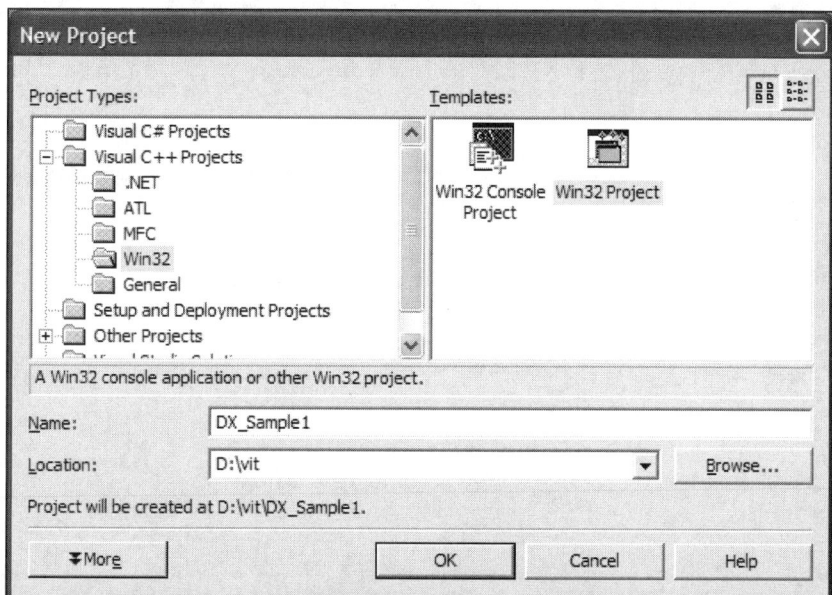

Fig. 7.3. Creating a new project in C++

Now you need to add a new CPP file to the project. To do this, select **Add New Item...** in the **Project** menu; from the various icons in the **Add New Item—DX_Sample** window, select the **C++ File** (**.cpp**) icon. The file also needs to be given a name (e.g., hello.cpp). Now you can start fleshing it out with code.

Setting Up the Environment, Header Files, and Libraries

First, you need to ascertain that the Visual Studio environment is properly set up for compiling programs that use DirectX 9.0 SDK components. To do this, select the **Options** item in the **Tools** menu; among the folders in the left panel of the **Options** window, find the **Projects** folder. Open it and select the **VC++ Directories** item.

Make sure that there is a path to the corresponding DirectX SDK folder among the list of the paths to the header files (**Include files**). If this path is not in the list, you will have to add it. In Fig. 7.4, this is G:\dx9sdk\include.

The path to the DirectX libraries is set in the same way. To do this, you have to select the **Library files** item from the dropdown list and add the **Lib catalog** path to the path list.

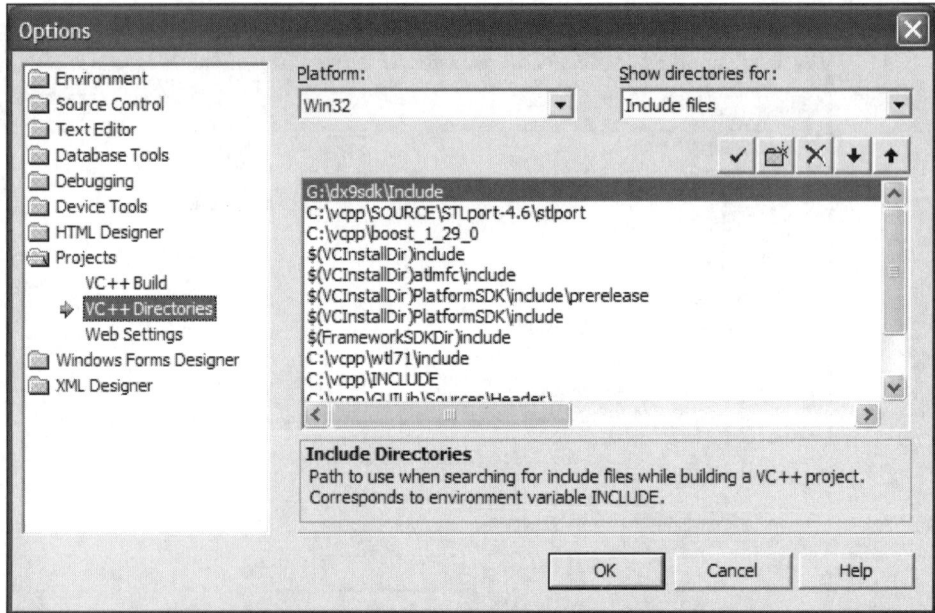

Fig. 7.4. Setting paths to the DirectX header files and libraries

Chapter 7: Using Direct3D Tools to Work with Graphics

Make sure that the paths to the **dx9sdk include** and **lib** folders are placed in the path list before analogous folders (e.g., from the platform SDK).

Now the compiler will know where to look for the header and library files. It is time to specify them. Add the following lines to the hello.cpp file:

```
#include <d3d9.h>
#include <d3dx9mesh.h>

#pragma comment(lib, "d3d9.lib")
#pragma comment(lib, "d3dx9.lib")
```

The code means that you will be using both the Direct3D library and the Direct3D Extension (D3DX) auxiliary components library that contains functions facilitating graphics programming.

The Application Class and the WinMain Function

In building the programs, you will be using the object-oriented approach. Create an application class and place the DirectX initialization and cleanup functions and the code to draw images. Call the class `SampleApplication` (Listing 7.1).

Listing 7.1. Defining the application class [C++]

```cpp
class SampleApplication
{
  IDirect3D9       *pD3D;
  IDirect3DDevice9 *pDevice;
  ID3DXMesh        *pTeapot;
  HWND             hWnd;

  static LRESULT WINAPI MsgProc(HWND, UINT, WPARAM, LPARAM);
  bool   CreateMainWindow();
  void   CreateTeapot();

public:

  SampleApplication():
    pD3D(NULL), pDevice(NULL), pTeapot(NULL), hWnd(NULL){}
  bool InitD3D();
  void CleanupD3D();
  void Render();
  void MessagePump();
};
```

The class holds the Direct3D resources it will need for its work and the descriptor of the main application window. In addition, it provides the auxiliary initialization, cleanup, and Windows message queue control functions.

Note that the MsgProc method is static, which is necessary for correct processing of Windows messages within the class. However, class fields cannot be referenced from within a static method because it cannot be known, which class instance is referenced. The solution to this problem is simple: define a global instance of the SampleApplication object. All external references will be to the fields of this object.

For all its simplicity, this method suffers from a significant shortcoming: there can be only one instance of this class in the program. However, this is not too important for the application class. As you will see later, developers of .NET software must not resort to this type of trick for processing messages.

Thus, declarations of a global application class instance and of the WinMain function are added to the code (Listing 7.2).

Listing 7.2. Application entry point: WinMain [C++]

```
static SampleApplication g_App;

int WINAPI WinMain(HINSTANCE, HINSTANCE, LPSTR, int)
{
  if(g_App.InitD3D())
  {
    g_App.MessagePump();
    g_App.CleanupD3D();
  }
  return 0;
}
```

The execution of WinMain starts with an attempt to initialize Direct3D. If this attempt is successful, the program enters the message processing cycle and cleans up Direct3D after its completion.

This is the only global function in the program; all the other functions in the file will be methods of the SampleApplication class.

Creating a Window

As you will see shortly, the InitD3D method first creates the main application window by calling CreateMainWindow. The source code of this method is given in Listing 7.3.

Chapter 7: Using Direct3D Tools to Work with Graphics 245

Listing 7.3. Function to create the main window [C++]

```
bool SampleApplication::CreateMainWindow()
{
  // Registering the window class
  WNDCLASSEX wc = { sizeof(WNDCLASSEX), CS_CLASSDC,
                    MsgProc, 0L, 0L,
                    GetModuleHandle(NULL), NULL, NULL,
                    NULL, NULL,
                    "Direct3D Class", NULL };

  RegisterClassEx( &wc );

  // Creating the application window
  hWnd = CreateWindow( "Direct3D Class",
                       "Direct3D for dummies",
                       WS_OVERLAPPEDWINDOW,
                       100, 100, 400, 300,
                       GetDesktopWindow(), NULL,
                       wc.hInstance, 0 );
  if(!hWnd)
  {
    MessageBox(0, "Error Creating Main Window",
               0, MB_OK|MB_ICONSTOP);
    return FALSE;
  }
  return TRUE;
}
```

Just like in a typical Window application, the window class is first registered. During the registration, the message processing procedure needs to be indicated (the `MsgProc` static method comes handy), as well as the class name (`Direct3D Class` in the example). Afterward, a 400 × 300-pixel main application window is created. A window creation error produces a diagnostic message.

Processing Messages

The `MessagePump` method pumps through Windows messages entering the program. In addition to reacting to the necessary program events (e.g., window closure), this makes it possible for the program to be a part of the Windows cooperative multitasking and to lower the processor workload. The method's source code is shown in Listing 7.4.

Listing 7.4. Application message cycle [C++]

```
void SampleApplication::MessagePump()
{
  MSG msg;
  while(GetMessage(&msg, 0, 0, 0))
  {
    TranslateMessage(&msg);
    DispatchMessage(&msg);
  }
}
```

The `MsgProc` method for the simplest application processes only two messages: WM_DESTROY (sent to the window when it is closed) and WM_PAINT (signaling that the window or part of it must be redrawn).

Listing 7.5. Application window function [C++]

```
LRESULT WINAPI SampleApplication::MsgProc(
  HWND hWnd, UINT msg, WPARAM wParam, LPARAM lParam )
{
  g_App.hWnd = hWnd;
  switch( msg )
  {
    case WM_DESTROY:
      PostQuitMessage( 0 );
      return 0;

    case WM_PAINT:
    {
      PAINTSTRUCT ps;
      BeginPaint(hWnd, &ps);
      g_App.Render();
      EndPaint(hWnd, &ps);
```

```
        return 0;
      }
   }
   return DefWindowProc( g_App.hWnd, msg, wParam, lParam );
}
```

To the standard processing of the `WM_PAINT` message, only a call of the `Render` method to draw 3D images was added.

However, before the Direct3D library can be used, it needs to be initialized. The methods of the `SampleApplication` class used for this purpose are considered in the next section.

Initializing the Library and Cleaning Up

First, the code in the `InitD3D` method creates the main application window by calling `CreateMainWindow`. If the window creation attempt is successful, the program begins to initialize the DirectX library.

For starters, try to create a *Direct3D object* to serve as a starting point for a convenient initialization of the Direct3D components. For this, call the `Direct3Dcreate9` functions with the `D3D_SDK_VERSION` constant as its parameter. If this call fails, it means that DirectX 9.0 is not supported on your computer and there is no sense in continuing.

If the function returns a created Direct3D object, use it to create and initialize a graphics device. For this, call the object's `CreateDevice` method, supplying it with the necessary parameters. (We will return to the initialization further on in this chapter.)

You also need an object to display. For our example, we used the `D3DXCreateTeapot` function from the D3DX library, which creates a 3D object that looks like a teapot.

Finally, having successfully initialized DirectX objects, show the main window. Using Direct3D, the application can now correctly redraw its contents.

The source code of the initialization function is shown in Listing 7.6.

Listing 7.6. DirectX initialization function [C++]

```
bool SampleApplication::InitD3D()
{
  if(!CreateMainWindow())
```

```
    return FALSE;

pD3D = Direct3DCreate9(D3D_SDK_VERSION);

if(!pD3D)
  return FALSE;

D3DPRESENT_PARAMETERS params;
ZeroMemory( &params, sizeof(params) );
params.Windowed = TRUE;
params.SwapEffect = D3DSWAPEFFECT_DISCARD;
params.BackBufferFormat = D3DFMT_UNKNOWN;

HRESULT hr = pD3D->CreateDevice(
  D3DADAPTER_DEFAULT, D3DDEVTYPE_HAL, hWnd,
  D3DCREATE_SOFTWARE_VERTEXPROCESSING,
  &params, &pDevice);
if(FAILED(hr))
{
  pD3D->Release();
  pD3D = 0;
  return FALSE;
}

D3DXCreateTeapot(pDevice, &pTeapot, 0);

ShowWindow(hWnd, SW_SHOWDEFAULT);
UpdateWindow(hWnd);

return TRUE;
}
```

After the window is closed, the function calls the application method to properly clean up all allocated DirectX resources. As you will see in the next section, DirectX objects follow COM rules, and the `Release` method must be used to release them (Listing 7.7).

Listing 7.7. The `CleanupD3D` method [C++]

```
void SampleApplication::CleanupD3D()
{
  if(pTeapot)
    pTeapot->Release();
  if(pDevice)
    pDevice->Release();
  if(pD3D)
    pD3D->Release();
}
```

As we have already mentioned, installing the Debug version of the DirectX library, which is included in the DirectX 9.0 SDK, can be useful for debugging complex DirectX applications. This library not only makes it possible to ensure correct method parameters but also issues a diagnostic message upon the program's completion if some object has not been deleted.

Constructing an Image

To construct an image, the `WM_PAINT` message handler calls the `Render` method, so it is time to get acquainted with it.

First, fill the output area with blue by calling the `Clear` device method. Next, before drawing the image, you need to do some preparatory work.

All instructions to output graphics objects must be enclosed in the `BeginScene`/`EndScene` operation brackets to process the output pipeline properly.

First, the light source for the scene and the characteristics of the teapot material are specified. Next, a world transformation matrix is applied to the device (the teapot is slightly zoomed-out and shifted along the Z-axis). Finally, the long-awaited image is output. The `Mesh` objects of the D3DX library can render themselves in Direct3D devices; all that is needed for this is to call the `DrawSubset` method. As you will see later, they comprise multiple minute 3D primitives (triangles, as a rule), but grouping primitives into an object makes the task of setting the world stage much easier.

After the scene is output, the `EndScene` method needs to be called. This will create the image in the secondary buffer. The device `Present` method allows the contents of the secondary buffer to be output to the screen.

The complete source code of the `Render` method is shown in Listing 7.8.

Listing 7.8. The `Render` method [C++]

```cpp
void SampleApplication::Render()
{
  if(pDevice)
  {
    // Filling the output area with dark blue
    pDevice->Clear( 0, NULL,
      D3DCLEAR_TARGET,
      D3DCOLOR_XRGB(0, 0, 128), 0.0f, 0 );

    // Drawing the scene
    if( SUCCEEDED( pDevice->BeginScene() ) )
    {
      // Creating the light source
      D3DLIGHT9 light =
        { D3DLIGHT_DIRECTIONAL,    // Infinite source
          {1, 1, 0, 0},            // Diffused lighting — Yellow
          {0, 0, 0, 0},
          {0.1f, 0.1f, 0.1f, 1},   // Scattered light — Dim white
          {0, 0, 0},
          {7, -2, 1}               // Direction vector
        } ;

      pDevice->SetLight( 1, &light ) ;
      pDevice->LightEnable( 1, TRUE ) ;

      // Creating the material
      D3DMATERIAL9 material = {
          {1, 1, 1, 1},
          {1, 1, 1, 1},
          {1, 1, 1, 1},
          {0, 0, 0, 0},
          1
        } ;
      pDevice->SetMaterial( &material ) ;

      float scale = 0.4f;
      D3DMATRIX transform = {
```

```
        scale,      0.0f,       0.0f,       0.0f,
        0.0f,       scale,      0.0f,       0.0f,
        0.0f,       0.0f,       scale,      0.0f,
        0.0f,       0.0f,       1.0f,       1.0f
    };

    pDevice->SetTransform(D3DTS_WORLD, &transform);

    pTeapot->DrawSubset(0);
    pDevice->EndScene();
  }

  // Outputting contents of the secondary buffer
  pDevice->Present( NULL, NULL, NULL, NULL );
 }
}
```

All necessary functions have been implemented. Compile the resulting program. If the compilation produces no errors (does this ever happen on the first try?), run the compiled program. The fruit of your labors is shown in Fig. 7.5.

You will enhance this example; but for now, familiarize yourself more closely with the alpha and omega of the DirectX library: COM.

Fig. 7.5. Window of the first program

7.3.2. Component Object Model: An Overview

In this section, consider in brief the features of the COM, which the implementation of DirectX for Windows platform is based on. Programmers familiar with COM can skip this section without negative effects on their understanding of the following material.

Programming using classes and objects has long become a common practice. The C++ language has acquired great popularity because of its support of object-oriented programming. Numerous class libraries have been built for C++ in its lifetime.

However, the modern world abounds in diverse technologies, and software compatibility on the source code level is no longer sufficient. What if you need to use an object created by a different compiler version or in a different language? A way to solve this problem has long been available in the Windows operating system.

DLLs make it possible to create code ready to be loaded and executed. Functions exported from a DLL become available to the calling program as if they were implemented in the program. Crossing these two ideas, you obtain a way to do *component programming*.

Component programming is a logical development of the object-oriented programming concepts. It solves the problems of reusing code from different programming environments and lowers the maintenance costs of different software-code versions. This is achieved by *compartmentalization:* separating *object interfaces* from their *implementation*.

Object Interface and Implementation

Object interface is the description of functions (methods, properties, etc.) in a high-level language. In component environments (such as COM), it is possible to reference objects only through their interfaces. What is the reason for such restrictions? Take a look.

If a software object can be referenced through a certain interface, the object is said to implement, or support, this interface. An object can support several interfaces at the same time.

In C++, an interface is usually defined as a class containing only a set of abstract virtual functions. For example, a two-method interface for handling pets is defined in Listing 7.9.

Listing 7.9. Pseudodefinition of a pet interface [C++]

```
// Interface names usually begin with "I"
interface IPet // Pet
{
  int  GetNumberOfLegs() = 0; // Abstract method — Number of legs
  void Speak() = 0;           // Abstract method — Make sound
};
```

If you are not familiar with how interfaces are defined in C++, note that `interface` is not a new keyword but only a macrodefinition (`#define`) of the familiar keyword `struct`, created to provide a graphic example.

```
// Somewhere in the system header files...
#define interface struct
```

You may ask, why `struct` and not `class`? The answer is simple: All structure members are public by default; therefore, it will not be necessary to specifically apply the `public` access modifier when defining the interface. Note that an interface is always designed to have a complete access: Either you can access the entire interface or you cannot access it at all.

Also note that it has been explicitly stated that all methods of the `IPet` structure (or interface) are purely virtual. This means that the `IPet` object cannot be created directly; it must be inherited from this type of an abstract class and all abstract methods implemented in the child object. In such cases, this type of object is called the *interface implementation*. An example of such an implementation is given in Listing 7.10.

Listing 7.10. Implementing the IPet interface for the Dog object [C++]

```
class CDog: public IPet
{
  int  GetNumberOfLegs();
  void Speak();
};

int CDog::GetNumberOfLegs()
{
  return 4;
```

```
}

void CDog::Speak()
{
  MessageBeep(-1); //Make the Windows system sound
}
```

Now, think about how this interface could be used in a C++ program. Suppose you want to create a Dog object and control it using the IPet interface. This can be done with the code fragment in Listing 7.11, which is similar to how COM objects are used (including the DirectX components).

Listing 7.11. Using the IPet interface [C++]

```
IPet *pDog = CreatePet("Dog");

// Determine whether this is a four-legged creature.
int nLegs = pDog->GetNumberOfLegs();

// If less than four legs, make the dog bark.
if( nLegs != 4 )
  pDog->Speak();
```

As you can see, the code for using the interface is similar to that used for usual work with C++ objects. The main difference lies in that the program does not use the CDog object directly (it does not even know about it); instead, it does all the work through the pointer to the IPet interface. For the same reason, the example calls the hypothetical CreatePet function that would know the particulars of how the interface is implemented and would be able to create an instance of the Dog object.

These limitations slightly complicate work with the components but make the program extremely flexible. Now, you can build and use ready components in any language, not only C++. Generally, having examined the memory image created by the interface, you can reproduce this binary image with any other tools (e.g., in C, which does not even have classes and virtual functions).

Some other programming environments have COM support built in, such as Delphi and Visual Basic. This allows you to create binary versions of components: to compile the component DLL written in one language and then call and use this object in other programming language.

Chapter 7: Using Direct3D Tools to Work with Graphics

However, there is one problem concerning the latter statement: The mechanisms for object creation and destruction differ from one programming environment to another. The hypothetical `CreatePet` function must take all these specifics into consideration to be able to create objects contained in compiled binary libraries and request support of the necessary interface from them.

The `CoCreateInstance` and `CoGetClassObject` functions are normally used to build COM components. These functions are made available by the COM library; therefore, it must be initialized before calling these functions.

Some DirectX objects can also be built in this way, but usually a less complicated method is used. The library makes available special functions for creating the necessary program components. For example, to create a Direct3D 9.0 object, the `Direct3DCreate9` function exists, which is defined in the d3d9.h header file. It is exactly this method that we used in the example.

The IUnknown Interface

The `IPet` interface described in the previous section is not a COM-style interface. To satisfy the requirements of the COM specification, all interfaces, including the DirectX interfaces, must be inherited from the special `IUnknown` interface. Despite its name, this interface is well known. A somewhat simplified definition of the `IUnknown` interface for C++ is given in Listing 7.12.

Listing 7.12. The `IUnknown` interface [C++]

```
interface IUnknown
{
  virtual HRESULT QueryInterface( const IID& iid, void** ppv ) = 0;
  virtual ULONG   AddRef() = 0;
  virtual ULONG   Release() = 0;
};
```

Consider the methods of the `IUnknown` interface.

The QueryInterface Method

Any given COM object can only be said to support the `IUnknown` interface. The function of the `QueryInterface` method is to determine whether the given object supports any other interface. Remember the `IPet` interface example? Had it been created following the COM specification, then any COM object could be queried for being a pet:

```
IUnknown *pUnk = ... // Obtaining a pointer to the object
IPet *pPet = 0;
if(SUCCEEDED(pUnk->QueryInterface(IID_IPet, (void**)&pPet))
{
   ... // Yes, this object is a pet.
}
```

We will explain two pieces in this example.

Usually, COM functions and methods return a special value of the HRESULT type to indicate the success or failure of the call. The SUCCEEDED and FAILED macros are the recommended method to check the result of the call.

To distinguish one interface from another (and to request support), a simple line with the name will not suffice. Names such as IPet are common, and there is a chance of the same name being used by more than one developer. To avoid the conflicts this would cause, the COM designers decided to use a special 128-bit GUID to identify interfaces and objects. When creating a new interface, the developer simply creates a new GUID and defines it in the header file or in the object type library. It was assumed in our example that such a GUID was defined in the interface header file under the name IID_IPet.

The AddRef and Release Methods

A regular instance of a C++ class is created in a program by calling a constructor and is removed when leaving the scope or by calling the delete operator if the object was created in the dynamic memory. In COM, an object typically implements several interfaces at once and the pointers to these interfaces are stored in the clients.

In this situation, keeping track of all these pointers becomes a difficult task. What if an object has been deleted but references to it remain? Continued use of these references will cause a program error. Another frequent problem is the need to remove an object after all references to it have been deleted. If a useless object cannot be deleted, it will be wasting system memory and other valuable resources.

The AddRef and Release methods are used to control the lifetime of objects. Having obtained an object interface for use, the AddRef method must be called. This will guarantee that the object will not be destroyed while at least one of its interfaces is being used.

The object must be notified when it is no longer used. The Release method must be called for each interface received from the object.

Chapter 7: Using Direct3D Tools to Work with Graphics 257

Usually, an object is destroyed if there are no more external references to it. But implementing this behavior is under control of the component's programmer.

The returned value of the `AddRef` and `Release` methods most often is the current value of the object's internal pointer counter, but it is recommended that you ignore this value because there are no well-defined specifications for it. Nevertheless, one of us happened to see a dubious way of ensuring removal of a DirectX object:

```
while(p->Release()); // (C) 1999, 2000 NVIDIA Corporation
```

As you can see, large companies sometimes ignore recommendations of the COM specification.

NOTE

This code was called right before an abnormal program termination, which somewhat justifies the developers' desire to remove the object. Nevertheless, there is a chance that this code will produce an endless loop.

We hope that this short introduction to the COM will be sufficient to understand the examples used in this book. If you want to learn more about it, we recommend that you read *Inside COM* by Dale Rogerson.

7.3.3. Managed DirectX and .NET Programming

.NET programmers can easily build DirectX applications now. Starting with the 9.0 version, the DirectX SDK includes *Managed DirectX,* a software interface for the DirectX library for the .NET platform. It comprises .NET assemblies implementing DirectX components, program examples, and documentation.

To be able to develop software using Managed DirectX, in addition to the runtime DirectX environment you will need the latest version of the .NET Framework (1.1 at publication) installed on your computer and the latest collection of the Managed DirectX assemblies. Here is the list of these files:

Microsoft.directx.audiovideoplayback.dll
Microsoft.directx.diagnostics.dll
Microsoft.directx.direct3d.dll
Microsoft.directx.direct3dx.dll
Microsoft.directx.directdraw.dll

Microsoft.directx.directinput.dll
Microsoft.directx.directplay.dll
Microsoft.directx.directsound.dll
Microsoft.directx.dll

We will build a test project using the Visual Studio 2003 environment. However, a simple DirectX application can easily be created without resorting to this development environment: As with GDI+, a simple word processor and the csc.exe command line compiler will suffice.

Well then, create a new project (Fig. 7.6). Select the **Visual C# Projects** from the **Project Types** list; from the list of projects that appears, select the **Windows Application** item. Enter the new project name, select the folder, in which to store it, and press the **OK** button.

The form designer window containing the form for the main window of the future application appears. Do not use the designer; instead, enter the source code of the entire program in a text editor. To do this, click the right mouse button on the designer window and from the popup menu that appears, select the **View Code** item.

Replace all the code in there with the code in Listing 7.13.

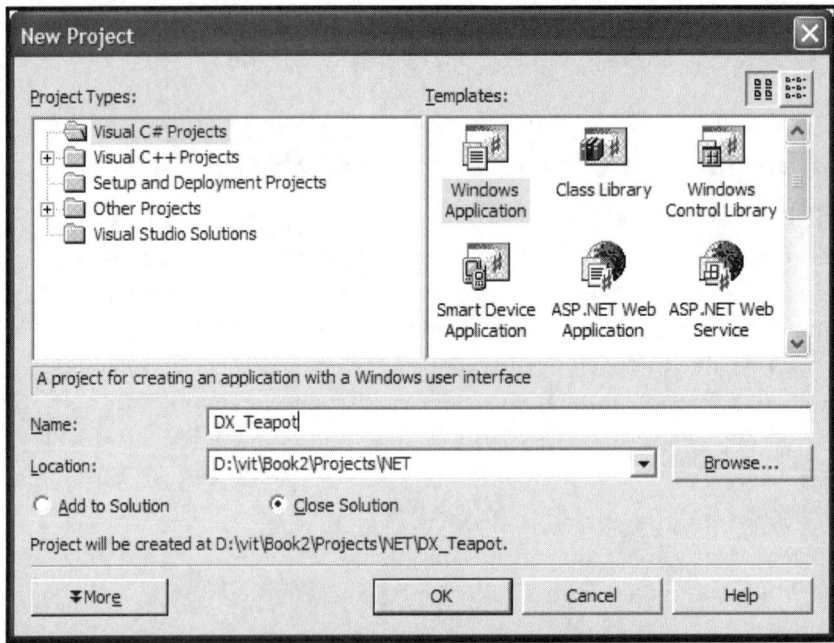

Fig. 7.6. Creating a new .NET platform application

Chapter 7: Using Direct3D Tools to Work with Graphics

Listing 7.13. Source code of the managed DirectX program [C#]

```
using System;
using System.Windows.Forms;
using Microsoft.DirectX;
using Microsoft.DirectX.Direct3D;

class TestForm: Form
{
  static void Main()
  {
    TestForm form = new TestForm();
    form.Text = "Direct3D for .NET";
    form.Width = 400;
    form.Height = 300;
    form.InitD3D();
    form.Show();
    while(form.Created)
    {
      form.Render();
      Application.DoEvents();
    }
  }

  Device device;
  Mesh teapot;

  public void InitD3D()
  {
    PresentParameters parameters = new PresentParameters();
    parameters.Windowed = TRUE;
    parameters.SwapEffect = SwapEffect.Discard;

    device = new Device(0, DeviceType.Hardware, this,
      CreateFlags.SoftwareVertexProcessing, parameters);
    teapot = Mesh.Teapot(device);
  }

  public void Render()
  {
```

```
device.Clear(ClearFlags.Target,
   System.Drawing.Color.Blue, 1.0f, 0);
device.BeginScene();
try
{
  device.RenderState.Lighting = TRUE;
  device.Lights[0].Type = LightType.Directional;
  device.Lights[0].Direction = new Vector3(7, -2, 1);
  device.Lights[0].Diffuse = System.Drawing.Color.Yellow;
  device.Lights[0].Commit();
  device.Lights[0].Enabled = TRUE;

  Material material = new Material();
  material.Ambient = System.Drawing.Color.White;
  material.Diffuse = System.Drawing.Color.White;
  material.Specular = System.Drawing.Color.White;
  device.Material = material;

  Matrix matrix = new Matrix();
  matrix.Scale(0.4f, 0.4f, 0.4f);
  matrix.M43 = 1; // Move along the Z-axis
  device.Transform.World = matrix;

  teapot.DrawSubset(0);
}
finally
{
  device.EndScene();
}
device.Present();
```

This program builds the same scene as its C++ equivalent, but the source code is noticeably shorter. This is because you did not have to spend time taking care of the low-level details such as registering the window class and message handling. Note that even though the interface concept is supported in .NET, when creating a managed API for DirectX interfaces they are packaged into "wrapper" classes, which makes their use appreciably easier.

To successfully compile the program, references to the following Managed DirectX assemblies need to be added to the project:

Microsoft.directx.dll
Microsoft.directx.direct3d.dll
Microsoft.directx.direct3dx.dll

To do this, select **Add Reference** in the **Project** menu and in the list of assemblies that appears, select all three assemblies by double-clicking them (Fig. 7.7).

By default, when Managed DirectX is installed, these files are placed into the <windows>\microsoft.net\manageddirectx\v4.09.00.0900\ folder. If the installer has not placed these files into the global assemblies cache, you can find them in this folder and add references to them to your project.

Now, the project should compile with no problems. Build the program and see whether it outputs to the screen the image output in the previous example in C++.

Now you can start to study Direct3D in a greater detail. Start by examining the initialization issues.

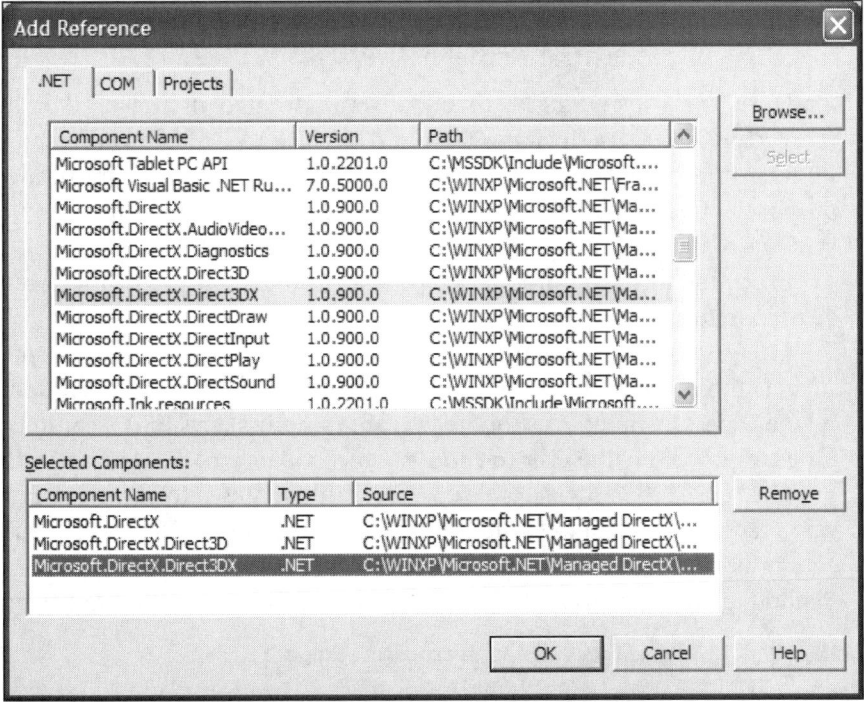

Fig. 7.7. Adding Direct3D assemblies to the C# project

7.4. Getting Started and Initializing Direct3D

As a rule, any library contains data structures that must be properly initialized; DirectX is no exception.

In this section, we describe the initialization specifics of the Direct3D component, the issues of selecting available graphics devices, and the video modes setup.

7.4.1. Initializing and Enumerating Graphics Devices Using C++ Tools

As already mentioned, in the C++ version, the library is properly prepared for work by creating the Direct3D object. This object implements the IDirect3D9 COM interface whose main function is to perform further initialization and to set up the modes of the graphics device.

In the example, the following source code is used to create the Direct3D object:

```
IDirect3D9 *pD3D;
...
pD3D = Direct3DCreate9(D3D_SDK_VERSION);
```

Here, D3D_SDK_VERSION is a constant defined in the d3d9.h header file. (DirectX 9.0 SDK also includes the old d3d8.h header file, in which this constant is set to a different value, so you have to be careful to use the right header file.) The purpose of this constant is to ascertain that the program is compiled using the same versions of the header files and the libraries.

Executing this code produces a pointer to the IDirect3D9 interface, which can be used to further configure the graphics equipment.

Lately, PCs equipped with more than one video adapter have become common, such as those configured with an integrated "office" video card and an additional "game" one. Obtaining a list of the available graphics devices is a common task that, for example, allows the user to choose, which video card to use for a virtual battle.

The IDirect3D9::GetAdapterCount() method is used to obtain the number of the video cards available in the system. Further enumeration of the available video adapters can be performed by sequentially calling the IDirect3D9::GetAdapterIdentifier method, incrementing the Adapter sequential number in the process:

```
HRESULT GetAdapterIdentifier(UINT Adapter,
  DWORD Flags,
  D3DADAPTER_IDENTIFIER9 *pIdentifier );
```

For the `Flags` value, 0 can be passed for regular enumeration, or the D3DENUM_WHQL_LEVEL constant can be passed to enumerate only those adapters whose drivers have the Microsoft Windows Hardware Quality Labs certification. In the latter case, do not be surprised if the computer attempts to connect to the Internet to load the most up-to-date certificates.

The last parameter is a pointer to the D3DADAPTER_IDENTIFIER9 structure, into which the information about the selected video adapter is stored. The source code using this information to output to the console data about the all installed adapters is shown in Listing 7.14.

Listing 7.14. Enumerating installed adapters [C++]

```cpp
#include <stdio.h>
#include <d3d9.h>

#pragma comment(lib, "d3d9.lib")

int main()
{
  IDirect3D9 *pD3D = Direct3DCreate9(D3D_SDK_VERSION);
  if(!pD3D)
  {
    printf("Direct3DCreate9 failed!\n");
    return 1;
  }
  int nCount = pD3D->GetAdapterCount();
  for(int i=0; i < nCount; i++)
  {
    D3DADAPTER_IDENTIFIER9 info;
    pD3D->GetAdapterIdentifier(i, 0, &info);
    printf("Adapter %d: \n"
           "\tDriver: %s\n"
           "\tDescription: %s\n"
           "\tDeviceName: %s\n",
           i, info.Driver, info.Description,
           info.DeviceName);
  }
  return 0;
}
```

The following is an example of the output produced by this program on a computer with one video card:

```
Adapter 0:
        Driver: ati2dvag.dll
        Description: RADEON 9600 SERIES
        DeviceName: \\.\DISPLAY1
```

And here is the output produced on a machine equipped with three video cards:

```
Adapter 0:
        Driver: nv4_disp.dll
        Description: NVIDIA GeForce DDR
        DeviceName: \\.\DISPLAY1
Adapter 1:
        Driver: perm2dll.dll
        Description: Appian Graphics Jeronimo Pro
        DeviceName: \\.\DISPLAY2
Adapter 2:
        Driver: perm2dll.dll
        Description: Appian Graphics Jeronimo Pro
        DeviceName: \\.\DISPLAY3
```

Another task in this area, enumerating the video modes available to the given video adapter, is solved in a similar way. To enumerate the video modes, the `IDirect3D9` interface makes the `GetAdapterModeCount` and `EnumAdpaterModes` methods available.

However, unlike the limited number of available video adapters, there are many combinations of resolution, color format, and screen refreshing frequency. Therefore, when enumerating the available video modes, it is also necessary to specify the valid pixel formats (defining the color depth and the order of the color components). The format constants are defined in the `D3DFORMAT` enumeration.

7.4.2. Enumerating Devices and Video Modes for Managed Direct3D

In the Direct3D version for .NET, the library does not have to be initialized explicitly. The `Direct3DCreate9` function is called automatically in the static constructor of the `Microsoft.DirectX.Direct3D.Manager` class.

Information about the available graphics devices can also be easily obtained using this class. Its `Adapters` property returns the `AdapterInformation` structures

Chapter 7: Using Direct3D Tools to Work with Graphics

list, containing all the necessary data. An example of a C# program that also outputs a list of installed adapters is shown in Listing 7.15.

Listing 7.15. Enumerating installed adapters [C#]

```
using System;
using System.Windows.Forms;
using Microsoft.DirectX;
using Microsoft.DirectX.Direct3D;

class TestForm: Form
{
  static void Main()
  {
    foreach(AdapterInformation adapterInfo in Manager.Adapters)
      Console.WriteLine("Adapter: \n\tDriver: {0}\n\t" +
        "Description: {1}\n\tDeviceName: {2}\n",
        adapterInfo.Information.DriverName,
        adapterInfo.Information.Description,
        adapterInfo.Information.DeviceName);
  }
}
```

The task of obtaining the list of video modes available to each video adapter is easy to solve: The `AdapterInformation` structure has the `SupportedDisplayModes` property that provides the list of all available video modes.

As previously mentioned, this list can contain hundreds of combinations; therefore, it is advisable to select from it only those that have the appropriate color format. For this purpose, the `SupportedDisplaysModes` property supports indexing by the code of the format defined in the `Microsoft.DirectX.Direct3D.Format` class: All you have to do is insert the format code in the square brackets after the property name.

The following is an example of the source code to output all video modes available to the first video adapter that have High Color 5-6-5 color depth (5 bits each to represent red and blue, and 6 bits to represent yellow).

```
foreach(DisplayMode mode in
  Manager.Adapters[0].
  SupportedDisplayModes[Format.R5G6B5])
    Console.WriteLine("{0}x{1}, {2} Hz, Format: {3}",
      mode.Width, mode.Height, mode.RefreshRate, mode.Format);
```

You have probably noticed that the task is once again made easier by a .NET Framework feature: All enumeration constants, for example, the names of various color formats, return their names in a human-legible format when output.

7.4.3. Initializing the Graphics Mode for C++

To output images in Direct3D, the `Device` object is used. This handles the interaction with the video adapter's hardware. When creating this object, several parameters need to be specified.

Recall the code fragments for creating the Direct3D device in the first program:

```
HRESULT hr = pD3D->CreateDevice(
   D3DADAPTER_DEFAULT, D3DDEVTYPE_HAL, hWnd,
   D3DCREATE_SOFTWARE_VERTEXPROCESSING,
   &params, &pDevice);
```

The first parameter of the `IDirect3D9::CreateDevice` method defines the adapter, for which the `Device` object is created. Either the adapter number received in the enumeration (as shown in Listing 7.14) or the `D3DADAPTER_DEFAULT` constant can be specified. In the latter case, the default adapter will be used.

The next parameter defines the device type and can take one of the following three values: `D3DDEVTYPE_HAL`, `D3DDEVTYPE_REF`, or `D3DDEVTYPE_SW`. The second and third modes perform all Direct3D operations by software emulation, and it makes sense to use them only for debugging because they are slow.

The `hWnd` parameter is needed to specify the descriptor of the Windows window, to which the created device will be bound.

The next parameter was introduced in DirectX 8.0 because of the hardware support of the Transform and Lighting (T&L) feature in the latest generation video adapters. We specified the `D3DCREATE_SOFTWARE_VERTEXPROCESSING` value to process primitive apexes by software. To enable hardware T&L support, use `D3DCREATE_HARDWARE_VERTEXPROCESSING`. This will greatly reduce the central processing unit workload in calculating apexes but will also limit the number of video cards capable of supporting your program.

Next, pass the pointer to the `D3DPRESENT_PARAMETERS` structure containing additional initialization parameters. The complete field list of this structure is given in the Direct3D reference. As you have seen, to initialize the window video mode, simply initialize the structure with zeros and specify only three parameters:

```
D3DPRESENT_PARAMETERS params;
ZeroMemory( &params, sizeof(params) );
```

```
params.Windowed = TRUE;
params.SwapEffect = D3DSWAPEFFECT_DISCARD;
params.BackBufferFormat = D3DFMT_UNKNOWN;
```

Here is another advantage of installing the Debug version of DirectX Runtime: Specifying the D3DSWAPEFFECT_DISCARD value in the SwapEffect field helps when debugging Direct3D applications. With this done, before building the scene, each output frame is filled with random noise. You will easily notice when the output image does not fill the entire frame area.

The initialization of the full-screen video mode requires a minimum of four more fields to be specified: BackBufferWidth, BackBufferHeight (screen resolution), BackBufferFormat (color format), and FullScreenRefreshRateInHz (screen refresh frequency). An example of initializing the 1024 × 768, TrueColor, default frame rate video mode is given in Listing 7.16.

Listing 7.16. Initializing the full-screen video mode [C++]

```
D3DPRESENT_PARAMETERS params;
ZeroMemory( &params, sizeof(params) );
params.Windowed = FALSE;
params.SwapEffect = D3DSWAPEFFECT_DISCARD;
params.BackBufferWidth = 1024;
params.BackBufferHeight = 768;
params.BackBufferFormat = D3DFMT_A8R8G8B8;
params.FullScreen_RefreshRateInHz = D3DPRESENT_RATE_DEFAULT;

HRESULT hr = pD3D->CreateDevice(
  D3DADAPTER_DEFAULT,
  D3DDEVTYPE_HAL, hWnd,
  D3DCREATE_SOFTWARE_VERTEXPROCESSING,
  &params, &pDevice);
```

If the video adapter does not support the specified color format, calling CreateDevice will return an error. Otherwise, the pDevice variable will hold a pointer to the created IDirect3DDevice9 device.

7.4.4. Initializing the Graphics Mode for C#

Setting the video mode in Managed DirectX is similar to doing this in C++ with one important difference: The `Device` object is created by calling a constructor, which looks more natural from the programming standpoint. The following is the source code for this constructor:

```
public Device(
  int adapter,
  DeviceType deviceType,
  Control renderWindow,
  CreateFlags behaviorFlags,
  PresentParameters presentationParameters
);
```

The parameters mean the same thing they do in the C++ version. The values of the constants are stored in the `DeviceType`, `CreateFlags`, and other enumeration classes, which obviates the need for the programmer to memorize them. We have already given the source code for the initialization of the window device; an example of setting the full-screen mode (with the same parameters as in the C++ example) is given in Listing 7.17.

Listing 7.17. Initializing the full-screen video mode [C#]

```
PresentParameters parameters = new PresentParameters();
parameters.BackBufferWidth = 1024;
parameters.BackBufferHeight = 768;
parameters.BackBufferFormat = Format.A8R8G8B8;
parameters.FullScreenRefreshRateInHz =
  PresentParameters.DefaultPresentRate;
parameters.Windowed = FALSE;
parameters.SwapEffect = SwapEffect.Discard;

device = new Device(0, DeviceType.Hardware, this,
   CreateFlags.SoftwareVertexProcessing, parameters);
```

In .NET, specifying incorrect or unsupported video mode parameters will generate the `Microsoft.DirectX.Direct3D.InvalidCallException` exception.

7.5. Removing Hidden Details

In the sample programs, the cute teapot is drawn in a good perspective that hides some of its defects. For the first example, we chose the position of the object and its viewing angle carefully: We wanted you to get a ready image as soon as possible without bothering with the details unnecessary for the purposes of the given example.

However, it is time to move on and get down to the nuts and bolts of DirectX. Start by getting acquainted with the way to implement algorithms for removing hidden details in Direct3D. The theoretical foundations of these algorithms are considered in detail in *Appendix 2*; here, we will describe the practical aspects only.

7.5.1. The Visibility Pyramid

As soon as the scene parameters of the example image are changed slightly, strange things start happening to the teapot. In the C++ program, find the following code fragment:

```
D3DMATRIX transform = {
    scale,  0.0f,   0.0f,   0.0f,
    0.0f,   scale,  0.0f,   0.0f,
    0.0f,   0.0f,   scale,  0.0f,
    0.0f,   0.0f,   1.0f,   1.0f
};
```

Exchange it with the following code (note the text in bold):

```
D3DMATRIX transform = {
    scale,  0.0f,   0.0f,   0.0f,
    0.0f,   scale,  0.0f,   0.0f,
    0.0f,   0.0f,   scale,  0.0f,
    0.0f,   0.0f,   0.3f,   1.0f
};
```

The analogous part in the C# example looks as follows:

```
matrix.M43 = 1; // Shift along the Z-axis
```

Likewise, change only the constant in the following line:

```
matrix.M43 = 0.3f; // Shift along the Z-axis
```

In both programs, only one element of the transformation matrix has been changed: the element indexed (4,3).

We consider geometric transformations in Direct3D in detail in *Chapter 8*; for now, it will suffice to say that this element is responsible for moving the object to or from the coordinate system center along the Z-axis. In other words, you have placed the teapot not 1.0 unit from the camera, as in the first case, but 0.3 units. The results of this change are shown in Fig. 7.8.

The results are no less striking if the same matrix element is changed by only 0.05, from 1.00 to 1.05 units (Fig. 7.9).

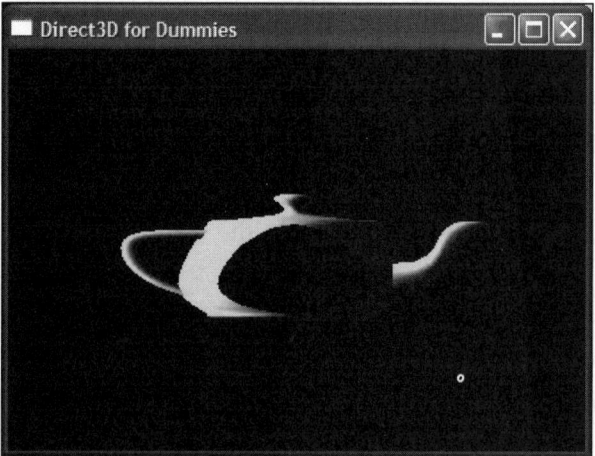

Fig. 7.8. Object is clipped in front

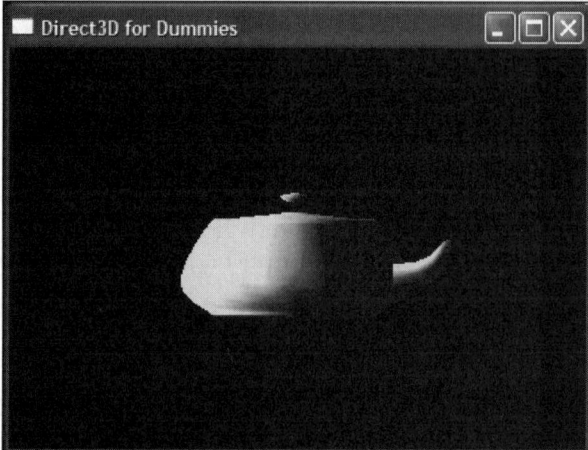

Fig. 7.9. Object is clipped in back

Chapter 7: Using Direct3D Tools to Work with Graphics

As can be seen from the illustrations, all details of the object that extend beyond certain boundaries are neatly clipped. If you experiment with the matrix elements (4,1) and (4,2), which control the object's translation along the other two coordinate axes, you will see that the output also gets clipped in these axes. The previous examples demonstrate the Direct3D clipping mechanism. But why are these restrictions needed?

If you draw four imaginary lines from the viewing point to the screen corners, you will get a pyramid with a rectangle (the screen) as its base. Continuing the lines farther into the virtual world, the world that projects onto the screen, you will get what is called the *viewing frustum:* the volume within the pyramid bound by the screen in front (the front clipping plane) and some plane in back (the back clipping plane). Everything outside of this viewing frustum is outside of the projection area, so why waste time drawing those details?

Distant objects do not have to be drawn either. You have to stop at the right distance because in most cases, sooner or later, some obstacle will interrupt the view anyway. Moreover, the human eye cannot see a teapot located, say, tens of miles away. The same is true of the objects located, for example, in the virtual world behind us or in front of the screen. This is why objects in DirectX are clipped by the viewing frustum's six planes (Fig. 7.10).

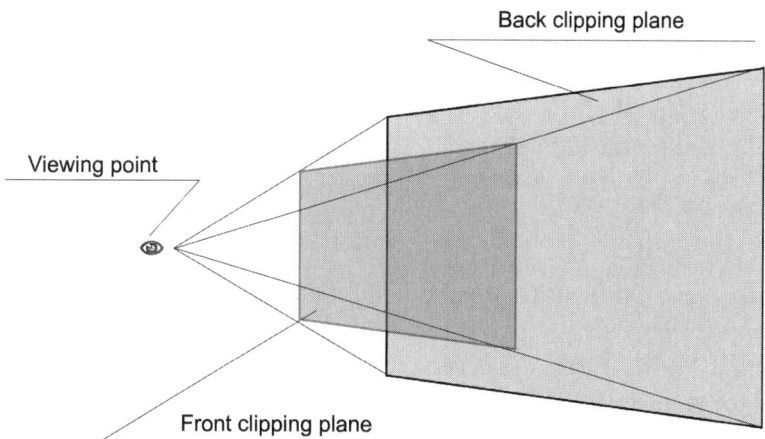

Fig. 7.10. Image projection and the viewing frustum

As you can see, this is a useful functionality, which makes it possible to save time when processing complex scenes and, consequently, to improve performance. How to configure the viewing frustum, you are going to learn in *Chapter 8* when you get a closer look at the Direct3D transformation matrices; for now, simply disconnect this mechanism because we do not care about speed in the tutorial examples.

To disable clipping in the C++ program, add the following line before the code outputting the object:

```
pDevice->SetRenderState(D3DRS_CLIPPING, FALSE);
```

The code to do this in the C# program looks as follows:

```
device.RenderState.Clipping = FALSE;
```

You can check it: If you move the object around the scene, it remains intact.

7.5.2. The Z-Buffer

To illustrate another problem arising when projecting complex objects (or groups of objects), add some dynamics to the scene.

Let the teapot rotate at a constant speed around the Y-axis. The first thing you need to do for this is to make the program constantly refresh (redraw) the scene. Because the C++ program calls the `Render` method in the `WM_PAINT` handler, for continuous refreshing, call the `InvalidateRect` function after you finish drawing:

```
case WM_PAINT:
{
  PAINTSTRUCT ps;
  BeginPaint(hWnd, &ps);
  g_App.Render();
  EndPaint(hWnd, &ps);
  InvalidateRect(hWnd, 0, TRUE);
  return 0;
}
```

To make the object rotate, use the D3DX utilities library, postponing closer study of Direct3D geometry until the next chapter. The `D3DXMatrixRotationY` function, which creates the necessary rotation-angle matrix, will help. To use it, you need to create the `D3DXMATRIX` object and pass to it the rotation angle in radians.

The `D3DXMATRIX` class, which is also made available by the D3DX library, is a simple container for the already-familiar `D3DMATRIX` structure. This class implements several useful mathematical operations and operations for comparing matrices.

To form the final matrix, the `rotation` matrix is multiplied by the initial `transform` matrix in the initial version of the program. The edited fragment of the `Render` method code is shown in Listing 7.18.

Listing 7.18. Implementing object rotation in the `Render` method [C++]

```
float scale = 0.4f;
D3DXMATRIX transform(
    scale,      0.0f,       0.0f,       0.0f,
    0.0f,       scale,      0.0f,       0.0f,
    0.0f,       0.0f,       scale,      0.0f,
    0.0f,       0.0f,       1.0f,       1.0f
);
D3DXMATRIX rotation;
D3DXMatrixRotationY(&rotation, GetTickCount()/1000.0f);
rotation *= transform;
pDevice->SetTransform(D3DTS_WORLD, &rotation);
pDevice->SetRenderState(D3DRS_CLIPPING, FALSE);
pTeapot->DrawSubset(0);
pDevice->EndScene();
```

As you can see from the listing, to obtain the rotation angle monotone increasing with each frame, use the `GetTickCount` function, which returns the number of milliseconds elapsed from the program's start. This number is then divided by 1000, making the teapot rotate at a speed of 1 radian per second (Fig. 7.11).

Here is the promised defect: Some parts of the teapot are seen through its body even though they should be hidden by it. If the object is redrawn in the same scene using slightly different coordinates, these two parts again will not be depicted correctly.

Fig. 7.11. Image is drawn incorrectly: the teapot's spout is seen through the teapot

The reason for this is that the object is composed of triangular primitives and the order, in which they are drawn, is not defined. If the triangles that make up the teapot's spout are drawn after its body, they will erase the already created image.

One of the most effective ways of solving this problem has been used for a long time by all modern video cards and is called the *Z-buffer* (or *depth buffer*) *algorithm*. It is based on a simple principle: Each pixel of the frame is associated with a special value called *depth*.

With this mode enabled, when a primitive is output, in addition to the frame buffer the Z-buffer is filled with the depth values of the corresponding pixels (i.e., their distance from the viewing plane). A pixel is output only when it is closer to the screen than the distance specified by the current depth value in the Z-buffer, in which case its depth value overwrites the old one in the Z-buffer.

To enable the depth buffer when initializing the video mode, the following two additional fields of the D3DPRESENT_PARAMETERS structure must be filled:

```
params.EnableAutoDepthStencil = TRUE;
params.AutoDepthStencilFormat = D3DFMT_D16;
```

The first field enables use of the Z-buffer; the second defines its format (in this case, the depth of each pixel will be stored as a 16-bit value).

The depth buffer must be cleared before outputting each frame; otherwise, the old depth values will interfere with the output of the new frames. In this task, resort to the help of the already familiar `Clear` method, using the D3DCLEAR_ZBUFFER flag. The value of 1.0 (the maximum depth) must be passed to this method as the third parameter. In addition, the Z-test must be turned on, enabling writing to the depth buffer. The following code shows what the beginning of the `Render` method looks like:

```
pDevice->Clear( 0, NULL,
   D3DCLEAR_TARGET|D3DCLEAR_ZBUFFER,
   D3DCOLOR_XRGB(0,0,128), 1.0f, 0 );
pDevice->SetRenderState(D3DRS_ZENABLE, TRUE);
pDevice->SetRenderState(D3DRS_ZWRITEENABLE, TRUE);
```

After the program has been compiled, you can observe the overlapping parts of the object being drawn correctly (Fig. 7.12).

In the C# program, the rendering is already done continuously, so you only need to add the rotation code and turn on the Z-buffer. To avoid repetition, modify the program slightly so that the teapot not only will rotate but also will move along the Z-axis.

The complete source code of the modified program is shown in Listing 7.19.

Chapter 7: Using Direct3D Tools to Work with Graphics

Fig. 7.12. Correct image (after turning on the Z-buffer)

Listing 7.18. Outputting a rotating object with the Z-buffer turned on [C#]

```
using System;
using System.Windows.Forms;
using Microsoft.DirectX;
using Microsoft.DirectX.Direct3D;

class TestForm: Form
{
  static void Main()
  {
    TestForm form = new TestForm();
    form.Text = "Direct3D for .NET";
    form.Width = 400;
    form.Height = 300;
    form.InitD3D();
    form.Show();
    while(form.Created)
    {
      form.Render();
      Application.DoEvents();
    }
  }
```

```
Device device;
Mesh teapot;

public void InitD3D()
{
  try
  {
    PresentParameters parameters = new PresentParameters();
    parameters.Windowed = TRUE;
    parameters.SwapEffect = SwapEffect.Discard;
    parameters.EnableAutoDepthStencil = TRUE;
    parameters.AutoDepthStencilFormat = DepthFormat.D16;

    device = new Device(0, DeviceType.Hardware, this,
      CreateFlags.SoftwareVertexProcessing, parameters);
    teapot = Mesh.Teapot(device);
  }
  catch(Exception e)
  {
    MessageBox.Show(e.Message);
    return;
  }
}

public void Render()
{
  try
  {
    device.Clear(ClearFlags.Target|ClearFlags.ZBuffer,
      System.Drawing.Color.Blue, 1.0f, 0);
    device.RenderState.ZBufferEnable = TRUE;
    device.RenderState.ZBufferWriteEnable = TRUE;
    device.BeginScene();
    device.RenderState.Lighting = TRUE;
    device.Lights[0].Type = LightType.Directional;
    device.Lights[0].Direction = new Vector3(7, -2, 1);
    device.Lights[0].Diffuse = System.Drawing.Color.Yellow;
    device.Lights[0].Commit();
    device.Lights[0].Enabled = TRUE;
```

```
      Material material = new Material();
      material.Ambient = System.Drawing.Color.White;
      material.Diffuse =  System.Drawing.Color.White;
      material.Specular = System.Drawing.Color.White;
      device.Material = material;

      Matrix matrix = new Matrix();
      matrix.Scale(0.7f, 0.7f, 0.7f);
      matrix *= Matrix.RotationY(
        System.Environment.TickCount / 300.0f );
      float move = (float)Math.Sin(
        System.Environment.TickCount/2000.0f)*4+6;
      matrix.M43 = move;
      Text = move.ToString("##.##");
      device.RenderState.Clipping = FALSE;
      device.Transform.World = matrix;
      device.Transform.Projection = Matrix.PerspectiveFovLH(
        (float)Math.PI / 4, 1.0f, 1.0f, 100.0f );

      teapot.DrawSubset(0);
      device.EndScene();
      device.Present();
    }
    catch(Exception e)
    {
      return;
    }
  }
}
```

7.5.3. Removing Back Faces

Another method to optimize the output of complex scenes involves dividing all object primitives into front faces and back faces (those facing the viewer and those turned from him, respectively). If an object has no holes in it, then only the front faces can be seen in whatever position it may be placed. Consequently, doing away with outputting back faces, the time to construct a scene can be reduced by about 50%. This method is called *culling*.

Fig. 7.13. Image drawn with back faces

The culling mode is enabled in Direct3D by default. Triangles are considered front faces if their vertices are numbered counterclockwise (on their screen projection). As you have seen, the D3DX library creates objects with this mode taken into account. If the opposite culling mode is set, only the internal cavities of the object will be drawn, producing a weird image (Fig. 7.13).

To set the reverse culling mode in C++, the `SetRenderState` method is used:

```
pDevice->SetRenderState(D3DRS_CULLMODE, D3DCULL_CW);
```

In C#, the following syntax is used:

```
device.RenderState.CullMode = Cull.Clockwise;
```

If the object has holes or semitransparent areas, then you must be able to see the back faces through them. For this, the culling mode needs to be disabled (using `D3DCULL_NONE` and `Cull.None` for C++ and C#, respectively).

7.6. Conclusion

In this chapter, you learned the basics of the Direct3D library and how to build simple 3D images. We invite you to study 3D graphics capabilities in more detail in *Chapter 8*.

Chapter 8: Looking Closer at Direct3D

In this chapter, the following are considered:

- ❐ Direct3D geometric transformation
- ❐ Using primitives and mesh objects to build 3D images
- ❐ Coloring polygons using textures, light sources, and materials
- ❐ Vertex and pixel shader technologies

8.1. Application of Geometric Transformations

In the previous chapter, you learned the principles of displaying Direct3D objects. This section is devoted to their detailed study.

A complex 3D object usually consists of many elements, and its designers do not know beforehand the screen position, in which it will be displayed. Therefore, 3D model designers (modelers) pick a convenient coordinate system, in which to design objects, with the object's center most often at the point with the (0, 0, 0) coordinates.

Before an object is output to the screen, all its points undergo the following series of transformations:

- If an object (e.g., a spaceship in a game) is moving in its virtual world, the coordinates of all points that form it (polygon vertices) must be updated. In addition to the straight-line movement, an object can rotate; sometimes, its scale can change (either proportionally in all axes or independently in each axis). These coordinate transformations are called *world* transformations.
- Even if all objects (e.g., buildings) in a 3D scene are stationary, the observer (the camera) can be moving. This behavior is often practised in car-racing and aircraft simulators. Consequently, before depicting all objects on the screen, their vertices must undergo analogous *(view)* transformations, reflecting the position of the observer.
- The image must be projected onto the screen, with the potential perspective effects taken into account. In perspective transformations, objects located farther from the camera appear smaller than their copies located closer, parallel lines intersect at the horizon line, etc. These transformations depend on the characteristics of the virtual camera. For example, when a wide-angle lens is modeled (called a *fish-eye* lens by photographers), perspective distortions will be greater. Consequently, there is a need for *projective* transformations.

To solve these tasks, Direct3D employs *transformation matrices,* a concept long known in mathematics. For each of the mentioned transformations, Direct3D has its own 4 × 4 matrix. The way transformations are carried out is simple: the new object coordinates are obtained by multiplying the object's coordinate vector by the corresponding transformation matrix.

You may have noticed an incongruity in the last phrase: In a 3D space, an object coordinate vector must have three components: (x, y, z). But for a multiplication by a 4 × 4 matrix, a four-element vector is needed. A four-element vector, in which the last element always equals one, is used for transformations.

8.1.1. Direct3D Coordinate Transformation Matrices for C++

When describing matrix elements, the D3DMATRIX structure is used. Elements are stored in it sequentially as a 4 × 4 array; therefore, such a structure can be initialized by a simple list of values:

```
D3DMATRIX matrix = {
    1.0f,      0.0f,      0.0f,      0.0f,
```

```
           0.0f,    1.0f,    0.0f,    0.0f,
           0.0f,    0.0f,    1.0f,    0.0f,
           0.0f,    0.0f,    0.0f,    1.0f
};
```

The matrix in the example is called the *unitary matrix* in mathematics: All its elements on the main diagonal equal one; all other elements equal zero. Its other name is the *identity matrix*, because the product of a vector multiplied by this matrix equals the original vector. Multiplying any other matrix by it produces the same result: the original matrix.

If only D3DMATRIX structures are used for transformations, their elements have to be calculated manually. However, as you already know from *Chapter 7*, you can take advantage of the D3DX library. It provides the following convenient methods for obtaining coordinate transformation matrices:

- The first method is based on using the D3DMATRIX class. As already noted, this class inherits from the D3DMATRIX structure; therefore, it can be passed to all methods or functions that require a pointer to this structure. D3DX contains functions that create matrices for the necessary transformations or solve specific mathematical problems (e.g., multiply matrices or find their determinants). These matrices are called D3DXMatrix*XXXXXX*, where *XXXXXX* is the particular matrix extension (e.g., AffineTransformation). Moreover, the class contains matrix algebra methods.
- The other method is available through the ID3DXMatrixStack interface. This interface is intended for manipulating transformations connected to each other. For example, to depict a turning tank turret, the transformations taking into account the location of the tank need to be performed first. Only after this is the turret rotation taken into account. The ID3DXMatrixStack interface can be used to apply a series of transformations (defined by its methods) to the entire set of stored matrices at once. To create such a set of stored matrices, use the D3DXCreateMatrixStack function.

In addition to the methods for performing simple geometric transformation, the D3DX library contains service methods for solving certain application tasks. In particular, a view matrix is often constructed by pointing out the object being observed. For example, in a car-race simulator, a view matrix of the observation camera may need to be created that reflects looking at a racing car.

To construct such a matrix, it is not necessary to solve an equation system: This problem is solved by calling the D3DXMatrixLookAtLH function. The LH suffix means that a matrix for the left-handed coordinate system (Direct3D's default coordinate system) is being constructed. The source code to construct a view matrix with the camera located at the (1, 0, 0) point and looking at a target with the (10, –5, 3) coordinates is given in Listing 8.1.

Listing 8.1. Creating a look-at target view matrix [C++]

```
D3DXMATRIX matView;
D3DXMatrixLookAtLH( &matView,
    &D3DXVECTOR3( 1.0f, 0.0f, 0.0f ),
    &D3DXVECTOR3( 10.0f, -5.0f, 3.0f ),
    &D3DXVECTOR3( 0.0f, 1.0f, 0.0f ) );
```

The last parameter defines the direction vector upward from the camera and usually coincides in direction with the Y-axis (unless the camera is also rotating along the view axis).

Finally, consider how to construct a projective transformation matrix that takes the perspective into account. There are various ways in the D3DX library to construct such a matrix. To specify the characteristics of the perspective distortion, either the *field of view* (FOV) or the dimensions of the viewing frustum (with which you are familiar from *Chapter 7*) can be employed. Quake players must be familiar with the FOV parameter, which can be adjusted in the game configurations. The FOV value for a projective matrix with the regular perspective distortions is 90 degrees ($\pi/4$). This matrix can be constructed in the LH coordinate system using the D3DXMatrixPerspectiveFovLH function (Listing 8.2).

Listing 8.2. Creating a projective matrix with FOV = 90 degrees [C++]

```
float fov = D3DX_PI/4;
int bufferWidth = 1024;
int bufferHeight = 768;
float aspectRatio = bufferWidth / (float)bufferHeight;
D3DXMATRIX matProj;
D3DXMatrixPerspectiveFovLH(&matProj, fov,
   aspectRatio, 1.0f, 100.0f);
```

The fourth and fifth parameters of the D3DXMatrixPerspectiveFovLH function define the distance from the viewer to the front and back clipping planes of the viewing frustum.

8.1.2. Transformation Matrices: The Managed DirectX Version

To work with transformation matrices, Managed DirectX makes the `Microsoft.DirectX.Direct3D.Matrix` class available.[i] It has both static methods (for obtaining various transformation matrices) and instance methods (for applying transformations to existing matrices). For example, to create a matrix for rotation around the X-axis, use the static `RotationX` method:

```
Matrix m = Matrix.RotationX(angle);
```

To rotate an existing matrix around the X-axis, make a call to its `RotateX` method:

```
m.RotateX(angle);
```

In both cases, remember that the `angle` rotation angle is specified in radians.

The microsoft.directx.direct3d.dll library also has the `MatrixStack` class that allows you to operate with a set of matrices and apply transformations to the entire set at once.

The `Matrix` class also contains service methods—such as obtaining a view matrix from the position of the target. In Listing 8.3, the source code is given for constructing a view matrix for looking at a target with the (2, 2, 2) coordinates from the (3, 3, 3) point.

Listing 8.3. Creating a look-at target view matrix [C#]

```
Matrix view = Matrix.LookAtLH(
  new Vector3( 3.0f, 3.0f, 3.0f ),
  new Vector3( 2.0f, 2.0f, 2.0f ),
  new Vector3( 0.0f, 1.0f, 0.0f ) );
```

To construct a projective transformation matrix taking FOV into account, a `Matrix` object has the `PerspectiveFovLH` static method available:

```
Matrix matProj = Matrix.PerspectiveFovLH((float)Math.PI/4, 1.0f,
  1.0f, 100.0f );
```

The function of its parameters is analogous to that of the C++ version.

---

[i] Do not confuse this class with its namesake in another namespace: `System.Drawing.Drawing2D.Matrix`. This class was considered in *Chapter 3*.

8.1.3. Applying Transformations to the Output Device

When initializing a Direct3D device, matrices for all three types of transformations considered previously are identity matrices. To set a proper transformation matrix, the `IDirect3DDevice9::SetTransform` method is used in C++ programs as follows:

```
HRESULT SetTransform(D3DTRANSFORMSTATETYPE State,
  CONST D3DMATRIX *pMatrix );
```

The `State` parameter defines the transformation type. To specify the world, view, and perspective transformations, use the `D3DTS_WORLD`, `D3DTS_VIEW`, and `D3DTS_PROJECTION` constants, respectively.

The `pMatrix` parameter must contain a pointer to the prepared matrix (as already noted, this can also be a pointer to the inherited `D3DXMATRIX` class).

The Managed Direct3D `Device` object implementation also has the `SetTransform` method. However, a simpler syntax for assigning a value to the `Transform` property exists:

```
device.Transform.World = myMatrix;
```

The preceding expression is equivalent to the following call:

```
device.SetTransform(TransformType.World, myMatrix);
```

Finally, you may need to use transformations for hidden processing of the target coordinates. For this, such D3DX functions as `D3DXVec3Transform`, `D3DXVec3TransformCoord`, and `D3DXVec3TransformNormal` can be employed. The managed `Matrix` class also has the `TransformPoins` and `TransformVectors` methods available for this purpose.

8.2. Working with Polygons

A *polygon* is traditional 3D-graphics name for a geometrical plane figure with three or more straight sides calculated in 3D space and output to the screen. Complex 3D objects (polygonal models) are built from hundreds and even thousands of such polygons; consequently, the number of polygons a video card can put out per second is one of its important performance characteristics.

Triangles are the most often used polygons, because all triangle vertices lie in one plane. Complex geometric figures are created by breaking their surface into triangles; the practice is called *triangulation*. This technique is also used to generate the D3DX built-in objects, as you shall now see.

Add the following call code to the `Render` method of the program before the object output code (the C++ version):

```
pDevice->SetRenderState(D3DRS_FILLMODE, D3DFILL_WIREFRAME);
```

The equivalent command for C# looks as follows:

```
device.RenderState.FillMode = FillMode.WireFrame;
```

The result is shown in Fig. 8.1.

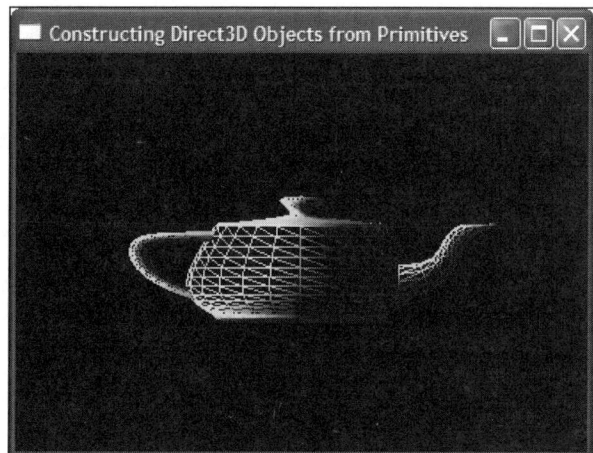

Fig. 8.1. Outputting an object using the wireframe mode

As you can see, for constructing objects of any complexity, the Direct3D library uses triangular element primitives. Therefore, in this section you will learn how to use 3D primitives and how the D3DX library can make this task easier.

8.2.1. Format of Vertices

Each polygon is defined by a set of *vertices*. In Direct3D, a vertex is not just a point in a 3D space but is also a flexibly-configured data structure (flexible vertex format, or FVF) that can carry other information necessary to depict a polygon: the vertex color, coordinates of the overlaid textures, lighting parameters (surface normals), etc. These data can be processed by both the built-in Direct3D mechanisms and the external vertex processing procedures *(shaders)*.

In C++ and C#, structures are convenient tools for defining vertex formats (and for accessing their data). An example of a definition of such a structure is shown in Listing 8.4.

Listing 8.4. Definition of colored cube vertices [C++]

```cpp
#pragma pack(1) // Important: Disable compiler data alignment.

// Data format of a simple vertex
struct Vertex
{
  float x, y, z;   // 3D coordinates
  DWORD color;     // Vertex color

};

// Vertex format definition constant
const DWORD VertexFVF = ( D3DFVF_XYZ | D3DFVF_DIFFUSE );

// Array defining eight cube vertices
static Vertex vertexSamples[] =
{
  { 0, 0, 0,   D3DCOLOR_XRGB(255,   0,   0) },
  { 1, 0, 0,   D3DCOLOR_XRGB(255, 127, 127) },
  { 1, 1, 0,   D3DCOLOR_XRGB(255, 127,   0) },
  { 0, 1, 0,   D3DCOLOR_XRGB(127, 127, 127) },
  { 0, 0, 1,   D3DCOLOR_XRGB(127, 127, 255) },
  { 1, 0, 1,   D3DCOLOR_XRGB(  0, 127, 127) },
  { 1, 1, 1,   D3DCOLOR_XRGB(  0,   0, 255) },
  { 0, 1, 1,   D3DCOLOR_XRGB(255,   0, 127) }
};

const UINT vertexCount =
  sizeof(vertexSamples)/sizeof(vertexSamples[0]);
```

For representing vertex data, a `Vertex` structure is created, in which the vertex coordinates and its color are stored. The library cannot recognize the structure definition created in a high-level language. To specify the vertex format, a combination of the D3DFVF enumeration flags is used. This enumeration is described in detail in the Direct3D documentation. In this example, the format is stored in the VertexFVF constant.

Chapter 8: Looking Closer at Direct3D 287

NOTE In Direct3D 9.0, with FVF, a new way of defining vertex format was introduced. It is called *vertex declaration* and is represented by the `IDirect3DVertexDeclaration9` interface. More information about this technique can be found in the DirectX 9.0 SDK documentation.

Later in the example, an array of eight such structures is created, each of which stores descriptions of the side 1 cube vertices with different colors for each vertex. Fig. 8.2 shows a diagram for constructing such a cube and its placement relative to the coordinate axis.

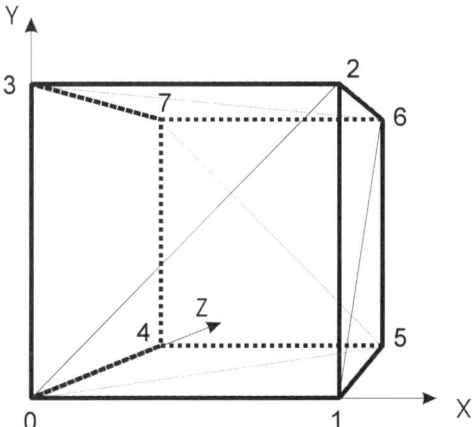

Fig. 8.2. Defining side 1 cube vertices

Each side of the cube is defined by 2 triangles. Consequently, descriptions of eight vertices and 12 triangles will be needed.

In Managed DirectX, definitions of vertex formats are constructed in a similar way, but for the most common vertex formats this library has ready-made structures defined within the `CustomVertex` class. In particular, for the example here, the `CustomVertex.PositionColored` structure can be used (Listing 8.5).

Listing 8.5. Definition of colored cube vertices [C#]

```
CustomVertex.PositionColored[] vertexSamples =
{
  new CustomVertex.PositionColored( 0, 0, 0, 0xFF0000 ),
  new CustomVertex.PositionColored( 1, 0, 0, 0xFF7F7F ),
```

```
    new CustomVertex.PositionColored( 1, 1, 0, 0xFF7F00 ),
    new CustomVertex.PositionColored( 0, 1, 0, 0x7F7F7F ),
    new CustomVertex.PositionColored( 0, 0, 1, 0x7F7FFF ),
    new CustomVertex.PositionColored( 1, 0, 1, 0x007F7F ),
    new CustomVertex.PositionColored( 1, 1, 1, 0x0000FF ),
    new CustomVertex.PositionColored( 0, 1, 1, 0xFF007F )
};
```

To obtain the vertex format constant in this case, use the `CustomVertex.PositionColored.Format` static field.

8.2.2. Creating and Filling a Vertex Buffer

In Direct3D, a contiguous block of memory, called a *vertex buffer*, is used to store a set of object vertices. This allows the vertex information to be compactly stored and uniformly processed.

The C++ Version

To create a vertex buffer in C++, the `IDirect3DDevice9::CreateVertexBuffer` device method needs to be called. It needs to be informed of the buffer size, the format of the vertices, and the parameters of the buffer's location in memory (Listing 8.6).

Listing 8.6. Creating a vertex buffer [C++]

```
IDirect3DVertexBuffer9 *pVertices;
// ...
if(FAILED(pDevice->CreateVertexBuffer(sizeof(vertexSamples),
  D3DUSAGE_SOFTWAREPROCESSING, VertexFVF,
  D3DPOOL_DEFAULT, &pVertices, NULL)))
{
  MessageBox(0, "Failed to create vertex buffer",
    "Direct3D Error", MB_OK);
  pD3D->Release();
  return FALSE;
}
```

As can be seen, the previously described `VertexFVF` constant is used to specify the format of the vertices. Execution of this code places a pointer to the

`IDirect3DVertexBuffer9` interface into the `pVertices` variable; this pointer can be used to manipulate the contents of the vertex buffer.

Use the `Lock` method of this interface to gain access to the vertex buffer data, after which the prepared definitions of the vertices (in the example, they are stored in the `vertexSamples` array) can be copied into the obtained address as shown in Listing 8.7.

Listing 8.7. Filling a vertex buffer with data [C++]

```
LPVOID pData = NULL;
pVertices->Lock(0, 0, &pData, D3DLOCK_DISCARD);
CopyMemory(pData, vertexSamples, sizeof(vertexSamples));
pVertices->Unlock();
```

After a vertex buffer is filled with data, its `Unlock` method must be called; otherwise, it cannot be used to output primitives.

The C# Version

In the C# program, the vertex buffer is represented by the `VertexBuffer` object. Use one of the three overloaded constructors to initialize it (Listing 8.8).

Listing 8.8. Creating and filling a vertex buffer [C#]

```
VertexBuffer vertices;
// ...
vertices = new VertexBuffer(
  typeof(CustomVertex.PositionColored),
vertexSamples.Length, device,
Usage.WriteOnly,
  CustomVertex.PositionColored.Format,
  Pool.Default);

// Gaining access to the vertices

CustomVertex.PositionColored[] pVertices =
  (CustomVertex.PositionColored[])vertices.Lock(0, 0);
// Copying data
for(int i=0; i < vertexSamples.Length; i++)
  pVertices[i] = vertexSamples[i];

vertices.Unlock();
```

As can be seen, in the C# version, the access to the vertex data is also gained by using the Lock and Unlock methods.

8.2.3. Outputting Primitives and Using the Index Buffer

Direct3D supports two primitive-output modes: *direct* and *index*.

The first mode is represented by the DrawPrimitive device method (or DrawPrimitives in the C# version). It allows the primitives defined in the current vertex buffer to be output. The primitive type is specified by the D3DPRIMITIVETYPE enumeration (it is called PrimitiveType in C#).

The simplest primitive type is a single triangle. When such primitives are used, the vertex buffer must hold a triangle list with three vertices for each triangle. This method is shown in Fig. 8.3.

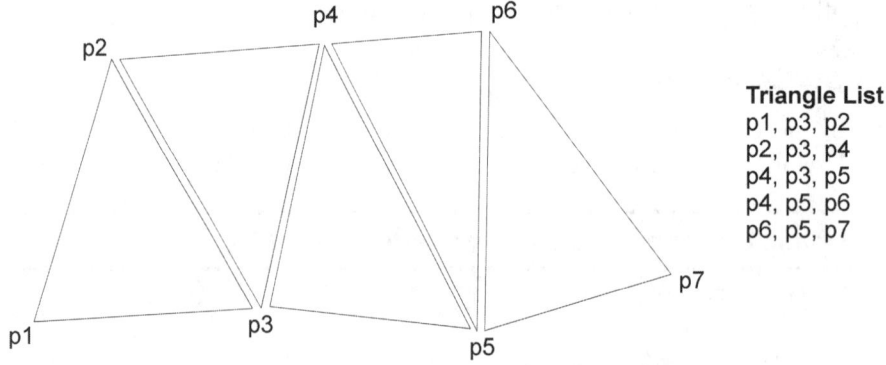

Fig. 8.3. Outputting a set of individual triangles

It is not difficult to see that this is a wasteful method. In this case, the adjacent triangles have common points—*p2, p3, p4, p5,* and *p6*—that will have to be doubled in the vertex buffer.

To display this type of objects, another primitive type is more suitable: a *triangle strip*, in which adjacent triangles are connected to each other by their sides. Output of this type of primitives is shown in Fig. 8.4.

As you can see, in this case the side-doubling problem has been eliminated. If all triangles have one common point, you can take advantage of the primitive type called a *triangle fan*. Fig. 8.5 shows four triangles sharing one common point, *p1*.

Nevertheless, when constructing complex objects, it is often impossible to eliminate doubling and to group triangles by the primitive types described previously.

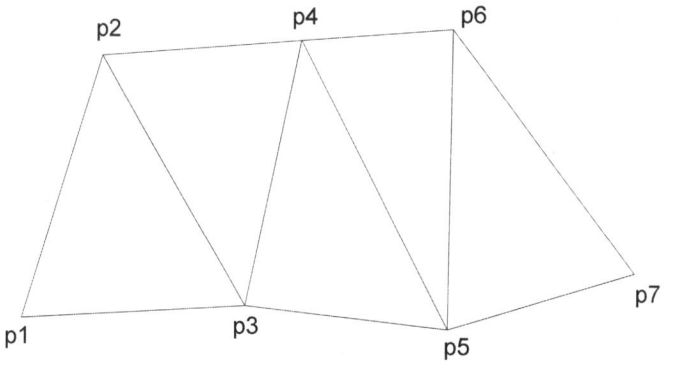

Fig. 8.4. Triangle strip output

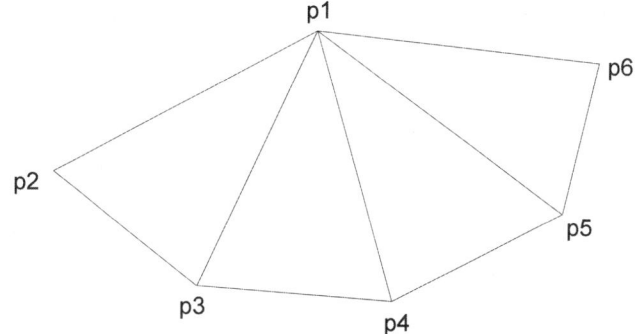

Fig. 8.5. Triangle fan output

This problem is solved using another, index primitive-output method. In this method, not the vertices but their indexes—sequence numbers in the vertex buffer—are used to define triangles. This makes it possible not only to eliminate the doubling of vertex data but also to save memory because integer indices take up much less space than vertex data.

To use the index mode, an additional data buffer, called an *index buffer,* needs to be created and filled with data. In the C++ version, the index buffer is represented by the `IDirect3DIndexBuffer9` interface. Listing 8.9 shows how to create this type of buffer and fill it with data.

Listing 8.9. Creating an index buffer and filling it with data [C++]

```
// Array defining six cube sides (12 triangles)
static WORD indexSamples[] =
{
```

```
    0, 2, 3,    0, 1, 2,
    3, 2, 6,    3, 6, 7,
    1, 6, 2,    1, 5, 6,
    0, 3, 7,    0, 7, 4,
    5, 4, 7,    5, 7, 6,
    0, 4, 5,    0, 5, 1
};
const UINT indexCount =
  sizeof(indexSamples)/sizeof(indexSamples[0]);
// ...
// Defining the variable for storing the index buffer
IDirect3DIndexBuffer9  *pIndices;
// ...
// Creating the index buffer
if( FAILED( pDevice->CreateIndexBuffer( sizeof(indexSamples),
  D3DUSAGE_WRITEONLY,
  D3DFMT_INDEX16,
  D3DPOOL_DEFAULT,
  &pIndices, NULL ) ) )
{
  MessageBox(0, "Failed to create index buffer",
    "Direct3D Error", MB_OK);
  pD3D->Release();
  return FALSE;
}
pIndices->Lock(0, sizeof(indexSamples), &pData, 0);
CopyMemory(pData, indexSamples, sizeof(indexSamples));
pIndices->Unlock();
```

This code is similar to the code for creating a vertex buffer, so you should have no problems understanding it.

In Managed DirectX, the index buffer is controlled by the IndexBuffer class. A fragment of the equivalent code for creating an index buffer and filling it with data in C# is shown in Listing 8.10.

Listing 8.10. Creating an index buffer and filling it with data [C#]

```
// Array defining six cube sides (12 triangles)
int[] indexSamples =
{
```

```
    0, 2, 3,    0, 1, 2,
    3, 2, 6,    3, 6, 7,
    1, 6, 2,    1, 5, 6,
    0, 3, 7,    0, 7, 4,
    5, 4, 7,    5, 7, 6,
    0, 4, 5,    0, 5, 1
};
// ...
IndexBuffer  indices;
//...
// Creating an index buffer and filling it with data
indices = new IndexBuffer(typeof(int), indexSamples.Length, device,
    Usage.WriteOnly, Pool.Default);
int[] pIndices = (int[])indices.Lock(0, LockFlags.Discard);
for(int i=0; i < indexSamples.Length; i++)
    pIndices[i] = indexSamples[i];
indices.Unlock();
```

To output primitives using an index buffer, the `Device` object has the `DrawIndexedPrimitive` method available (it is called `DrawIndexedPrimitives` in the C# version). Before outputting primitives, the following operations must be executed:

- Set the current vertex buffer in the device (the one defining the necessary vertex data)
- Convey to the device the format of the vertices defined in the vertex buffer (using the FVF enumeration constants)
- Set the current index buffer

Examples of the C++ and C# source code used to output the cube are given in Listings 8.11 and 8.12, respectively.

Listing 8.11. Outputting primitives using the index buffer [C++]

```
pDevice->SetStreamSource(0, pVertices, 0, sizeof(Vertex));
pDevice->SetFVF(VertexFVF);
pDevice->SetIndices(pIndices);
pDevice->DrawIndexedPrimitive(D3DPT_TRIANGLELIST, 0, 0,
    vertexCount, 0, indexCount/3);
```

Listing 8.12. Outputting primitives using the index buffer [C#]

```
device.SetStreamSource(0, vertices, 0);
device.VertexFormat = CustomVertex.PositionColored.Format;
device.Indices = indices;
device.DrawIndexedPrimitives(PrimitiveType.TriangleList, 0, 0,
   vertexSamples.Length, 0, indexSamples.Length/3);
```

If you insert the code fragments described in this section into your version of the program, you should get on the screen a rotating cube whose vertices are different colors (Fig. 8.6).

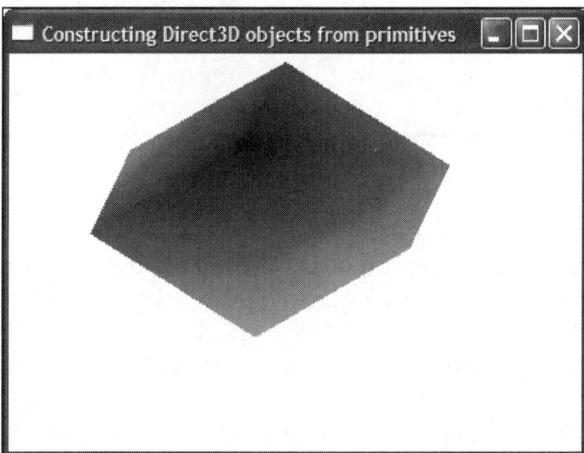

Fig. 8.6. Outputting a cube with colored vertices

Complete source codes of the corresponding C++ and C# programs can be found on the accompanying CD-ROM.

8.2.4. Using Mesh Objects

As you learned in *Chapter 7*, the D3DX library provides a tool that makes working with polygons easy: Mesh objects. They hide from the programmer the tiresome working with vertex and index buffers, making it possible to handle numerous polygons as a single object.

The `ID3DXBaseMesh` interface provides basic functionality for working with meshes: displaying, enumerating elements and vertices, and accessing the vertex and index data. Two other interfaces that inherit from it, `ID3DXMesh` and `ID3DXPMesh`, implement additional capabilities: optimizing meshes to improve performance and automatically adjusting objects to the required level of detail. In Managed DirectX these interfaces, as a rule, are wrapped into the `BaseMesh`, `Mesh`, and `ProgressiveMesh` classes.

In a device, `Mesh` objects are displayed by the `DrawSubset` method, which you used in the previous chapter to draw objects. That example was a bit simplistic, because a `Mesh` object can consist of several parts, each with different characteristics. Consequently, in actual applications, the `DrawSubset` method is usually iterated to display all compound object components, as shown in Listing 8.13.

Listing 8.13. Displaying a compound `Mesh` object [C#]

```
for( int i=0; i < mesh.AttributeTable.Length; i++ )
{
  device.Material = meshMaterials[i];
  device.SetTexture(0, meshTextures[i]);
  mesh.DrawSubset(i);
}
```

`Mesh` objects can be stored in files with the X extension (yes, they are called *X files* in the SDK documentation). Meshes are loaded from files using the `D3DXLoadMeshFromX` function or the `Mesh.FromFile` static method. The DirectX 9.0 SDK has more than 30 of these files: they can be found in the samples\media folder.

There also are methods for creating `Mesh` objects from scratch (the `Mesh` managed class constructor and the `D3DXCreateMesh` function), but they are normally used only in modeling-related applications. 3D objects used in games are created in professional design packages—such as 3DStudio Max or Maya—and then exported into the X format.

The source codes for plug-ins for exporting models from these applications can be found on the MSDN Web site in the **DirectX SDK "Extras" download** section.

8.3. Modeling Visual Effects

This section provides information on some Direct3D tools that allow you to obtain some interesting visual effects.

8.3.1. Light Sources and Materials

To make the scene look more realistic, the lighting must be taken into account. The Direct3D light model keeps track of the color, the propagation direction and distance of the light source, the location of the camera (the view matrix), and the characteristics of the current material to calculate color components for each vertex on the object's surface. The color of each vertex is obtained from the following components: the current color of the material, the specified color of the vertex (given in vertex data), and the color and intensity of the light emitted by the scene's light sources.

There are three types of Direct3D light sources:

- Directional
- Point
- Spotlight

To add lighting to a scene, first enable it and then add the required number of light sources. The latter are defined by the `D3DLIGHT9` structure (the `Light` class in the Managed DirectX version). Remember that each additional light source slows the scene construction.

The source code for creating a directed source of red light with a spatial rotation direction vector is given in Listing 8.14. Note that the `RenderState.Lighting` property must be used to enable or disable the lighting.

Listing 8.14. Creating a rotating light source [C#]

```
device.RenderState.Lighting = TRUE;
Light light = new Light(); // Void constructor
light.Type = LightType.Directional;
light.Diffuse = System.Drawing.Color.Red;
light.Direction = new Vector3(
   (float)System.Math.Cos(System.Environment.TickCount / 250.0f),
   1.0f, (float)System.Math.Sin(Environment.TickCount / 250.0f));
device.RenderState.Lighting = TRUE;
```

As already noted, when calculating vertex lighting, the characteristics of the material being modeled are taken into account: the diffuse, ambient, and emissive colors and the reflection characteristics.

To specify the material parameters, use the `D3DMATERIAL9` structure in Direct3D. To set in the device the current material, use the `IDirect3DDevice9::SetMaterial` function.

8.3.2. Fog Effects

Fog is often used when modeling 3D images, especially when constructing open scenes. There are two reasons for this:

- Putting haze over remote objects makes the image more natural and closer to the reality. A human's subconscious takes fog density into account when automatically estimating distances to objects.
- Fog makes it possible to efficiently regulate the scene-drawing depth and to clip the objects located beyond the fog boundary to speed up the scene drawing.

The Direct3D fog implementation assumes that a proper projective matrix[i] is installed in the device and the fog color specified. The intensity of the 3D-scene elements assuming the fog color will be greater the farther they are from the viewing point.

To take fog into account in C++, use the `SetRenderState` method with the `D3DRS_FOGENABLE` parameter:

```
pDevice->SetRenderState(D3DRS_FOGENABLE, TRUE);
```

In C#, use the `FogEnable` property:

```
device.FogEnable = TRUE;
```

To set, for example, white fog in C++, the following call can be used:

```
pDevice->SetRenderState(D3DRS_FOGCOLOR, 0x00FFFFFF);
```

In C#, this is done by setting the following property:

```
device.RenderState.FogColor = System.Drawing.Color.White;
```

There also are capabilities to adjust the distribution law, fog boundaries, and other parameters. Details on them can be found in the DirectX SDK documentation and in the source code of the **MFCFog** example.

---

[i] A detailed description of the requirements for this matrix can be found in the *W-Friendly Projection Matrix* section of the DirectX documentation.

8.3.3. Applying Textures

Textures are bitmap images applied to the polygons being output; they are an indispensable attribute of almost any 3D scene. Even a coarsely-reproduced object surface will look more realistic if a texture is applied to it. This technique is widely used in computer games.

Some other effects, such as mirror reflections, are modeled with the help of textures. For this, an additional buffer is used, in which the entire scene is reflected. Then the "mirror" surface is overlaid with the texture obtained from this buffer. Modern video cards allow *multitexturing* (i.e., applying several textures to a polygon in one output operation). Multitexturing can also be used to obtain other reflecting surfaces, such as a polished marble floor.

Textures also are Direct3D objects that support the `IDirect3DTexture9` interface. The D3DX library contains a family of handy methods, called `D3DXCreateTextureXXXX`, for creating textures and loading them from the graphics files of popular formats, bitmap resources, etc.

In Managed DirectX, textures are manipulated by the `Texture` class. Textures can be loaded from graphics files by either the `TextureLoader` class or the `Texture` class: it has a constructor that takes as a parameter an instance of the `Bitmap` class, described in *Chapter 5*.

To output polygons with textures applied, the vertex data must be used with the texture coordinates specified. Use the `D3DFVF_TEX0`.. `D3DFVF_TEX8` flags in C++ programs and the corresponding `CustomVertex` classes in C# programs (e.g., colored texture vertices are defined by the `CustomVertex.PositionColoredTextured`-type structure).

Before outputting textured polygons, the necessary textures in the Direct3D device are set using the `SetTexture` method.

8.3.4. Sprites

Sprites are rectangular bitmap images with transparent and semitransparent areas. Sprites are normally used to output small objects, stylized labels, and other bitmaps (e.g., background images).

DirectX graphics have no direct sprite support, and DirectDraw interfaces have been declared obsolete. In Direct3D, sprite output can only be simulated by constructing two textured triangles.

But the D3DX library comes to the rescue again, making the `ID3DXSprite` interface available (in the Managed DirectX version, it is represented by the `Sprite` class).

Its `Draw` method makes sprite output a simple matter. The `DrawTransform` method performs output, taking coordinate transformation matrices (considered in *Section 8.1*) into account.

8.4. Shaders

The size for this book was limited, and we carefully sorted the topics we wanted to present as an introduction to Direct3D. We could not pass over the new 3D graphics technology that was a revolutionary breakthrough in image quality and reality: the shader technology.

What are shaders? They are short procedures that manipulate vertex descriptions or image pixels to achieve supplementary effects. For example, vertex shaders can be used to imitate an image swaying deep under water or to calculate vertex lighting that takes shadows cast by the objects into account. Pixel shaders can color a cartoon image or transform all colors into shades of black and white. Shader use is limited only by the developer's imagination.

What is the difference between shaders and regular code that manipulates vertex and pixel data? Shader code is executed not by the central processing unit (CPU) but by the special block of the modern video cards. This allows the following:

- It dispenses with the standard calculation of the lighting, texturing, geometry, and other scene parameters, implementing instead custom processing logic (e.g., the Phong lighting model, which provides more realistic metallic surfaces).
- It unburdens the CPU from raw graphics calculations, allowing it to perform more "intellectually" demanding tasks, such as modeling the artificial intelligence of the game characters while the shader block is doing its job.
- It speeds up calculations by multisequencing them (several shader blocks can work with the CPU at the same time).

To provide effective instruction on shader use, we would have to write a separate book. Unfortunately, we have limited ourselves to only a brief introduction to this technology. If you would like to learn more about shaders, we advise you to study the DirectX SDK documentation and examples and examine the materials referenced at the end of this chapter.

8.4.1. Vertex Shaders

A vertex shader is a procedure for processing a single vertex. Its input parameters are the vertex data and a set of constants (shader parameters). Its execution modifies the values of the vertex coordinates, its color, and the texture coordinates. Consequently, shaders cannot clip vertices or change their number. Moreover, either the built-in vertex processing or a shader can be used: These processing techniques cannot be combined.

When vertex shaders are enabled, the vertex data described in *Section 8.2* are ignored by Direct3D. A vertex becomes a simple set of data whose format is determined by the program and shader procedure logic.

If vertex shaders are not supported by the video card, they can be successfully simulated by the Direct3D environment software. The performance drop in this case is noticeable, but for most applications it can be tolerated.

8.4.2. Pixel Shaders

Pixel shaders, as follows from their name, operate on individual pixels, or rather on their characteristics: texture coordinates and color and transparency values. The execution result of such a shader is the color of the frame buffer pixel, which can undergo further transformations (e.g., to take fog into account).

Unlike vertex shaders, pixel shaders cannot be simulated with acceptable speed using software; therefore, when selecting a Direct3D hardware device, you must rely on the selected video adapter's support of pixel shaders. Pixel shaders can be simulated by software, but the drastic performance drop (it can take several seconds to calculate just one frame) makes this simulation sensible for debugging only.

8.4.3. The Development Tools: Assembler and HLSL

Shader instructions are binary data loaded into a Direct3D device. Theoretically, it is possible to create your own block of the necessary data. But machine code programming is passé in the 21st century, so more convenient tools exist for shader construction.

Since DirectX 8.0, a special Assembly-level language for developing shaders has been available to programmers. The SDK includes two utilities for compiling vertex and pixel shaders: *vsa.exe* and *psa.exe*, respectively.

Constructing shaders in such a low-level language is rather difficult, so a high-level language, similar to C, was introduced in DirectX 9.0. It is called Microsoft High-Level Shader Language (HLSL).

By a strange coincidence, not long before DirectX 9.0 came out, Nvidia announced a new shader development language called Cg, whose instruction syntax is identical to HLSL. These names designate the same product developed jointly by Microsoft and Nvidia. Because Nvidia video cards support not only Direct3D but also its competitor, OpenGL API, the company included the support of Cg shaders in its OpenGL implementation.

But return to Direct3D. There are three main ways to use HLSL code in your program:

- Compile the shader's source code into a binary pixel or vertex module using the fxc.exe command line compiler (located in the bin folder of the DirectX 9.0 SDK installation folder). This method makes it possible to use HLSL shaders even in DirectX 8.0 (if the video card supports them). To use these modules, they have to be loaded into the device using the CreatePixelShader and CreateVertexShader methods.
- The D3DX library has an auxiliary function, D3DXAssembleShader, that allows compilation to be done on the fly. Afterward, the data created by this function need to be loaded using the CreatePixelShader and CreateVertexShader methods.
- The easiest way is to use the D3DXCreateEffectFromFile and D3DXCreateEffectFromResource functions. They automatically compile the shader's source code from an external file or resource and load it into the device.

In addition, the Direct3D SDK has an effectedit.exe utility, a simple HLSL shader development environment. It includes a text editor window and compilation, parameter setting, and preview tools (Fig. 8.7).

There are other shader procedure development and debugging tools. For example, ATI Technologies' *RenderMonkey* is a handy product (Fig. 8.8). Despite its jocular name, this is a serious package for game and 3D-effects developers. It includes an HLSL editor with the syntax highlighting feature, a shader disassembler, and an extensive effects library.

You can download this package from the **http://www.ati.com/developer** site for free.

Part IV: Using the DirectX 9 Library

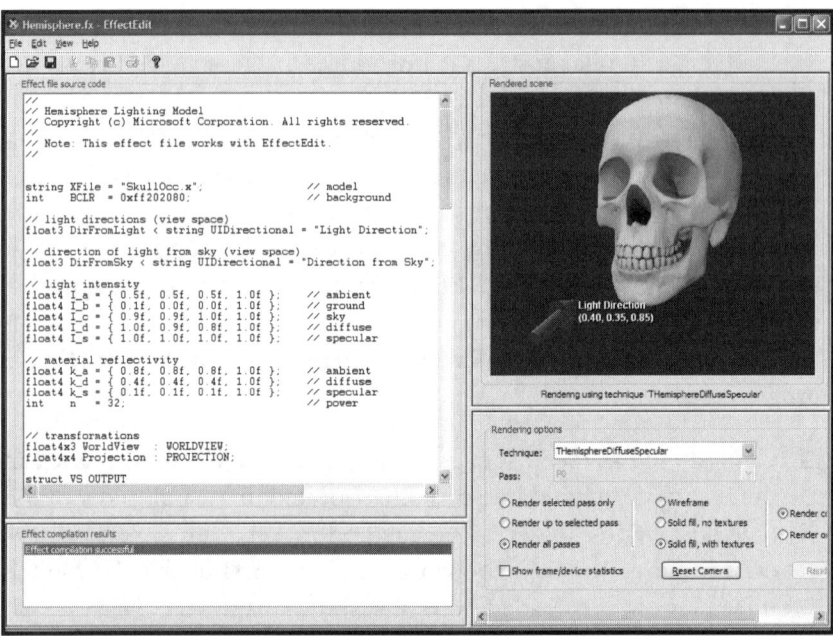

Fig. 8.7. EffectEdit visual shader development environment

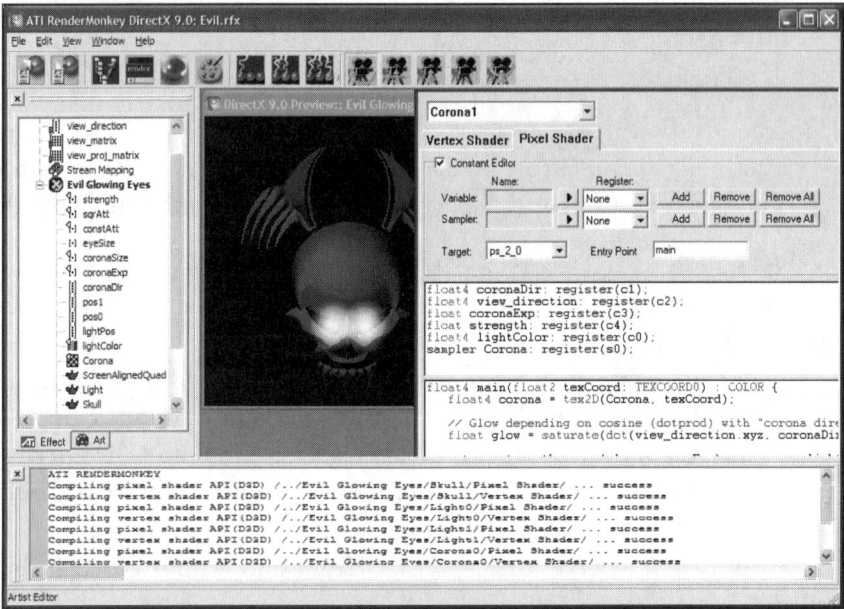

Fig. 8.8. RenderMonkey package

8.5. Conclusion

This concludes the second chapter devoted to exploring the rich capabilities of the Direct3D library. We tried to make mastering this library easy for beginners, but to move on you will need more study. To help you, we provide references to some of the online resources we consider most useful to developers of Direct3D graphics and especially games.

8.5.1. Internet Resources

- http://msdn.microsoft.com/directx/

    DirectX Developers Center—The heart of the Microsoft DirectX documentation. Articles, examples, and updates for DirectX programming packages.
- http://www.ati.com/developer/techpapers.html

    ATI Developer: Technology Papers and Presentations—An ATI site for 3 graphics developers.
- http://developer.nvidia.com/page/documentation.html

    Nvidia Developers Documentation—Developers' manuals, the newest Nvidia product SDKs, and answers to FAQs.
- http://gamedev.net/

    GameDev.net—An international game developers' site. Many interesting Direct3D and OpenGL materials.

Good luck mastering 3D graphics.

APPENDIXES

Appendix 1: Mathematical Fundamentals of Spline Construction 307

Appendix 2: Mathematical Fundamentals for Plane and 3D Transformations 315

Appendix 3: General Information about Raster Graphics 339

Appendix 1: Mathematical Fundamentals of Spline Construction

A1.1. Definitions

First, a few general definitions need to be given.

- A *spline* is a curve that meets certain smoothness criteria.
- Fixed *anchor points* form a set of points, upon which the spline is constructed.
- *Interpolation* is the construction of a curve that passes through a set of anchor points.
- *Approximation* is the construction of a smooth curve that passes not necessary through but near a set of anchor points.
- *Extrapolation* is the construction of a line beyond the limits of the interval specified by a set of anchor points.

In the simplest case, interpolation can be implemented by connecting the anchor points with straight line segments (Fig. A1.1); this method is called *linear interpolation*. This curve passes through the set of anchor points and is suitable, for example, for depicting currency exchange rate dynamics. However, if a set of anchor points was obtained as a result of some experimentation, linear interpolation may not reflect exactly the behavior of the experiment's object on the intervals between the anchor points. Moreover, this type of interpolation is often deficient from the aesthetic viewpoint. Therefore, interpolation using some smooth curve may be more acceptable.

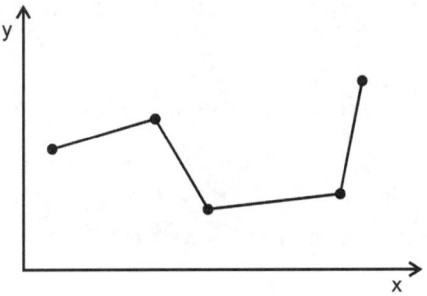

Fig. A1.1. Linear interpolation

The smoothness criterion is determined by the derivatives of the function describing the curve: The order of a curve's smoothness is the maximum order of the continuous derivative of the curve. A function is usually considered smooth if it has a continuous first- or second-order derivative.

A smooth interpolation curve of $n + 1$ anchor points can be constructed with the help of the nth degree polynomial.

A *polynomial* is a function of the type given in the following equation:

$$f(x) = a_n x^n + a_{n-1} x^{n-1} + \ldots + a_1 x + a_0 = y \qquad \text{A1.1}$$

In A1.1, the unknowns are the a_i coefficients of the polynomial, in which $i = (0, 1, \ldots, n)$. To find them, coordinates from the anchor points set are substituted into the equation $n + 1$ times. This produces a system of $n + 1$ equations linear with respect to a_i.

For example, if the set consists of three points, the polynomial degree will be $n = 2$ and the a_i coefficients can be obtained from the following system of equations:

$$\begin{cases} a_2 x_1^2 + a_1 x_1 + a_0 = y_1 \\ a_2 x_2^2 + a_1 x_2 + a_0 = y_2 \\ a_2 x_3^2 + a_1 x_3 + a_0 = y_3 \end{cases}$$

Appendix 1: Mathematical Fundamentals of Spline Construction

When constructing the equation system, it is important that no two points have identical coordinates in the set; otherwise, the system will have no solution.

The shortcomings of the method when the entire anchor points set is defined by one function are the following:

- Graphs of high-degree polynomials typically swing widely in the intervals between the anchor points.
- Beyond the anchor points' interval limits, polynomials have a tendency to increase or decrease infinitely.
- The more points in a set (the higher the degree of the polynomial), the more equations in the system to find the coefficients.

To avoid these complications, smooth curves are constructed from separate segments.

A second-order smoothness compound curve can be formed from regular third-degree polynomial arcs. Four anchor points are needed to calculate the coefficients of such a polynomial. Consequently, each segment of a compound curve is built on the control of four points. To provide a smooth transition between the segments, only the part of the curve lying between the two inside points of each 4-tuple is used. The 4-tuples are chosen so that they overlap each other—that is, the second point of the previous 4-tuple is chosen as the first point of the next 4-tuple. For example, segment 1 (Fig. A1.2) is constructed on the anchor points 0, 1, 2, and 3; segment 2 is constructed on the anchor points 1, 2, 3, and 4, and so on. With this approach, to build a curve beginning at the first point and ending at the last point of the control set, these endpoints are doubled.

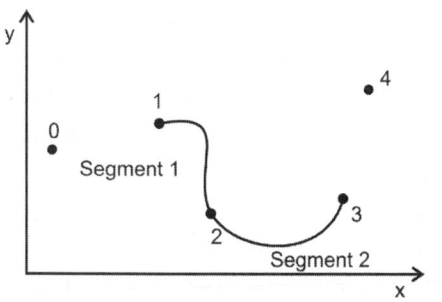
Fig. A1.2. A cardinal spline

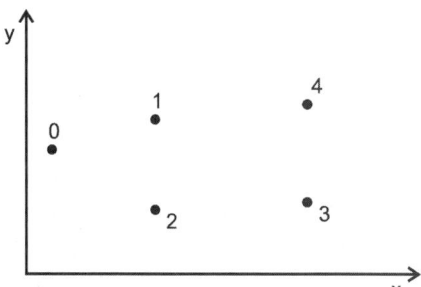
Fig. A1.3. An unacceptable set of points

The preceding description of curve construction assumes that the coordinates of the anchor points are given as $y_i(x_i)$ and are located in the ascending order of the value of their abscissas. For example, different points with coinciding abscissas (Fig. A1.3) are not allowed. Consequently, it is convenient to describe complex curves (closed or self-intersecting) with the help of parametric equations.

A1.2. Specifying Curves Parametrically

Equations of the following type are *parametric* representations of a curve (in 3D space in the given case):

$$x = x(t), y = y(t), z = z(t), \alpha \leq t \leq \beta \qquad \text{A1.2}$$

The variable t is the parameter.

Denote functions $x(t)$, $y(t)$, and $z(t)$ by vector R: $R(t) = (x(t), y(t), z(t))$; the anchor points array will be denoted by vector P: $P = \{P_i = (x_i, y_i, z_i), i = 0, 1, 2, ..., n\}$. An individual spline is calculated for each coordinate. The position of a point corresponding to a given t on each of the $x(t)$, $y(t)$, $z(t)$ parametric curves is the position of an (x, y, z) point on the spline. The value $t = \alpha$ corresponds to the spline's starting point, and the value of $t = \beta$ corresponds to the spline's endpoint. Stepping through the values from α to β, the t parameter specifies the location of each spline's point.

In practice, a spline is usually constructed from individual segments defined by elementary, and as a rule third-degree, equations. The procedure is as follows:

1. To build a curve on the interval between points i and $i + 1$, a 4-tuple of points numbered $i - 1$, i, $i + 1$, and $i + 2$ is taken.
2. The parameter range of values is specified as $0 \leq t \leq 1$. The parameter value of $t = 0$ corresponds to the starting point of the curve segment between points i and $i + 1$. The parameter value of $t = 1$ corresponds to the endpoint of this curve segment. The range $0 < t < 1$ corresponds to the inner points of the given segment.
3. The parameter range is broken into m parts (e.g., $m = 10$).
4. Based on the values of the corresponding coordinates of the anchor points 4-tuple and the t_k value, $k = (0, 1, ..., m)$, m inner points of the spline are calculated on the segment between the anchor points numbered i and $i + 1$.
5. The points calculated in the previous step are connected by straight lines. Consequently, the higher the m value, the more closely approximated the spline will be.

Appendix 1: Mathematical Fundamentals of Spline Construction

The advantages of this approach are the following:

- Calculations are simplified.
- Low-order equations are used.
- When a point is added to the anchor points set, only four segments of the curve need to be recalculated.

In building compound curves, it is important to meet certain smoothness conditions in their joint points. Only then will the compound curve have reasonably good geometric characteristics. This requirement can be met by using the class of *geometrically continuous* curves.

A compound curve is geometrically continuous if along this curve the unit vector of its tangent changes continuously; a curve is called *doubly geometrically continuous* if its curvature vector also changes continuously.

A1.3. Spline Varieties

There are many splines possessing different properties. Here are examples of some of them.

A1.3.1. The Catmull-Rom Interpolation Spline

For an array of points P_0, P_1, P_2, and P_3, a Catmull-Rom spline is defined by the following type of equation:

$$R(t) = \frac{1}{2}\left(-t(1-t)^2 P_0 + (2 - 5t^2 + 3t^3)P_1 + t(1 + 4t - 3t^2)P_2 - t^2(1-t)P_3\right), \quad \text{A1.3}$$

$$0 \leq t \leq 1$$

A compound Catmull-Rom spline has the following properties:

- It passes through the anchor points.
- It is geometrically continuous.
- The curve is uniquely defined by the basis function set; that is, its shape cannot be adjusted.

Because a Catmull-Rom spline is of the interpolation type, it passes through each of the anchor points. However, when a compound spline is built, each segment is calculated based on the interval between the two inner points of the next

4-tuple of the set. Therefore, to construct a compound interpolating spline starting in the first anchor point and ending in the last anchor point, it is enough to add to the control-points set the copies of the first and last points. The copy of the first anchor point is added at the beginning of the set, and the copy of the last anchor point is added at the end of the set.

A closed interpolated spline can be built by adding points $P_{n+1} = P_0$, $P_{n+2} = P_1$, and $P_{n+3} = P_2$ to the n-point control-points set.

A1.3.2. The Basic Beta-Spline

For a specified array of P_0, P_1, P_2, and P_3 points, a Beta-spline is defined by the following equation:

$$R(t) = b_0(t)P_0 + b_1(t)P_1 + b_2(t)P_2 + b_3(t)P_3,$$
$$0 \leq t \leq 1$$

A1.4

The functional coefficients $b_0(t)$, $b_1(t)$, $b_2(t)$, and $b_3(t)$ are specified by the following equations:

$$b_0(t) = \frac{2\beta_1^3}{\delta}(1-t)^3$$

$$b_1(t) = \frac{1}{\delta}\left(2\beta_1^3 t(t^2 - 3t + 3) + 2\beta_1^2(t^3 - 3t + 2) + 2\beta_1(t^3 - 3t + 2) + \beta_2(2t^3 - 3t^2 + 1)\right)$$

$$b_2(t) = \frac{1}{\delta}\left(2\beta_1^2 t^2(-t + 3) + 2\beta_1 t(-t^2 + 3) + 2\beta_2 t^2(-2t + 3) + 2(-t^3 + 1)\right)$$

$$b_3(t) = \frac{2t^3}{\delta}$$

Here, $\beta_1 > 0$, $\beta_2 \geq 0$, and $\delta = 2\beta_1^3 + 4\beta_1^2 + 4\beta_1 + \beta_2 + 2$.

The numeric β_1 and β_2 parameters are called the *Beta-spline shape* parameters; the β_1 parameter is the *slope* (displacement) parameter, and the β_2 parameter is the *tension* parameter.

The properties of a Beta-spline are as follows:

- It lies inside the convex hull specified by the anchor points.
- It is a doubly geometrically continuous spline.
- Its shape can be adjusted by the β_1 and β_2 parameters.

A compound Beta-spline, as a rule, does not pass through any of the anchor points. However, it is known that the starting point of a curve lies in the triangle formed by the first three anchor points and that the endpoint lies in the triangle formed by the last three anchor points. Consequently, to construct a compound Beta-spline starting in the first anchor point and ending in the last anchor point, it is sufficient to add two copies of the first point and two copies of the last point to the control-points set.

A closed Beta-spline can be built by adding points $P_{n+1} = P_0$, $P_{n+2} = P_1$, and $P_{n+3} = P_2$ to the n-point control-point set.

A1.3.3. The Bezier Spline

For a specified array of anchor points, an elementary cubic Bezier spline is defined by the following equation :

$$R(t) = (((1-t)P_0 + 3tP_1)(1-t) + 3t^2P_2)(1-t) + t^3P_3,$$

$$0 \le t \le 1$$

A1.5

An elementary spline starts at point P_0 and ends at point P_3, touching the P_0P_1 and P_2P_3 segments.

The Bezier spline properties are as follows:

❐ It lies within a convex hull specified by the anchor points.
❐ The spline is uniquely defined by a set of basic functions; that is, its shape cannot be adjusted.

For a compound Bezier spline to be geometrically continuous, the three points in the joint (the connection point and the two adjacent points) must lie on one straight line. For example, suppose there are six anchor points: P_0, ..., P_5. To build a geometrically continuous compound spline, this set is supplemented by an auxiliary point, P_*, taken at the middle of the P_2P_3 segment (Fig. A1.4). A compound spline is constructed from two elementary cubic Bezier splines for the P_0, P_1, P_2, P_* and P_*, P_3, P_4, P_5 anchor points 4-tuples.

Cubic Bezier splines are popular in computer graphics. For example, in Corel-Draw, Bezier splines serve as the basis, on which all other types of lines are built. The **Curve** mode can be enabled for any line segment. This is done by selecting the second node of the segment and issuing the **convert to Curve** command. In the **Curve** mode, two points equidistant from the segment's end *anchor points* (P_* and P_{**}) are added to the segment (Fig. A1.5). The 4-tuple of the P_0, P_*, P_{**}, P_1 points defines the Bezier spline. The position of the points can be changed, with CorelDraw calculating the spline's shape (Fig. A1.6).

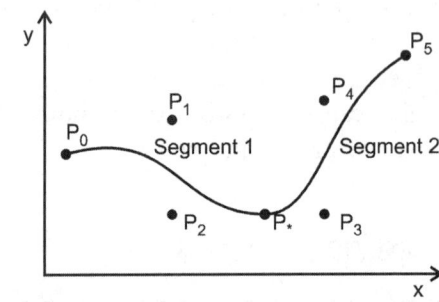

Fig. A1.4. Constructing a compound Bezier curve

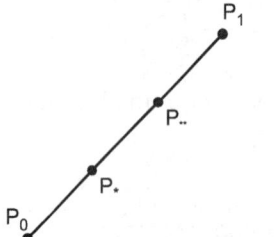

Fig. A1.5. Converting a segment into a curve

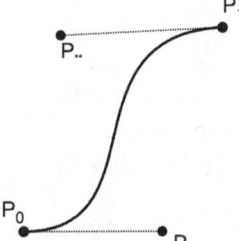

Fig. A1.6. Changing the curve's shape

The material considered here is implemented in the *Bezier* program, which can be found on the accompanying CD-ROM.

The Bezier splines were not forgotten in the GDI+ library. Building splines with the help of GDI+ is considered in *Section 2.2.3*.

Appendix 2: Mathematical Fundamentals for Plane and 3D Transformations

A2.1. Vectors

A *vector* is a directed straight-line segment.
Vectors and their parts are designated by the following conventional symbols:

- P, Q—Segment endpoints
- **a**, **b**, **c**—Vectors
- **0**—A zero-length vector
- |**a**|—The vector length that equals the distance between the endpoints
- −**a**—An |**a**|-length vector whose direction is opposite that of **a**
- p, q—Real numbers

A2.1.1. Vector Properties

Vectors are not modified by parallel translation (Fig. A2.1).
Summing two vectors produces a vector: **a** + **b** = **c** (Fig. A2.2).
A p**a** product is a vector of the |p||**a**| length; if $p = 0$ or **a** = 0, then p**a** = 0 (Fig. A2.3).

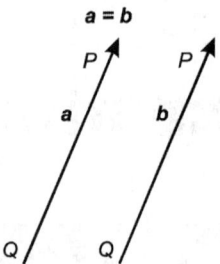

Fig. A2.1. Parallel translation of vectors

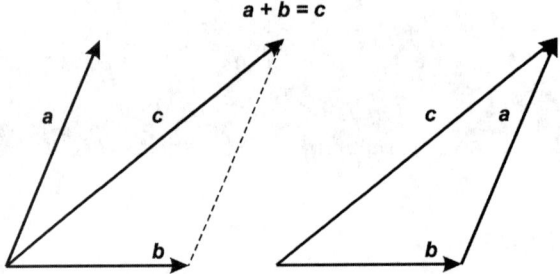

Fig. A2.2. Addition of two vectors

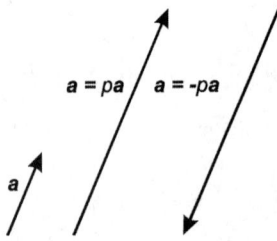

Fig. A2.3. Multiplication of a vector by a real number

If $p > 0$, the direction of the resulting vector coincides with the direction of **a**; if $p < 0$, the direction of the resulting vector is opposite the direction of **a**.

The following rules are true for vectors:

- $\mathbf{a} + \mathbf{b} = \mathbf{b} + \mathbf{a}$
- $(\mathbf{a} + \mathbf{b}) + \mathbf{c} = \mathbf{a} + (\mathbf{b} + \mathbf{c})$
- $\mathbf{a} + 0 = \mathbf{a}$
- $\mathbf{a} + (-\mathbf{a}) = 0$
- $p(\mathbf{a} + \mathbf{b}) = p\mathbf{a} + p\mathbf{b}$

Appendix 2: Mathematical Fundamentals for Plane and 3D Transformations

- $(p + q)\mathbf{a} = p\mathbf{a} + q\mathbf{a}$
- $1\mathbf{a} = \mathbf{a}$
- $0\mathbf{a} = \mathbf{0}$

In the orthogonal 3D coordinate system, the direction of the axes is specified by three perpendicular unit vectors **i**, **j**, and **k**.

In the *right-handed* coordinate system, when a right-hand screw is turned so that its head slot moves from lining up with the **i** vector to lining up with the **j** vector in the shortest way, the direction of the **k** vector coincides with its forward movement (Fig. A2.4). The starting point of the vectors is denoted by the letter O.

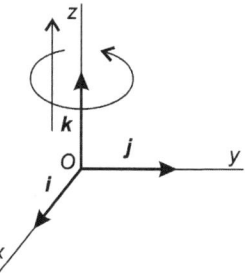

Fig. A2.4. Right-handed coordinate system

Any vector, **V**, can be written as an **i**, **j**, **k** linear combination:

$$\mathbf{V} = x\mathbf{i} + y\mathbf{j} + z\mathbf{k}$$

Here, x, y, and z are the linear coordinates of the vector's $\mathbf{V} = OP$ endpoint P. Vector **V** can be represented as follows:

$$\mathbf{V} = [x \ y \ z] \text{ or } \begin{bmatrix} x \\ y \\ z \end{bmatrix}$$

A2.1.2. The Vector Dot Product

The *dot product* of two vectors, **a** and **b**, is represented as $\mathbf{a} \cdot \mathbf{b}$: $p = \mathbf{a} \cdot \mathbf{b}$ and is defined as shown in the equation below.

$$\mathbf{a} \cdot \mathbf{b} = |\mathbf{a}||\mathbf{b}|\cos\gamma \qquad \text{A2.1}$$

Here, γ is the angle between **a** and **b**. The dot product is a real number. Applying A2.1 to unit vectors **i, j**, and **k** produces the following:

$$\mathbf{i}\cdot\mathbf{i}=\mathbf{j}\cdot\mathbf{j}=\mathbf{k}\cdot\mathbf{k}=1; \quad \mathbf{i}\cdot\mathbf{j}=\mathbf{j}\cdot\mathbf{i}=\mathbf{j}\cdot\mathbf{k}=\mathbf{k}\cdot\mathbf{j}=\mathbf{k}\cdot\mathbf{i}=\mathbf{i}\cdot\mathbf{k}=0 \qquad \text{A2.2}$$

The properties of the dot product are the following:

- $p(q\mathbf{a}\cdot\mathbf{b}) = pq(\mathbf{a}\cdot\mathbf{b})$
- $(p\mathbf{a} + q\mathbf{b})\cdot\mathbf{c} = p\mathbf{a}\cdot\mathbf{c} + q\mathbf{b}\cdot\mathbf{c}$
- $\mathbf{a}\cdot\mathbf{b} = \mathbf{b}\cdot\mathbf{a}$
- $\mathbf{a}\cdot\mathbf{a} = 0$, if $\mathbf{a} = \mathbf{0}$

The dot product of two vectors, $\mathbf{a} = [a_1\ a_2\ a_3]$ and $\mathbf{b} = [b_1\ b_2\ b_3]$, is the sum of the products of the components of the vector:

$$\mathbf{a}\cdot\mathbf{b} = a_1 b_1 + a_2 b_2 + a_3 b_3 \qquad \text{A2.3}$$

A2.3 follows from $\mathbf{a}\cdot\mathbf{b} = (a_1\mathbf{i} + a_2\mathbf{j} + a_3\mathbf{k})\cdot(b_1\mathbf{i} + b_2\mathbf{j} + b_3\mathbf{k})$, with the dot product properties and A2.2 taken into account.

A2.1.3. The Vector Cross Product

The *cross product* of two vectors, **a** and **b**, is represented as $\mathbf{c} = \mathbf{a} \times \mathbf{b}$. The result of the cross product of two vectors is a vector. The length of vector **c** is as follows:

$$|\mathbf{c}| = |\mathbf{a}||\mathbf{b}|\sin\gamma \qquad \text{A2.4}$$

Here, γ is the angle between the **a** and **b** vectors. The direction of the **c** vector is perpendicular to the plane, in which the **a** and **b** vectors lie, and is such that the **a**, **b**, and **c** vectors form a right-handed 3-tuple in the order they are listed. This means that if vector **a** is turned toward vector **b** through an angle less than 180 degrees, the direction of the **c** vector coincides with the forward direction of a right-handed screw turned in the same direction.

The properties of the cross product of vectors are the following:

- If $\mathbf{a} = p\mathbf{b}$, p being a real number, then $\mathbf{c} = \mathbf{a} \times \mathbf{b} = \mathbf{0}$ — follows from A2.4.
- With p being a constant, the following equalities hold:

$$(p\mathbf{a}) \times \mathbf{b} = p(\mathbf{a} \times \mathbf{b})$$

Appendix 2: Mathematical Fundamentals for Plane and 3D Transformations

$$\mathbf{a} \times (\mathbf{b} + \mathbf{c}) = \mathbf{a} \times \mathbf{b} + \mathbf{a} \times \mathbf{c}$$

$$\mathbf{a} \times \mathbf{b} = \overline{\mathbf{b} \times \mathbf{a}}$$

In the general case, $\mathbf{a} \times (\mathbf{b} \times \mathbf{c}) \neq (\mathbf{a} \times \mathbf{b}) \times \mathbf{c}$

For the right-handed orthogonal coordinate system defined by vectors $\mathbf{i}, \mathbf{j}, \mathbf{k}$, the following equalities hold:

$$\mathbf{i} \times \mathbf{i} = \mathbf{j} \times \mathbf{j} = \mathbf{k} \times \mathbf{k} = 0;\ \mathbf{i} \times \mathbf{j} = \mathbf{k};\ \mathbf{j} \times \mathbf{k} = \mathbf{i};$$

$$\mathbf{k} \times \mathbf{i} = \mathbf{j};\ \mathbf{j} \times \mathbf{i} = -\mathbf{k};\ \mathbf{k} \times \mathbf{j} = -\mathbf{i};\ \mathbf{i} \times \mathbf{k} = -\mathbf{j}$$

Accounting for these equalities in the vector cross product produces the following equation:

$$\mathbf{a} \times \mathbf{b} = (a_1\mathbf{i} + a_2\mathbf{j} + a_3\mathbf{k}) \times (b_1\mathbf{i} + b_2\mathbf{j} + b_3\mathbf{k})$$

From this, the following is obtained:

$$\mathbf{a} \times \mathbf{b} = (a_2 b_3 - a_3 b_2)\mathbf{i} + (a_3 b_1 - a_1 b_3)\mathbf{j} + (a_1 b_2 - a_2 b_1)\mathbf{k} \quad \text{A2.5}$$

The right-hand part of A2.5 is the expression of a third-order *determinant* (see A2.11). Consequently, A2.5 can be written in a matrix notation.

$$\mathbf{a} \times \mathbf{b} = \begin{vmatrix} \mathbf{i} & \mathbf{j} & \mathbf{k} \\ a_1 & a_2 & a_3 \\ b_1 & b_2 & b_3 \end{vmatrix} \quad \text{A2.6}$$

A2.2. Determinants

Consider the following system of equations:

$$\begin{cases} a_1 x + b_1 y = c_1 \\ a_2 x + b_2 y = c_2 \end{cases} \quad \text{A2.7}$$

If $a_1 b_2 - a_2 b_1 \neq 0$, then to solve the system of A2.7, the first equation is multiplied by b_2, and the second one is multiplied by $-b_1$. The products are then summed, producing the following: $(a_1 b_2 - a_2 b_1)x = b_2 c_1 - b_1 c_2$. Then, the first equation is multiplied by $-a_2$ and the second one is multiplied by a_1. The products are summed, producing the following: $(a_1 b_2 - a_2 b_1)y = a_1 c_2 - a_2 c_1$.

If $a_1b_2 - a_2b_1 \neq 0$, then the following is true:

$$x = \frac{b_2c_1 - b_1c_2}{a_1b_2 - a_2b_1}; \qquad y = \frac{a_1c_2 - a_2c_1}{a_1b_2 - a_2b_1} \qquad \text{A2.8}$$

The expression in the divisor can be written as follows:

$$D = \begin{vmatrix} a_1 & b_1 \\ a_2 & b_2 \end{vmatrix} = a_1b_2 - a_2b_1 \qquad \text{A2.9}$$

A2.9 is called the second-order determinant.
Using determinants, A2.7 can be written as follows:

$$x = \frac{D_1}{D}, \; y = \frac{D_2}{D}, \text{ with } D \neq 0 \qquad \text{A2.10}$$

Here, $D_1 = \begin{vmatrix} c_1 & b_1 \\ c_2 & b_2 \end{vmatrix}$, $D_2 = \begin{vmatrix} a_1 & c_1 \\ a_2 & c_2 \end{vmatrix}$.

D_i ($i = 1, 2$) is obtained by replacing the ith column with the right-hand part of the system of A2.7. This method is called *Cramer's rule*, and it can be used to solve systems of more than two equations.

The third-order determinant looks as follows:

$$D = \begin{vmatrix} a_1 & b_1 & c_1 \\ a_2 & b_2 & c_2 \\ a_3 & b_3 & c_3 \end{vmatrix} = a_1 \begin{vmatrix} b_2 & c_2 \\ b_3 & c_3 \end{vmatrix} - a_2 \begin{vmatrix} b_1 & c_1 \\ b_3 & c_3 \end{vmatrix} + a_3 \begin{vmatrix} b_1 & c_1 \\ b_2 & c_2 \end{vmatrix} \qquad \text{A2.11}$$

Higher-order determinants are written in the same way.

A2.2.1. Properties of Determinants

Transposing columns and rows does not affect the determinant's value, as shown here:

$$\begin{vmatrix} a_1 & b_1 \\ a_2 & b_2 \end{vmatrix} = \begin{vmatrix} a_1 & a_2 \\ b_1 & b_2 \end{vmatrix}$$

Appendix 2: Mathematical Fundamentals for Plane and 3D Transformations

Switching the places of rows or columns changes the determinant's sign as follows:

$$\begin{vmatrix} a_1 & b_1 & c_1 \\ a_2 & b_2 & c_2 \\ a_3 & b_3 & c_3 \end{vmatrix} = - \begin{vmatrix} a_1 & b_1 & c_1 \\ a_3 & b_3 & c_3 \\ a_2 & b_2 & c_2 \end{vmatrix}$$

Multiplying any row or column by a number multiplies the determinant's value by the same number, as shown here:

$$\begin{vmatrix} pa_1 & pb_1 \\ a_2 & b_2 \end{vmatrix} = p \begin{vmatrix} a_1 & a_2 \\ b_1 & b_2 \end{vmatrix}$$

Modifying a row (or column) by adding corresponding elements of another row (or column) multiplied by a constant will not change the value of the determinant, as shown here:

$$\begin{vmatrix} a_1 & b_1 & c_1 \\ a_2 & b_2 & c_2 \\ a_3 + pa_1 & b_3 + pb_1 & c_3 + pc_1 \end{vmatrix} = \begin{vmatrix} a_1 & b_1 & c_1 \\ a_2 & b_2 & c_2 \\ a_3 & b_3 & c_3 \end{vmatrix}$$

If a row (or column) is a linear combination of other rows (or columns), the determinant's value equals zero, as follows:

$$\begin{vmatrix} a_1 & b_1 & c_1 \\ a_2 & b_2 & c_2 \\ pa_1 + qa_2 & pb_1 + qb_2 & pc_1 + qc_2 \end{vmatrix} = 0$$

Determinants make it possible to describe various geometric figures in a convenient form. For example, the equation of a straight line passing through points $P_1 = (x_1, y_1)$, $P_2 = (x_2, y_2)$ in a 2D space (R^2) can be written as follows:

$$\begin{vmatrix} x & y & 1 \\ x_1 & y_1 & 1 \\ x_2 & x_2 & 1 \end{vmatrix} = 0 \qquad \text{A2.12}$$

If, for example, $x = x_1$, $y = y_1$, then the first row is a linear combination; consequently, $D = 0$.

A plane passing through points $P_1 = (x_1, y_1, z_1)$, $P_2 = (x_2, y_2, z_2)$, $P_3 = (x_3, y_3, z_3)$ in a 3D space (R^3) can be defined as follows:

$$\begin{vmatrix} x & y & z & 1 \\ x_1 & y_1 & z_1 & 1 \\ x_2 & y_2 & z_2 & 1 \\ x_3 & y_3 & z_3 & 1 \end{vmatrix} = 0 \qquad \text{A2.13}$$

A2.3. Homogeneous Coordinates

Equation $aX + bY + c = 0$ defines a straight line in R^2. Substitute X for x/w and Y for y/w, you obtain the equation $a(x/w) + b(y/w) + c = 0$, which can be written as follows:

$$ax + by + cw = 0 \qquad \text{A2.14}$$

Equations of the A2.14 type are called *homogeneous* because the structure of their ax, by, and cw terms is the same; consequently, x, y, and w are called homogeneous coordinates of point (X, Y).

If $w = 1$ (in the x, y, w system, the 2D space lies in the $w = 1$ plane), then A2.14 describes a plane passing through the coordinate origin and the given straight line.

Assuming that (x, y, w) is another way of writing $(x/w, y/w)$, w must not equal zero. However, certain useful properties of homogeneous coordinates become apparent when no such requirement is made.

Consider the following system:

$$\begin{cases} 2x + 3y - 6 = 0 \\ 4x + 6y - 24 = 0 \end{cases} \qquad \text{A2.15}$$

This system defines two parallel lines and has no solution.

Changing the coordinates to homogeneous ones converts the system of A2.15 to that of A2.16.

$$\begin{cases} 2x + 3y - 6w = 0 \\ 4x + 6y - 24w = 0 \end{cases} \qquad \text{A2.16}$$

The system of A2.16 has at least one solution: $(x = 0, y = 0, w = 0)$.

The following system is equivalent to the system of A2.16:

$$\begin{cases} 2x + 3y = 0 \\ w = 0 \end{cases} \qquad \text{A2.16, a}$$

Therefore, A2.17 is valid:

$$\frac{x}{y} = \frac{-2}{3} \qquad \text{A2.17}$$

Consequently, a solution of the system of A2.16 consists of all points $(3p, -2p, 0)$, where p is any number. In the x, y, w space, these points form a straight line passing through points $(0, 0, 0)$ and $(3, -2, 0)$. The specific line is an infinity line; its points can be considered the $(3p, -2p, w)$ limit points when w approaches zero.

A2.4. Using Homogeneous Coordinates

In regular 2D coordinates, linear planar transformations can be written as follows:

$$[x' \; y'] = [x \; y] \mathbf{A}$$

Here, **A** is the following transformation matrix:

$$\mathbf{A} = \begin{bmatrix} a_1 & a_2 \\ b_1 & b_2 \end{bmatrix}$$

The **A** matrix maps points $[1 \; 0]$ and $[0 \; 1]$ onto points $[a_1 \; a_2]$ and $[b_1 \; b_2]$. However, regardless of the type of the **A** matrix, point $[0 \; 0]$ will be mapped onto the $[0 \; 0]$ point; therefore, this method cannot be used to perform the operation of translating points to a new position. In the homogeneous coordinates, a point in 2D space is specified by a 3-tuple (x, y, w) and transformations are written as $[x' \; y' \; w'] = [x \; y \; w]\mathbf{A}$:

$$\mathbf{A} = \begin{bmatrix} a_1 & a_2 & a_3 \\ b_1 & b_2 & b_3 \\ c_1 & c_2 & c_3 \end{bmatrix}$$

In this case, the following transformations take place:

$$[1 \ 0 \ 0]A = [a_1 \ a_2 \ a_3]$$
$$[0 \ 1 \ 0]A = [b_1 \ b_2 \ b_3]$$
$$[0 \ 0 \ 1]A = [c_1 \ c_2 \ c_3]$$

This means that the homogeneous coordinates can be used to express any transformations through matrix multiplication.

A2.5. Planar Transformations

Consider the following system:

$$\begin{cases} x' = x + a \\ y' = y \end{cases} \qquad \text{A2.18}$$

The system of A2.18 can mean either that all points in the $x - y$ plane are translated to the right over the a distance (Fig. A2.5) or that the coordinate axis is translated to the left over the same a distance (Fig. A2.6).

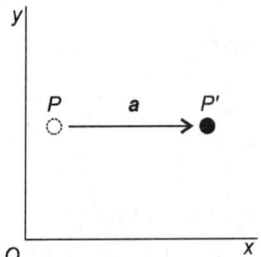
Fig. A2.5. Point translation

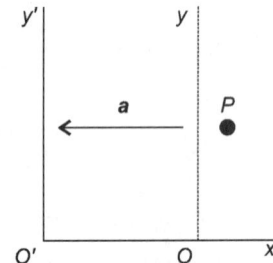
Fig. A2.6. Coordinate system translation

In more complex situations, the same transformation can be similarly considered as either changing the point coordinates or changing the coordinate system.

The general translation operation is given by A2.19.

$$\begin{cases} x' = x + a \\ y' = y + b \end{cases} \qquad \text{A2.19}$$

Appendix 2: Mathematical Fundamentals for Plane and 3D Transformations

Consider now the operation of rotating point $P = (x, y)$ through angle φ about the coordinate origin O to point $P' = (x', y')$ (Fig. A2.7). The new coordinates of the point are calculated with the help of the following system:

$$\begin{cases} x' = ax + by \\ y' = cx + dy \end{cases} \qquad \text{A2.20}$$

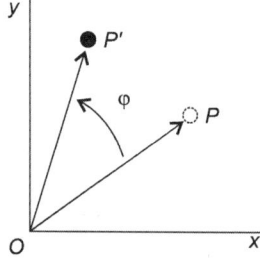

Fig. A2.7. Rotating point P through angle φ around the coordinate origin O to point P'

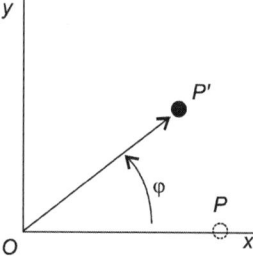

Fig. A2.8. Rotating point P through angle φ around the coordinate origin O to point P' for $P = (1, 0)$

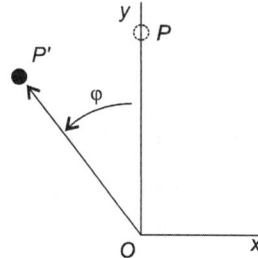

Fig. A2.9. Rotating point P through angle φ around the coordinate origin O to point P' for $P = (0, 1)$

Consider Fig. A2.8. When $P = (1, 0)$, then $x' = a$ and $y' = c$. From Fig. A2.8, find $a = \cos \varphi$, $c = \sin \varphi$.

Similarly, when $P = (0, 1)$: $b = -\sin \varphi$ and $d = \cos \varphi$ (Fig. A2.9).

Consequently, rotation about the coordinate origin O can be expressed as shown in the system of A2.21.

$$\begin{cases} x' = x \cos \varphi - y \sin \varphi \\ y' = x \sin \varphi + y \cos \varphi \end{cases} \quad \text{A2.21}$$

Often, rotation needs to be performed around some random point—that is, (x_0, y_0). The steps to carry out this transformation are as follows:

1. The coordinate origin point O is translated to the point with the (x_0, y_0) coordinates. All that needs to be done for this operation is to subtract the coordinates of the (x_0, y_0) point from the coordinates of the (x, y) point.
2. A rotation about the new coordinate origin point is performed as follows:

$$\begin{cases} x' = (x - x_0) \cos \varphi - (y - y_0) \sin \varphi \\ y' = (x - x_0) \sin \varphi + (y - y_0) \cos \varphi \end{cases} \quad \text{A2.22}$$

3. The coordinate system is returned to the original state by adding the coordinates of the (x_0, y_0) point to the coordinates of the (x', y') point as follows:

$$\begin{cases} x' = x' + x_0 \\ y' = y' + y_0 \end{cases} \quad \text{A2.23}$$

Consequently, a rotation through angle φ around random point (x_0, y_0) can be written as shown in the system of A2.24.

$$\begin{cases} x' = x_0 + (x - x_0) \cos \varphi - (y - y_0) \sin \varphi \\ y' = y_0 + (x - x_0) \sin \varphi + (y - y_0) \cos \varphi \end{cases} \quad \text{A2.24}$$

A2.6. Matrix Notation for 2D Transformations

Notation for a translation operation in homogeneous coordinates is as follows:

$$[x'\ y'\ 1] = [x\ y\ 1]\begin{bmatrix} 1 & 0 & 0 \\ 0 & 1 & 0 \\ a & b & 1 \end{bmatrix}$$

Notation for a rotation through angle φ about point O in homogeneous coordinates is as follows:

$$[x'\ y'\ 1] = [x\ y\ 1]\begin{bmatrix} \cos\varphi & \sin\varphi & 0 \\ -\sin\varphi & \cos\varphi & 0 \\ 0 & 0 & 1 \end{bmatrix}$$

Notation for rotation through angle φ around point (x_0, y_0) is as follows:

$$[x'\ y'\ 1] = [x\ y\ 1]\mathbf{R}$$

Here, **R** is a 3 × 3 matrix.
The following steps are carried out to find **R**:

1. As follows, the (x_0, y_0) point is translated to the coordinate origin—point O:

$$[u_1\ v_1\ 1] = [x\ y\ 1]\mathbf{T}',\ \text{where}\ \mathbf{T}' = \begin{bmatrix} 1 & 0 & 0 \\ 0 & 1 & 0 \\ -x_0 & -y_0 & 1 \end{bmatrix}$$

2. A rotation through angle φ about O is performed as follows:

$$[u_2\ v_2\ 1] = [u_1\ v_1\ 1]\mathbf{R}_0,\ \text{where}\ \mathbf{R}_0 = \begin{bmatrix} \cos\varphi & \sin\varphi & 0 \\ -\sin\varphi & \cos\varphi & 0 \\ 0 & 0 & 1 \end{bmatrix}$$

3. The coordinate origin is translated to the (x_0, y_0) point as follows:

$$[x'\ y'\ 1] = [u_2\ v_2\ 1]\mathbf{T},\ \text{where}\ \mathbf{T} = \begin{bmatrix} 1 & 0 & 0 \\ 0 & 1 & 0 \\ x_0 & y_0 & 1 \end{bmatrix}$$

Taking into account the associative property of matrix multiplication—that is, $(AB)C = A(BC) = ABC$—finds the following:

$$[x'\ y'\ 1] = [u_2\ v_2\ 1]T = \{[u_1\ v_1\ 1]R_0\}T =$$
$$\{[x\ y\ 1]T'\}R_0T = [x\ y\ 1]T'R_0T$$

Consequently, the following is true:

$$R = T'R_0T = \begin{bmatrix} \cos\varphi & \sin\varphi & 0 \\ -\sin\varphi & \cos\varphi & 0 \\ c_1 & c_2 & 1 \end{bmatrix}, \text{where} \begin{array}{l} c_1 = x_0 - x_0\cos\varphi + y_0\sin\varphi \\ c_2 = y_0 - x_0\sin\varphi - y_0\cos\varphi \end{array}$$

A2.7. Translation and Rotation in 3D Space

A translation in 3D space is called transforming the $P = (x, y, z)$ point to the $P' = (x', y', z')$ point according to the following system of equations:

$$\begin{cases} x' = x + a_1 \\ y' = y + a_2 \\ z' = z + a_3 \end{cases}$$

Here, a_1, a_2, a_3 are constants.

In matrix notation, this operation is expressed as shown below.

$$[x'\ y'\ z'\ 1] = [x\ y\ z\ 1]T,\ T = \begin{bmatrix} 1 & 0 & 0 & 0 \\ 0 & 1 & 0 & 0 \\ 0 & 0 & 1 & 0 \\ a_1 & a_2 & a_3 & 1 \end{bmatrix} \quad \text{A2.25}$$

Rotation about the coordinate axis can be written without resorting to the homogeneous coordinates. That's what you should do to keep your notations short. In the right coordinate system (Fig. A2.10), rotation through angle φ around the Z-axis is given by the following transformation matrix:

$$[x'\ y'\ z'\ 1] = [x\ y\ z\ 1]R_z,\ R_z = \begin{bmatrix} c & s & 0 \\ -s & c & 0 \\ 0 & 0 & 1 \end{bmatrix} \quad \text{A2.26}$$

Here, $c = \cos\varphi$ and $s = \sin\varphi$.

Appendix 2: Mathematical Fundamentals for Plane and 3D Transformations

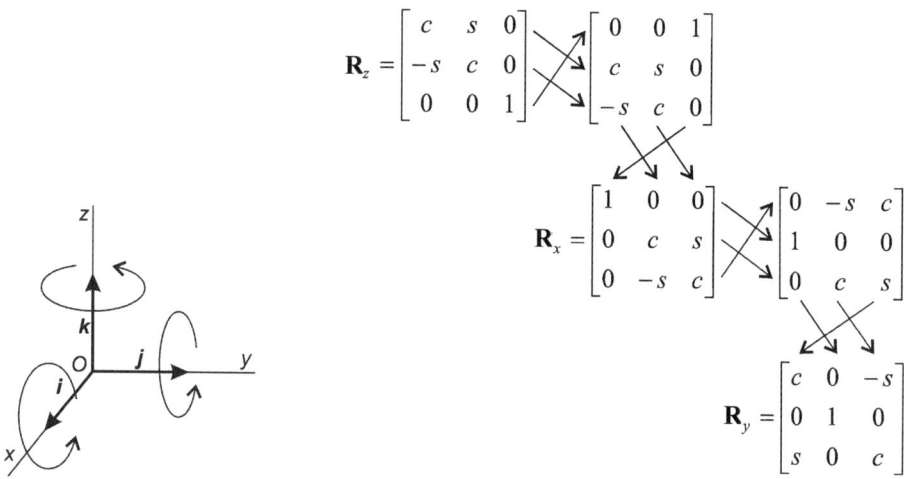

Fig. A2.10. Right coordinate system

Fig. A2.11. Matrix transformation arrangement

The $\mathbf{R}_z$ matrix can be used to construct rotation matrices about the X- and Y-axes (the $\mathbf{R}_x$ and $\mathbf{R}_y$ matrices). These matrices are obtained by cycling rows and columns according to the $\mathbf{R}_z \to \mathbf{R}_x \to \mathbf{R}_y \to \mathbf{R}_z$ arrangement (Fig. A2.11).

Inversion matrices are used when the coordinate system needs to be changed, as shown here:

$$\mathbf{T}^{-1} = \begin{bmatrix} 1 & 0 & 0 & 0 \\ 0 & 1 & 0 & 0 \\ 0 & 0 & 1 & 0 \\ -a_1 & -a_2 & -a_3 & 1 \end{bmatrix}, \quad \mathbf{R}_z^{-1} = \begin{bmatrix} c & -s & 0 \\ s & c & 0 \\ 0 & 0 & 1 \end{bmatrix}, \quad \text{A2.27}$$

$$\mathbf{R}_x^{-1} = \begin{bmatrix} 1 & 0 & 0 \\ 0 & c & -s \\ 0 & s & c \end{bmatrix}, \quad \mathbf{R}_y^{-1} = \begin{bmatrix} c & 0 & s \\ 0 & 1 & 0 \\ -s & 0 & c \end{bmatrix}$$

A2.8. Parallel Projection

Three components are necessary to perform transformations: the *viewpoint*, the *object*, and the *screen*. The screen is located between the viewer and the object (Fig. A2.12). If the camera (the eye) is in point E, then for each point P of the object, the straight line PE crosses the screen in point P'. The coordinate system, in which the locations of the object, viewpoint, and the screen, as well as the screen size, are defined is called the *world coordinate system*. The task is to convert the $P = (x, y, z)$ world coordinates of a set of points belonging to an object into the $P' = (X, Y)$ coordinates of the set of points of the image projected onto the screen; (x, y, z) are the world coordinates of the object's P point, and (X, Y) are the screen coordinates of this point's screen projection (the P' point). The necessary coordinate conversion steps are diagrammed in Fig. A2.13.

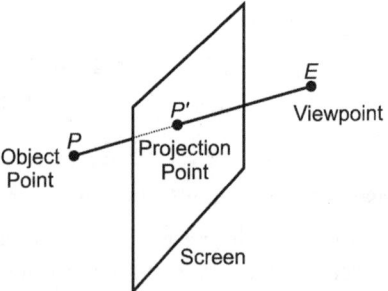

Fig. A2.12. Projecting an object point to the screen

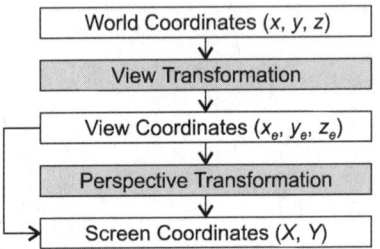

Fig. A2.13. Coordinate-conversion flowchart

First, the world coordinates are transformed into the view coordinates (with the origin in point E). Then, perspective transformation may be performed, adding the perspective effect depending on the distances of the object and the viewpoint to the screen. When constructing a parallel projection, perspective transformation is not performed and the (x_B, y_B) coordinates of the P point are used as the (X, Y) coordinates of the P' point.

A2.8.1. View Conversion

Assume you have a right-handed world coordinate system and its origin point O coincides with the object's center. The E point is specified as follows in spherical coordinates (ρ, θ, φ) relative to point O:

$$x_E = \rho \sin \varphi \cos \theta, \quad y_E = \rho \sin \varphi \sin \theta, \quad z_E = \rho \cos \varphi \qquad \text{A2.28}$$

The EO vector defines the observer's position (Fig. A2.14).

The view coordinate system is shown in Fig. 7.6. In addition to the location in space, it differs from the world coordinates because it is left-handed (the world coordinate system is right-handed). In the matrix notation, conversion of world coordinates into view coordinates looks as shown below.

$$\begin{bmatrix} x_e & y_e & z_e & 1 \end{bmatrix} = \begin{bmatrix} x & y & z & 1 \end{bmatrix} \mathbf{V} \qquad \text{A2.29}$$

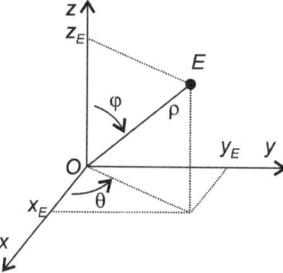
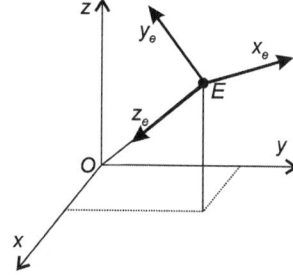

Fig. A2.14. Polar coordinates of point E **Fig. A2.15.** View coordinate system

To obtain matrix $\mathbf{V}$, four elementary transformation matrices need to be multiplied. In the process, the following actions are performed:

1. A translation is made from point O to point E (Fig. A2.16). Here is the matrix for this transformation:

$$\mathbf{T} = \begin{bmatrix} 1 & 0 & 0 & 0 \\ 0 & 1 & 0 & 0 \\ 0 & 0 & 1 & 0 \\ -x_e & -y_e & -z_e & 1 \end{bmatrix} \qquad \text{A2.30}$$

2. The coordinate system is rotated through the angle $\frac{\pi}{2} - \theta$ about the Z-axis (Figs. A2.16 and A2.17). This makes the direction of the Y-axis coinciding with the horizontal component of the *OE* vector with the X-axis perpendicular to this component. Because the direction of this rotation is negative, the matrix of this transformation will coincide with the matrix to rotate the *point* through the same angle in the *positive* direction, as follows:

$$\mathbf{R}_z = \begin{bmatrix} \cos(\pi/2-\theta) & \sin(\pi/2-\theta) & 0 \\ -\sin(\pi/2-\theta) & \cos(\pi/2-\theta) & 0 \\ 0 & 0 & 1 \end{bmatrix} = \begin{bmatrix} \sin\theta & \cos\theta & 0 \\ -\cos\theta & \sin\theta & 0 \\ 0 & 0 & 1 \end{bmatrix} \quad \text{A2.31}$$

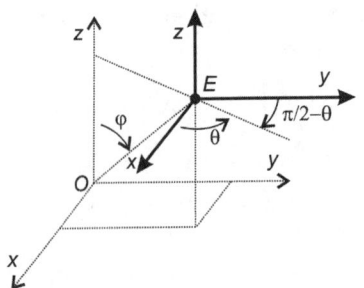

Fig. A2.16. Translation to point *E*

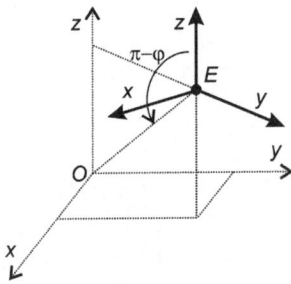

Fig. A2.17. Rotation about the Z-axis

3. The system is rotated in the positive direction through angle $\pi - \varphi$, which corresponds to rotating the point through angle $-(\pi - \varphi) = \varphi - \pi$ (Figs. A2.17 and A2.18). The matrix for this transformation is as follows:

$$\mathbf{R}_x = \begin{bmatrix} 1 & 0 & 0 \\ 0 & \cos(\varphi-\pi) & \sin(\varphi-\pi) \\ 0 & -\sin(\varphi-\pi) & \cos(\varphi-\pi) \end{bmatrix} = \begin{bmatrix} 1 & 0 & 0 \\ 0 & -\cos\varphi & -\sin\varphi \\ 0 & \sin\varphi & -\cos\varphi \end{bmatrix} \quad \text{A2.32}$$

4. The direction of the X-axis is changed: $x' = -x$ (Fig. A2.19). The matrix for this transformation is as follows:

$$\mathbf{M}_{yz} = \begin{bmatrix} -1 & 0 & 0 \\ 0 & 1 & 0 \\ 0 & 0 & 1 \end{bmatrix} \quad \text{A2.33}$$

Appendix 2: Mathematical Fundamentals for Plane and 3D Transformations

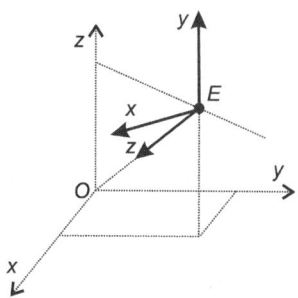

Fig. A2.18. Rotation about the X-axis

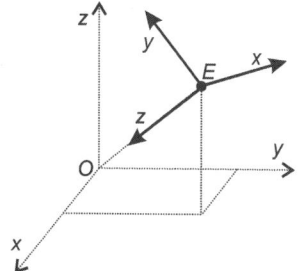

Fig. A2.19. Changing X-axis's direction

Matrix **V** is obtained by multiplying matrices of A2.30–A2.33 as follows:

$$\mathbf{V} = \mathbf{TR}_z^* \mathbf{R}_x^* \mathbf{M}_{yz}^* \quad \quad \text{A2.34}$$

(The $*$ character means expanding a 3×3 matrix to a 4×4 one by adding an extra row and column $[0\ 0\ 0\ 1]$).

The results of the A2.34 multiplication is a change of the world coordinates into the view coordinates transformation matrix, as follows:

$$\mathbf{V} = \begin{bmatrix} -\sin\theta & -\cos\varphi\cos\theta & -\sin\varphi\cos\theta & 0 \\ \cos\theta & -\cos\varphi\sin\theta & -\sin\varphi\sin\theta & 0 \\ 0 & \sin\varphi & -\cos\varphi & 0 \\ 0 & 0 & 0 & 1 \end{bmatrix} \quad \text{A2.35}$$

The view coordinates of a point are found by multiplying its world coordinates (in the homogeneous notation) by the **V** matrix (A2.35).

The (x_e, y_e) view coordinates are the orthogonal (parallel) projection of the point $P = (x, y, z)$. The (x_e, y_e) coordinates can be directly used to form an image on the screen.

A2.8.2. Perspective Transformations

Consider Fig. A2.20. Assuming the y coordinate of the P point equals zero, from the similarity of the ΔEPO and $\Delta EP'Q$ triangles follows A2.36, a:

$$\frac{P'Q}{EQ} = \frac{PO}{EO} \Rightarrow \frac{X}{d} = \frac{x}{z} \Rightarrow X = d\frac{x}{z} \quad \text{A2.36, } a$$

Y is determined similarly:

$$Y = d\frac{y}{z} \qquad \text{A2.36, b}$$

Because the Z-axis coincides with EO (the direction of the viewpoint toward the object's center in point O), the origin of the screen coordinate system will be in point Q, where EO crosses the screen. To place an object into the center of the screen, A2.36 can be supplemented with the corresponding offset as follows:

$$X = d\frac{x}{z} + \frac{W}{2}, \quad Y = d\frac{y}{z} + \frac{H}{2} \qquad \text{A2.37}$$

Here, W and H are the screen width and height, respectively.

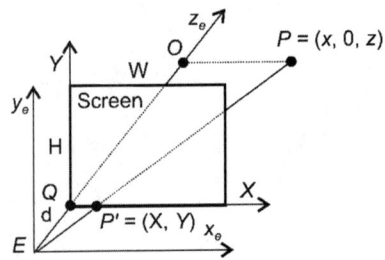

Fig. A2.20. Perspective transformation

A2.9. Two Approaches to Removing Hidden Lines and Surfaces

To construct realistic 3D images, hidden parts of objects (edges and surfaces) need to be removed. There are two main approaches to solving this task.

The first approach directly compares objects to determine, which of their parts are visible. In this case, the work is conducted in the object space. This approach is employed in the algorithms considered in *Sections A2.9.1 and A2.9.2*.

The other approach determines for each screen pixel the object closest to it (along the projection direction). In this case, the work is performed in the screen coordinates space. This approach is employed in the algorithms considered in *Sections A2.9.3, A2.9.4, and A2.9.5*.

A2.9.1. Algorithms for Culling Back Faces

Let an external unit normal vector be specified for each face of some shape. If the angle between the face normal and the projection direction (the viewpoint direction) is obtuse, such a face is hidden and is called a *back face*. If this angle is acute, the face is visible and is called a *front face* (Fig. A2.21).

When a 3D scene is just one convex polyhedron, culling back faces removes the hidden surfaces.

In general, the described check does not offer a complete solution but significantly reduces the number of the faces that need to be inspected.

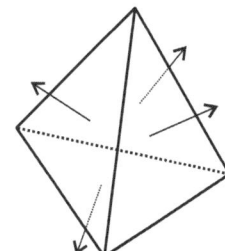

Fig. A2.21. Determining back faces

A2.9.2. The Roberts Algorithm

The prerequisite for this algorithm is for each face to be a convex polyhedron. Because this condition is the most easily met for triangular object faces, first break object faces into triangles. Then, make up a list of faces (triangles) and a list of edges. Next, test whether the edges of the polyhedron are visible by checking whether they are overlaid by the faces.

Now, discard all edges whose determining faces are both back faces. Test whether the remaining edges are overlaid by faces. The following cases are possible:

- ❏ An edge is not overlaid by a face (Fig. A2.22): Proceed to checking whether it is overlaid by the next face.
- ❏ An edge is completely overlaid by a face (Fig. A2.23): The visibility test for this edge is completed at this stage.
- ❏ An edge is only partially overlaid by a face (Fig. A2.24): Break the edge into several parts; remove the edge from the list but add its parts that are not overlaid by a face.

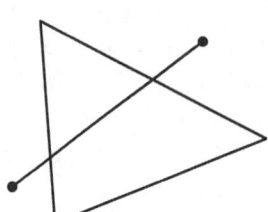
Fig. A2.22. An edge is not overlaid by a face

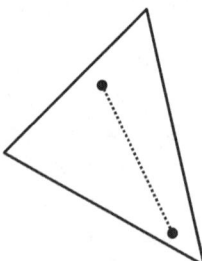
Fig. A2.23. An edge is completely overlaid by a face

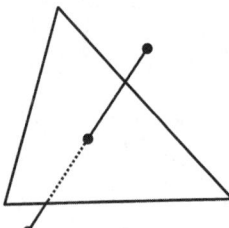
Fig. A2.24. Edges partially overlaid by faces

The number of tests can be significantly reduced by resorting to the "divide and conquer" method. The idea is as follows: The screen is divided into several equal parts. For each part, a list is made of only edges whose projections lie in this part of the screen. When performing the edge visibility check, first determine, into which parts of the screen its projection falls, and then check whether it is overlaid only by the faces in the lists of the given parts.

A2.9.3. The Z-Buffer Algorithm

Here, each screen pixel is associated to the distance to the object projected onto it (Z-buffer). To output a face to the screen, first convert it into its screen bitmap form and determine the depth of each pixel. If the depth value is less than the value stored in the Z-buffer ($+\infty$ initially), then this value replaces the old value in the Z-buffer. In the end, only the pixels that are projections of the closest to the screen objects are drawn.

Because this algorithm is simple yet laborious, it is prevalently implemented in hardware.

This algorithm is widely used in various graphics libraries to keep farther pixels from overriding closer pixels when working with concave objects (see, e.g., Section 7.5.2).

A2.9.4. Warnock's Algorithm

This algorithm is based on dividing the screen into several parts (Fig. A2.25). First, the screen is divided into four equal parts. The following situations are possible:

- Part of the screen is completely covered by the projection of the closest face.
- Part of the screen is not covered by any face projection.
- Part of the screen is partially covered by a face projection.

In the first case, the part of the screen is filled with the face color; in the second case, it is filled with the background color. In the third case, the given part of the screen is further subdivided into four parts, each of which is tested for these three conditions. The subdivision can be continued down to one pixel, in which case the pixel is filled with the color of the closest face.

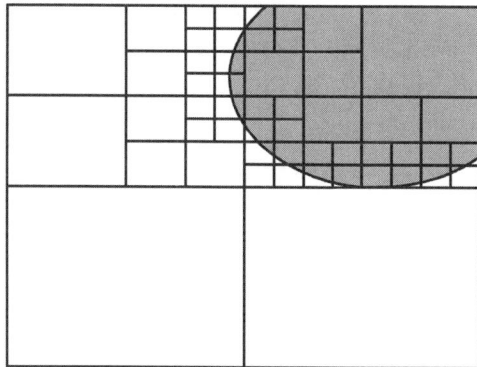

Fig. A2.25. Dividing screen into parts

A2.9.5. The Line Scanning Algorithm

Assume that the image on the screen is a set of vertical lines (pixel columns). Consider cutting a 3D scene by a plane passing through one such line and the projection center (the viewpoint). Such an intersection will produce a set of segments that have to be projected to the screen. The initial problem has come to removing the hidden segments on each line.

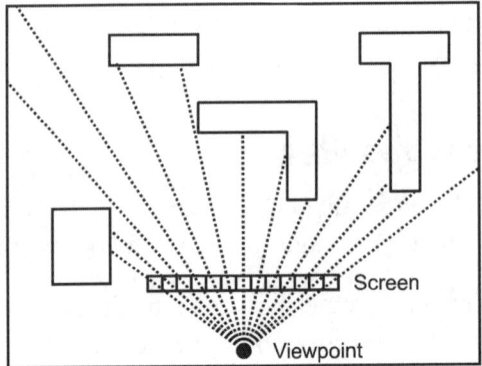

Fig. A2.26. A view from above the maze

This algorithm can be used to visualize movements in a maze (Fig. A2.26). If the distance between the floor and the ceiling is the same for the entire scene and the walls are vertical, the task can be considered a 2D one.

Draw straight lines through the viewpoint and the pixel columns. Only the closest intersections of the maze walls by these lines will be visible. Solving a 2D problem, determine the distance to the closest wall. The image in each pixel column can consist of three parts: the floor, a wall, and the ceiling. Part of the line is filled with the floor color, part with the wall color, and part with the ceiling color. Depending of the distance between the wall and the viewpoint, the color intensity can be varied.

Appendix 3: General Information about Raster Graphics

A3.1. Graphics Formats

A *graphics format* is the order (or structure), in which image-describing data are recorded in a file.

Graphics data are usually divided into two classes: vector and raster. Depending on the type of data that describe them, images are called vector or raster images.

Vector data represent lines, polygons, curves, etc., using numerically defined fixed (anchor, base, or key) points. Programs processing vector data reproduce lines by connecting the anchor points. With the information about anchor points, attributes (color, width, and other line parameters) and a set of output (or drawing) rules (or conventions) are stored. An example of a vector drawing is shown in Fig. A3.1.

Raster data are a set of numerical values defining the brightness and color of individual *pixels*. Pixels are the lowest-level elements (or color dots), from which raster images are formed. The term *raster* as used in computer graphics has several meanings different than those used in the printing trade. In this book, a raster is an array of pixels (also an array of numerical values). The term *bitmap* is often used to designate an array of pixels. In a bitmap, each pixel is assigned a certain number of bits; the same number is assigned for each of image pixel. This number is called the pixel's *bit depth* or the image's *color depth* because the number of colors depends on the number of bits assigned per pixel. The most used depths are 1, 2, 4, 8, 16, 24, and 32 bits.

Fig. A3.1. A vector image

Fig. A3.2. A raster image

Sources of raster data can be programs that form images on raster screens and various image-input devices (scanners, digital cameras, etc.).

An example of a raster image is shown in Fig. A3.2.

The type of a graphics file format is determined by the type of graphics data contained in the file and the way it is saved. The most widely used formats are the raster, vector, and metafile formats.

The *vector format* is most convenient for storing images that can be broken into simple geometric figures (e.g., drawings or text). Vector files hold mathematical descriptions of the image elements. The most common vector formats are Auto-CAD Drawing Exchange Format (DFX), and Microsoft SYmbolic LinK (SYLK).

The *raster format* is used to store raster data. Files of this type are especially suitable for storing real world images (e.g., digital photographs). Raster files hold the image bitmap and its specification data. The most common raster formats are bitmap (BMP), Tagged Image File Format (TIFF), GIF, PC Paintbrush Exchange (PCX), and Joint Photographic Experts Group (JPEG) formats.

The *metafile format* allows vector and raster data to be stored in one file. An example of such a format is CDR, the CorelDraw file format.

In addition, there are file formats for storing animation (video information), multimedia (audio, video, and graphics information), hypertext (not only text but also embedded reference links), hypermedia (hypertext plus graphical and video information), 3D images, fonts, etc.

A3.2. Graphics File Elements

Graphics files comprise sequences of data or data structures called *file elements* or *data elements*. These elements are subdivided into three categories: fields, tags, and streams.

- A *field* is a fixed-size data structure of a graphics file. The field's position in the file is usually determined either by an absolute offset from the file beginning or end or by an offset relative to another field.
- A *tag* is a data structure whose size and position vary from file to file. A tag's position can be specified absolutely or relative to another file element. Tags can contain other tags or sets of linked fields.
- A *stream* is a set of data intended to be read sequentially. Unlike fields and tags, a stream does not provide rapid access to the needed data because the location of these in file is determined during the reading process.

As a rule, combinations of these data elements are used in graphics files.

A3.3. Format Conversion

The need to exchange images among different programs often engenders a data-format conversion problem. Specialized programs exist for this purpose; moreover, common graphics editors can read and save images in different formats. Therefore, converting raster data in one format to raster data in another format usually is not difficult. Another matter is converting vector images into raster ones. In such conversions, some information is inevitable lost because of the move from the ideal mathematical description of the image to its discrete (raster) representation. The reverse conversion, from the raster into the vector format, is a formidable task that deals with image recognition.

A3.4. Pixels and Color

Pixels are differentiated into physical and logical types.

Physical pixels are the real dots displayed on the output device: the smallest elements on the imaging surface that can be manipulated. When output to the screen or printer, one physical pixel is usually formed from several smaller color dots. For example, one color pixel on the monitor is formed from three smaller red, green, and blue dots whose brightness determines the pixel color.

Logical pixels are like angels dancing on the head of a pin:[i] They have location and color but take no physical space (i.e., the height and width of logical pixels cannot be calculated). In essence, a logical pixel is just some number that specifies its color. The position of a logical pixel (its coordinates) when output to a physical device (e.g., a printer when the pixel is converted into a physical color dot) is determined by its location in the bitmap and the number of pixels per measurement unit (or its resolution).

When logical pixels are displayed on a physical screen, the numerical data characterizing their brightness and color are converted into the intensity of the physical pixel luminosity. To make this conversion, the size and location of physical pixels must be taken into account.

The number of colors a pixel can assume is directly connected to the number of bits assigned to it and equals 2^n, where n is the number of bits. Images whose pixels are assigned 1 bit are called *monochrome*, or single-color, images. Such images are suitable for depicting technical drawings and text. Images of 24-bit and greater

---

[i] The number of angels that "can dance on the head of a pin" is an old theological debate.

color depth are called *true color*. Each pixel of such images can take on more than 16 million colors. This number of colors is considered sufficient to depict reality reasonably accurately.

Displaying colors specified for logical pixels on an imaging device may produce a color-matching problem. For example, if the output device is capable of reproducing up to 16 million colors, it will have no problems displaying an 8-bit color depth (256 colors) image. But with the situation reversed, the visualization program will have to work hard to match image colors to the output device capabilities. In this event, some data loss and, as a consequence, image quality degradation are inevitable. Moreover, all sorts of side effects are possible: moiré, secondary outlines, and other artifacts.

A3.5. Color Palettes

The *color palette*, also called the *color map* or *color table*, is a one-dimensional array of color values. With the help of the color palette, colors are specified indirectly by indicating their position in the array. Using the color palette, pixel color information is saved in a file as a sequence of indices. In many cases, color palettes allow the volume of raster data to be significantly reduced.

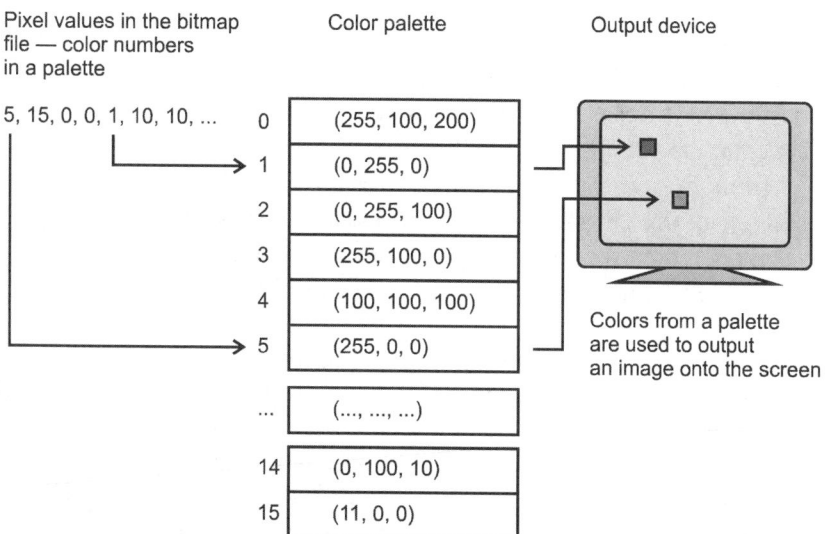

Fig. A3.3. Using a color palette to define colors

Most often, 16- and 256-bit color palettes are used with corresponding color depths of 4 and 8 bits; however, other sizes of color palettes are possible.

For example, each 4-bit color depth image pixel can take on 16 colors (2^4). These 16 colors are defined in a color palette, usually included in the same file as the raster data. Each pixel value is considered an index in this palette and has a value from 0 to 15. Color values in the palette are specified with the highest possible precision. Usually, a palette element takes 24 bits (3 bytes). This way, a palette element can specify one of 16,777,216 colors (2^{24}). An image-displaying program reads raster data, or indices in the color table, from a file and uses their corresponding colors to color screen pixels (Fig. A3.3). Color palettes of different images in most cases differ.

A3.6. Color and Color Models

Various mathematical systems (or models) are used to describe colors. No single existing color-representation system is superior to the rest. Different systems are used for different goals and tasks.

Graphics files usually use color models based on the three primary colors that cannot be obtained by mixing other colors. The gamut of colors that can be obtained by mixing the primary colors forms the *color space* or *spectrum*.

Color models can be divided into two categories: additive and subtractive. In the *additive models*, new colors are obtained by mixing primary colors of different intensity with black. The greater the intensity of the mixed colors, the closer to white the resulting color. White is obtained at the maximum intensity of each of the three primary colors; black is formed at the lowest intensity of the three primary colors. Additive color models are used in self-luminous devices (e.g., monitors).

In *subtractive models*, primary colors are subtracted from white. The greater the intensity of the subtracted colors, the closer to black is the resulting color. Subtractive models are used to form color images on reflective media (e.g., paper).

The most common color models are the following:

- The *RGB model* is additive and is the most widely used in graphics formats. Each pixel is represented as three numerical values of Red, Green, and Blue intensities. Each color is usually allocated 8 bits, which can record 256 intensity levels. Consequently, the (0, 0, 0) value represents black and the (255, 255, 255) value represents white.
- The *Cyan-Magenta-Yellow (CMY) model* is subtractive and is used to obtain color images on white surfaces. When a CMY image is illuminated, each of its

main colors absorbs its complementary color: cyan absorbs red, magenta absorbs green, and yellow absorbs blue. Theoretically, the highest intensity of all three main colors should produce black. In practice, however, this does not happen (because the characteristics of the real-life pigments are far from the mathematical ideals). Therefore, the fourth component is added to the model: black, denoted by the letter *K*. The result is the CMYK model, widely used in the printing trade. In a subtractive model image, each image pixel is composed of four main color dots.

Other color models exist that are not based on color mixing, such as hue–saturation–value. The *hue* is basically a pure spectral color: red, orange, blue, etc. The *saturation* determines the amount of white in the color. For example, a 100% saturated red hue contains no white and is considered a pure color. A 50% saturation defines a lighter hue, which will correspond to rose. The *value* specifies the color brightness intensity.

A3.7. Data Compression

Compression is a process of reducing the size of a data block. Because, as a rule, great amounts of data are used to describe images, image files are large. Therefore, graphics data are often compressed. Usually, each graphics file format supports one of the compression methods (or algorithms). In most cases, the compression replaces superfluous information with its more compact form. Compression can be logical or physical, the difference between the two being the method, in which data are compacted. Physical data compression does not take into account the information carried by the data. Logical compression, on the contrary, is based on logical analyses of the compressed data. An example of logical compression can be compressing the string "United States of America" into the abbreviation "USA." Logical compression is not employed for graphics data.

Compression methods can be *lossy* or *lossless*. After restoring (unpacking) previously compressed data, if the obtained data have a one-to-one correspondence to the source data, the compression is said to have been lossless.

In lossy compression methods, some image data are discarded to obtain the highest compression ratio.

The following are some of the most common compression methods:

- *Pixel packing* consists of storing 1-, 2-, or 4-bit pixels—8, 4, or 2 per byte, respectively.

- *Run-length encoding* is a common compression algorithm used in such raster formats as BMP, TIFF, and PCX.
- The *Lempel–Ziv–Welch* (LZW) algorithm is used in GIF and TIFF formats.
- The *JPEG algorithm,* developed by Joint Photographic Experts Group, comprises a set of compression methods. The basic JPEG implementation applies first the discrete cosine transformation algorithm to the image, then Huffman coding.
- *Fractal compression* is a mathematical process that encodes raster images into a collection of mathematical data describing fractal (similar or recurring) image properties.

Compression is usually applied to raster image data. When a compressed image is saved to a file, a header is added to the packed raster data describing image parameters and the compression method.

Vector files are seldom compressed. This is because vector formats already store data in a very compact form and the compression ratio is not worth the bother.

It is important to understand that compression algorithms do not specify any file format but simply define a data coding method.

A3.8. Comparison of Popular Graphics Formats

Compressed raster data are mainly saved in JPEG, GIF, PNG, and TIFF formats. Printing trade professionals have their own opinions about image storage formats and methods; they especially dislike JPEG for its lossy compression despite the high compression ratio. Without getting into useless arguments about the best format, a comparison of their capabilities is summarized in Table A3.1.

Table A3.1. Characteristics of Graphics Formats

Supported Property	JPEG	GIF	PNG	TIFF
True color images	Yes	No	Yes	Yes
Storage of several frames in one file	No	Yes	No	Yes

continues

Table A3.1 Continued

Supported Property	JPEG	GIF	PNG	TIFF
Transparency (color key)	No	Yes	Yes*	No
Transparency (alpha channel)	No	No	Yes	Yes (in 32-bit formats)
Lossless compression	No	Yes	Yes	Yes

* PNG is probably the unique format for transparency support. This format allows you to save semitransparent index images, grayscale images with alpha channel, etc. These capabilities, however, are not fully implemented in Microsoft products in general or in GDI+ in particular.

So, there you have it: further proof that you just cannot have it all—and even if you can, then not at the same time. There is no universal format, and you have to compromise in each case. Ultimately, the choice of which format to use is yours.

We will briefly describe GIF particularities. This is an index format—that is, the color of each pixel is defined by the pixel's index in the color palette. The maximum index size is 8 bits; therefore, an image cannot be more than 256 colors. This model implements the color key transparency; that is, one of the palette colors can be designated transparent. When GIF files are loaded by the GDI+ codec, they are converted into the native form for this library: 32-bit raster. Transparent color pixels in this process are simply given an alpha value equal to zero.

Moreover, it is worth remembering that GIF used to have license limitations because it used the patented LZW compression belonging to Unisys Corporation. However, according to published information at **http://www.unisys.com/about_unisys/lzw**, the patent has expired (the last country, in which it was in effect—until June 20, 2004—was Japan). Thus, developers using LZW[i] work libraries in their products no longer have to pay royalties to Unisys.

The same applies to the TIFF files compressed using the LZW method. TIFF is a container format and technically can hold several frames compressed using different methods (including JPEG).

---

[i] LZW is used in the GDI+ library. For more details, see the Knowledge Base article "*INFO: Unisys GIF and LZW Technology License Information*" (Q193543).

References

1. Aitken, Peter, and Scott Jarol. *Visual C++ Multimedia Adventure Set.* Coriolis Group Books, 1995—560 pp.

    This book considers practical application of Visual C++ for creating multimedia applications that support hypertext, output of graphics files, animation, and playback of audio and video files.

2. Angel, Edward. *Interactive Computer Graphics: A top-down approach with OpenGL.* Addison Wesley Publishing, 2002—613 pp.

    This book considers mathematical principles of 3D-object construction and programming principles of OpenGL. Modern tendencies for constructing interactive client–server graphics systems and principles of graphics program development are covered. It also describes the use of graphics tools for visualizing scientific calculations.

3. Lindley, Craig A. *Practical Image Processing in C: Acquisition, manipulation, storage.* John Wiley & Sons, 1990—533 pp.

    The author examines hardware and software for outputting images to the screen, classic image-processing methods and algorithms, and the implementation of C algorithms into programs.

4. Petzold, Charles. *Programming Windows with C#*, book and CD-ROM edition. Microsoft Press, 2001—1200 pp.

    This book is an extensive guide to programming .NET applications in C#. It considers in detail the program event architecture for WinForms and the issues of programming this platform using the GDI+ library.

5. Richter, Jeffrey. *Programming Applications for Microsoft Windows* (Microsoft Programming Series), book and CD-ROM edition. Microsoft Press, 1999—1056 pp.

   The author provides detailed coverage of using API Windows functions and virtual memory, controlling processes and threads, and developing DLLs.

6. Richter, Jeffrey. *Applied Microsoft .NET Framework Programming*. Microsoft Press, 2002—640 pp.

   This recent book from the well-known technical writer introduces professional programmers to the principles of the .NET platform organization from the "inside." Microsoft professionals declared this book the best introduction to the .NET environment.

7. Rogers, David F. *Procedural Elements for Computer Graphics*, 2nd edition. WCB/McGraw-Hill, 1998—711 pp.

   The author analyzes the algorithms and techniques of modern graphics systems, giving special attention to raster graphics techniques. The algorithms are pseudocode programs that can be easily converted into Pascal, Fortran, or Basic. The book abounds in illustrations and examples and refers to practice problems.

8. Rogers, David F., and J. Alan Adams. *Mathematical Elements for Computer Graphics*. WCB/McGraw-Hill, 1990—611 pp.

   This text is an introduction to the computer graphics principles and the main techniques of implementing graphics effects. The book is not tied to any specific platform or technology but examines the necessary principles and gives a useful mathematical mechanism.

9. Schildt, Herbert, and Frank Crockett. *MFC Programming from the Ground Up*, 2nd edition. Osborne/McGraw-Hill, 1998—663 pp.

   The book gives a detailed examination of MFC use.

10. Yuan, Feng. *Windows Graphics Programming*. Hewlett-Packard Professional Books, 2002—1280 pp.

    This is a thorough, meticulous, and detailed exploration of the Windows GDI. The author examines the principles of its internal architecture, the architecture of the graphics core, and the drivers of the graphics devices and print system. The reader will learn the difference between the Windows NT and the Windows 98 GDI implementations and will be introduced to the DirectX programming interface.

Internet Resources

1. **http://msdn.microsoft.com**—The Microsoft site offers lots of technical documentation, source code of example programs, articles, etc.
2. **http://www.codeguru.com**—This site is dedicated to Windows programming. It contains numerous program examples in different languages. There is also a computer graphics section.
3. **http://www.codeproject.com**—Although younger than the **CodeGuru** site, this has quickly reached the popularity of the latter. Among its materials are quite a few articles devoted to the GDI+ library.
4. **http://www.gotdotnet.com**—This site was created by Microsoft to advance its .NET framework initiative. It contains a large quantity of instructional materials, articles, program examples, and interviews with the creators of this platform.
5. **http://www.bobpowell.net/gdiplus_faq.htm**—Bob Powell provides GDI+ FAQ for .NET programmers.

CD Contents

Folder	Description	Applicable Chapter
\Sources	Source and executable files of the example programs.	
\Sources\Painter	The Painter program. Used for drawing shapes, polygons, surface transformations, 3D transformations, surfaces, and level lines. Has the capability to export images in BMP files.	4
\Sources\BMViewer	The BMViewer program. Used for viewing and editing bitmap images.	6
\Sources\Bezier	The Bezier program. Used for drawing splines of various types.	A1
\Pics\Painter	Images created by the Painter program.	4
\Pics\Samples	Examples of bitmap images processed by the BMViewer program.	6
\Sources\GDIPlus\DemoVC	The first C++ GDI+ program. Demonstrates loading and outputting GIF images and outputting semitransparent gradient text.	1
\Sources\GDIPlus\DemoCS	The first C++ .NET program. Demonstrates the same operations as the preceding C++ but does so using WinForms.	1
\Sources\GDIPlus\Clock	A C# clock program. Uses WinForms to demonstrate capabilities of vector primitives.	2
\Sources\GDIPlus\Curves	A program to construct cubic splines and Bezier curves using the GDI+ library.	2

continues

Continued

Folder	Description	Applicable Chapter
\Sources\GDIPlus\MetaGen	A C++ program that demonstrates writing an image to a metafile.	3
\Sources\GDIPlus\PlayMeta	A .NET (C#) example of metafile analyses and selective playback.	3
\Sources\GDIPlus\Codecs	A program to view the graphics formats supported by the library and the properties of their codecs.	5
\Sources\GDIPlus\Butterfly	A C++ program that demonstrates storing GIF images in the program resources, outputting animated images, and double buffering.	5
\Sources\GDIPlus\Animated	An example of working with animated GIF images in .NET.	5
\Sources\GDIPlus\RevFrame	A demonstration of direct access to bitmaps in the .NET environment.	5
\Sources\Direct3D\TeapotVC	An introduction to Direct3D: outputting a 3D object.	7
\Sources\Direct3D\TeapotNET	The use of Direct3D in .NET: outputting a 3D object using Managed DirectX.	7
\Sources\Direct3D\CubeVC	An example of controlling output of Direct3D primitives: vertex data, color, and coordinate transformation matrices.	8
\Sources\Direct3D\CubeNET	Demonstrates outputting primitives and working with vertex data using Managed Direct3D.	8

The DivX511Bundle.exe file shows a video about A-List Publishing books. To watch this file, install Standard DivX Codec(FREE) available for free download from **http://www.divx.com/divx/**.

Index

.NET Framework, 7, 8, 11, 18, 21, 24
.NET Framework SDK, 14

3

3D transformations:
   perspective, 333
   rotation, 328

A

Algorithm:
   backface culling, 335
   line scanning, 337
   Roberts, 335
   Warnock's, 337
   Z-buffer, 336
Alpha, 43, 45
Anchor points, 307, 339
Antialiasing, 58, 59
Applications:
   multiple document interface, 148
   single document interface, 148
Approximation, 307
AppWizard, 240, 241
Artificial intelligence, 299
Assembly, 11
Attributes, 11

B

Back faces, 277
Bezier curves, 54
Bit:
   depth, 340
   pattern, 43
BitBlt, 157
Bitmap, 339
Bitmap data transformations:
   frame-by-frame, 170
   geometric, 170
BlurMatrix, 213
BMP, 1, 20

C

C3DPolygon, 81
CBlur, 213
CBrightCont, 202
CContour, 215
CDocument, 148
CEmboss, 210
CFilter, 188
CInvertColors, 209
Class:
   document, 148
   view, 148

ClearType, 21
CMatrixFilter, 192
Color:
   additive model, 344
   depth, 340
   gradient, 44
   key, 347
   palette, 343
   space, 344
   subtractive model, 344
COM, 248, 252
Compression:
   logic, 345
   lossless, 345
   lossy, 345
   physical, 345
Coordinate system, 57, 60
   homogeneous, 322
   right-handed, 319
   view, 331
   world, 330
Cramer's rule, 320
CSharp, 216
Culling, 277
Curve:
   Beta-spline, 312
   Bezier, 313
   compound, 309
   geometrically continuous, 311
   segmented, 310
   spline, 310
CView, 148

D

D3DX, 243, 247, 249
Data:
   compression, 345
   raster, 339
   vector, 339
Delayed Loading, 30, 31
Delegate, 75

Delegates
   .NET, 33
Determinant, 320
Direct3D:
   Initialization, 262
   Extension, 243
DirectX, 237
   Graphics, 238, 241
   Runtime, 238
   SDK, 239
Document, 148
Document/View, 148
dpi, 231
Dynamically Loaded Library, 11

E

EMF, 1, 20
EMF+, 20
Enumerations, 22
Events:
   .NET, 33
Execution thread, 181
Exif, 1, 20
Extrapolation, 307

F

Field, 341
Filter:
   base class, 188
   blur, 212
   brightness/contrast, 202
   colors inversion, 209
   contour, 214
   denoise (entropy), 218
   denoise (median), 226
   emboss, 210
   Histogram, 195
   point, 191
   spatial, 192
Fog, 297

Format:
  BMP, 341
  CDR, 341
  GIF, 341
  graphics, 339
  JPEG, 341
  metafile, 341
  PCX, 341
  raster, 341
  TIFF, 341
  vector, 341
FOV, 282

G

Garbage collector, 9, 18, 40
GC, 40, 41
GDI heap, 38
GDI+, 18
GdiPlus.dll, 18, 21, 24
GetDeviceCaps, 231
GetHistogram, 171
GIF, 1, 20, 346, 347
Graphics, 39, 42, 53, 64, 65, 70, 72, 73

I

ICO, 1, 20
IDisposable, 41
Image:
  brightness, 202
  brightness histogram, 170
  contrast, 195
  monochrome, 342
  truecolor, 343
Index buffer, 291
Interface, 252
  MDI, 149
Interpolation, 58
Interpolation, 307
  linear, 307
IUnknown, 255

J, L

JPEG, 1, 20, 346
LIFO, 156
Linear combination, 321
LZW, 347

M

Managed code, 18
Managed DirectX, 239, 257
  assemblies, 261
Manifest, 11
Metadata, 11, 13
Metafile, 43, 57, 68, 70, 71, 72, 73, 74, 75, 77, 78
mscoree.dll, 9
MSIL, 9, 10
Multiple Document Interface (MDI), 148

N, O

Namespace, 13, 15, 29
Object
  Direct3D, 247
Objects
  graphics, 37, 39
OnPrint, 229

P

Path, 45, 63
Pattern, 45
Perspective, 80
Picture, 171
Pixel shader, 300
Pixels:
  logical, 342
  physical, 342
Planar transformations
  rotation, 325

Platform SDK, 21
PNG, 1, 20, 346, 347
POINT3D, 80
Polynomial, 308
Primitive, 37, 38, 39, 42, 46, 47, 59, 64
Projection:
   parallel, 330, 333
   perspective, 330
Projective transformations, 280

R

Raster, 339
Raster data tranformations:
   bit, 168
   spatial, 168
Reflection, 11, 69, 77
Region, 63
Removing hidden details, 269
Resource leak, 38
Resources, 40, 41

S

Shaders, 299
SharpDevelop, 15
Single Document Interface (SDI), 148
Slider, 171
Spline, 46, 51, 53, 307
Sprites, 298
Stateful model, 38
Stateless model, 39
Static, 171
Stream, 341
System.Object, 10, 12, 15

T

T&L, 266
Tag, 341
Texture, 43, 298
TIFF, 1, 20, 346
Transform and Lighting, 266
Transformation matrix, 280, 328
   inversion, 329
TransformPix, 191, 211, 216
Transparency, 347
Transposition, 320
Triangle:
   fan, 290
   list, 290
   strip, 290
Triangulation, 335

U, V

Using, 41
Vector, 315
   cross product, 318
   dot product, 317
Verbatim string, 69
Vertex buffer, 288
Vertex shader, 300
View transformations, 280
Viewing frustum, 271
Virtual screen, 157
Visibility pyramid, 269

W, Z

WHQL, 263
Windows Forms, 13, 16, 33
WMF, 1, 20
World transformations, 280
Z-buffer, 272